Christianity

A NEW LOOK
AT
ANCIENT WISDOM

David J. H. Hart

Christianity

A NEW LOOK
AT
ANCIENT
WISDOM

Northstone

Editor: Michael Schwartzentruber
Cover and interior design: Margaret Kyle
Proofreading: Dianne Greenslade
Cover illustration: www.photos.com

Unless otherwise noted, all scripture quotations are from Today's English Version (Good News)
copyright © 1992 by American Bible Society. Used by Permission.

Excerpt from *Good Will Hunting* used under license from Miramax Film Corp.
All rights reserved.

NORTHSTONE PUBLISHING is an imprint of WOOD LAKE BOOKS INC. Wood Lake Books
acknowledges the financial support of the Government of Canada, through the Book Publishing
Industry Development Program (BPIDP) for its publishing activities.

WOOD LAKE BOOKS is an employee-owned company, committed to caring for the environment
and all creation. Wood Lake Books recycles, reuses, and encourages readers to do the same.
Resources are printed on recycled paper and more environmentally friendly groundwood papers
(newsprint), whenever possible. The trees used are replaced through donations to the Scoutrees For
Canada Program. A percentage of all profit is donated to charitable organizations.

Library and Archives Canada Cataloguing in Publication
Hart, David J. H., 1955–
Christianity: a new look at ancient wisdom/David J. H. Hart.
Includes bibliographical references and index.
ISBN 1-896836-76-3
1. Christianity and culture. 2. Christianity – Forecasting.
I. Title.
BR121.3.H37 2005 261   C2005-904833-6

Published by Northstone Publishing
an imprint of WOOD LAKE BOOKS, INC.
9025 Jim Bailey Road, Kelowna, BC, Canada, V4V 1R2
250.766.2778
www.northstone.com
www.woodlakebooks.com

Printing 10 9 8 7 6 5 4 3 2 1
Printed in Canada
at Houghton Boston, Saskatoon, SK

Contents

Dedication

Dedication to my parents,
Elsie and Theodore Hoppner,
whose passion for God never faltered!

Acknowledgments

A book often begins as a solitary impulse, as passion of the heart, by its author. But before long, it turns into a shared enterprise, a collective undertaking by many people. This book was no different for me. I would like to acknowledge some of the very special people who have contributed to this project in a variety of ways.

First and foremost, I would like to thank the congregation of Bedford United Church located in Bedford, Nova Scotia. Not only has this remarkably thoughtful and open congregation explored with me the many ideas and concepts presented in this book, but the sabbatical time they allowed me in 2001 enabled me to get this project off the ground. Without their help then, and along the way, this book would never have been written.

To Terry Paul Choyce, the very first reader and editor of the initial manuscript, I owe a huge word of thanks. From the beginning, she believed in this project and nurtured it along with her warm enthusiasm, encouragement, and editorial insights. As the manuscript began to take shape, many other wonderful friends took the time and energy to read it. The thoughtful suggestions made by Marion Christie, Heather Clarke, Carolyn Crowell, Chris Davison, Don Farmer, Fay and Robert Jackson, Jill LeClair, Don Stewart, and Jeanann Tell have all helped to make this a much better book than it otherwise would have been. As the manuscript neared completion, it was Donna Sinclair whose friendship, encouragement, editorial expertise, and publication suggestions provided the final push to help this "baby be born." My prayer is that the universe will indeed return to her all the blessings she shares with others!

Once the manuscript moved to the publication phase, I found myself blessed with the support of Mike Schwartzentruber. Mike is not only a superb editor but also a deep thinker and profoundly spiritual human being. Without exception, his commentary and suggestions have always proved to be "right on the mark." His work has helped to make this a much better book than it otherwise would have been. Thank you, Mike!

Finally, I wish to thank my beloved spouse and partner, Daniele, who is my toughest critic, most thoughtful confidante, and a rock of support in the midst of our shared journey of life and all its projects; and, my daughter Kinza, whose pride and love for her dad makes my heart sing each and every day. I love you both!

Introduction

When I was five, my two older brothers – Roger, age nine; and Kye, age 12 – drowned in a rafting accident. That event changed my parents' lives, and my own life, forever. I had barely begun school, yet I needed to find answers to some very difficult questions. Maybe because I was so young, those questions didn't present themselves in words, or as ideas, but rather as feelings. Overnight, I went from being a happy-go-lucky little boy, without a care in the world, to being a child overwhelmed with loneliness and a fear of abandonment. The question these feelings generated was "Why?" Why had life become so sorrowful? And there were other, more obscure feelings and questions. Having been raised in a committed, church-going family, and having absorbed the message of the children's song *Jesus Loves Me*, I had always felt completely at home in the church. But now, this too changed. I no longer felt quite so secure in this home, or that I belonged there in the same way I had in the past. The message I had absorbed during my first years in church had been radically challenged by a new one: "Life can be brutal and love can be snatched away in an instant." The new feeling that accompanied this message was one of uncertainty and anxiety regarding the central learning I had acquired from the church. If I could have put into words the question my feelings raised, it would have been this: "Did Jesus *really* love me, if he could let this kind of thing happen to me?"

At the age of five, then, life placed before me some big questions. Regrettably, I found no answers in the church of my birth. Neither did my mother and it was her search that took us elsewhere.

One day, sometime after the death of my brothers, my mother poured out her grief to the pastor of the Pentecostal church our family had been attending. When she revealed to him the devastation of her soul, he replied, rather brusquely, "Don't you realize that your sons are much better off in heaven? God simply called them home."

9

My mother had realized no such thing. No doubt she would have *liked* to believe that God had simply called her sons to a better place. Indeed, in a previous time and for someone else she might have been able to *believe* it. But now she was not so sure. She struggled with the same dilemma that confronted Job in the Old Testament: How could God allow such terrible things to happen to good people, to people who loved God with their whole being? She needed more understanding.

In her despair, she turned to the minister of the local United Church of Canada congregation. From him, she received more effective pastoral care and a more thoughtful response to her questions. And so our family moved to a new spiritual home. Even there, however, my feelings of loss and separation found no resolution or healing. And, in time, they led to a full-blown questioning of my Christian faith.

I remember one event, in particular, which happened when I was a teenager. I was camping with some friends beside a beautiful river in northern Ontario. I woke up in the middle of the night, and, while my fellow campers slept, crawled out of my sleeping bag and slipped down to the river's edge. I can still vividly recall the beauty of the scene that awaited me. A full, white moon shone overhead. A light mist rose off the water. And two solitary loons swam by, calling to each other with their haunting cries. In that moment, a question surfaced within me: "Why am I not happy?"

I had loving, caring parents and everything I needed for my material well-being. I attended an excellent school and had several close friends. And here I was, surrounded by this most exquisite beauty, and yet all I could feel was a deep emptiness and unhappiness looming beneath the surface of my conscious life. Beside this beautiful river, in the middle of the night, this realization thrust itself into my conscious awareness for the very first time.

Existential angst filled my young soul and I struggled with depression for the next two years. Nothing I heard or experienced in my church over those years was able to touch, let alone heal, the deep unhappiness I felt. And so, like many others of my generation, I ceased attending church or looking to it for spiritual help.

These were the tumultuous days of the 1960s and 1970s. In the exploratory mood of that time, my spiritual quest first led me down the strange and unknown pathways of other world religions and alternative spiritual movements. But then, by one of life's unexpected surprises, my journey took a 360-degree turn back to my own Christian church and tradition. In time, I found not only the spiritual answers, but also the inner peace and serenity that had so eluded me in the years following the death of my brothers. Since then my mission has been to accompany other people, as they seek answers to their questions and peace for their restless souls.

Today, as the spiritual leader of a large, Christian congregation, I regularly meet people who are facing challenging circumstances. The onset of cancer, the death of a child, the breakdown of a relationship, the termination of employment – all of these are experiences that draw people to seek a spiritual perspective on life. I also meet people who are not experiencing any extraordinary stressors, but who, nonetheless, hunger for a sense of something more, something deeper and more meaningful in their lives. These people often tell me that they have drifted away from the Christian church because its teachings and practices no longer make sense to them, or fail to make any real difference to their lives or in the world.

Fortunately, there are today many voices seeking to articulate new understandings of Christianity. Some of these have emerged out of the biblical scholarship movement, others out of new spiritual and experiential pathways, and yet others out of contemporary science.

Drawing upon these many voices and upon my own experience, I hope to articulate in this book the core beliefs of the Christian faith, in a way that makes sense of and speaks to the experience of contemporary people, for whom the traditional expressions of Christian faith no longer hold meaning or purpose.

The rudder that sets the direction for the entire book is a new, or rather *reclaimed*, vision of God that is emerging today. Historically, much of Christian doctrine and dogma has been shaped by belief in a God who exists "up in the sky" beyond human life and existence. The truth, however, is that the biblical tradition also speaks of a God who is ever-present, who surrounds us on all sides, who lives within us, and who is the one in whom we live, breathe, and have our being. With this vision of God setting our course, we need not avoid any of the tough questions that arise from life's often painful and difficult circumstances.

In addition, the new approaches to God and to life that we will explore in this book are not ones we must simply believe, no questions asked. Ultimately, the Christian life is *not* about believing correct dogmas or ideas, but about testing within our own lives ideas, principles, and practices that have the power to transform us in positive and life-giving ways.

This desire to experience the living truth of God, which I felt as a child and which so many people experience today, warrants a brief discussion of the difference between spirituality and religion.

Spirituality and Religion

The Christianity of my youth was ill-equipped to address my spiritual longing and needs because it had become separated from its own spiritual origins. Without being rooted in the spirit, religion becomes empty and shallow, a form without substance. Mind you, without being rooted in a religious tradition and community, spirituality can become ungrounded and self-serving. The two need each other. Indeed, they are different sides of the same coin.

The term "spirit" refers to many different things. Primarily, as I use it, it refers to God as an immaterial reality that pervades the entire universe, and that gives life and vitality to creation. In English Bibles, Spirit is also the word used to translate the Hebrew word *ruach*, which means wind and breath. Like the wind, the Spirit's presence is not seen, but felt. In short, Spirit is a metaphor for that mysterious and invisible, sacred and life-giving dimension of existence.

Spirituality can be defined as the human need to experience this invisible, sacred dimension of life, which gives us our being, which holds us all together in a single unity, and which is the deepest source of our joy and serenity. Given that we experience so much of life as a crazy whirlwind of activity and stress, it's no wonder that we hunger for a deeper peace and joy. Given, too, that so much of life includes the inevitable suffering caused by broken dreams, boredom, sickness, loss, and death, it's no wonder that we yearn for a deeper connection with the source of life and with each other; a connection that can never be lost.

Sometimes we experience this joy or sense of connection in totally unexpected moments of grace and serendipity, when the sacred makes itself known and present to us. Lying under the stars at night, watching the sun come over the horizon in the early morning, basking in the afterglow of lovemaking – all of these can be moments when we experience a profound serenity, joy, and acceptance that enable us to feel more connected with each other and with the larger mystery of life. They can be moments when we cease to experience life as a problem and instead experience the sheer wonder of it.

But spirituality also consists of the vast collection of practices that enable people to intentionally and proactively connect with this divine reality. Different forms of prayer, meditation, worship, artistic expression, and even service, can enable us to enter into a deep sense of union with all of life, and to experience a profound sense of joy and meaning. In other words, spirituality consists of the experiential side of religion. It is less concerned with analyzing and talking about God and is more occupied with our actual experience of God, or the sacred dimension of life.

The term religion, on the other hand, refers to something different. Throughout human history, certain women and men have claimed and demonstrated in their personal lives an extraordinary connection with that mysterious, invisible dimension of life we call Spirit, the sacred, or God. In the chapter dealing with Jesus, I refer to them as spiritual geniuses. Abraham and Moses, the Buddha, Lao Tzu, Jesus, and Mohammed were all such people.

Obviously, something was at work in these people. They demonstrated a serenity, a personal power for living, a clarity of vision, and a love that was beyond anything their followers had previously experienced. In turn, their followers or disciples learned from them and imitated them and began to experience some of the same serenity, power for living, and love in their own lives. Soon a formal community and organization began to develop around the leader. Upon the death of the leader, these communities assumed responsibility for communicating the teachings of the founder, and for carrying out his or her other ministries of healing and renewal in the society at large. These organizations are what we refer to as religions.

With few exceptions, each is based on the experience and life of an original spiritual genius or luminary known for his or her exceptional spiritual clarity and power.

The dilemma for religious organizations has always been how to carry on the work of the original leader. As long as the original leader or spiritual genius is alive, he or she can oversee how the teaching is passed on to others. However, once that person has died, it becomes the task of the disciples to pass on his or her teaching and practice with integrity. As time passes, as the original disciples directly taught by the teacher die, the original teachings tend to evolve. They become shaped by influences that may or may not be in harmony with the founder's intent.

In the case of Jesus, who never wrote down a single word, whose ministry was based entirely in an oral tradition, and who actively taught for only a short time, this problem was especially pronounced. We see it developing in the New Testament, a collection of early Christian writings established in the decades following Jesus' death, and containing many different teachings, not all of which agree with each other. We see the problem in the life of St. Paul himself. Certainly, Paul had a profound conversion experience of the risen Christ, and became a brilliant promoter for the early Christian church. However, many scholars and contemporary Christians believe that Paul taught a form of Christianity that in many respects was not true to the teachings of Jesus at all. This is not so much a criticism of Paul as it is an example of how religious movements evolve and change after the death of the original founder.

Fortunately, today we have very powerful literary, historical, and anthropological tools with which to analyze and evaluate ancient texts and teachings. As a result, we are able to sift through the ancient writings and discern much more clearly the teachings of the original founder, and what was added by later disciples. This process has taken place not just in Christianity, but in all of the world's major religious traditions.

We are beginning to discover that all of the world's religious and spiritual geniuses have had profound experiences of the divine or sacred dimensions of life. Although their reflections on that experience may differ according to their cultural and intellectual background, they also agree in many ways. In addition, the experience of the sacred or divine has led all the world's religious luminaries to espouse similar moral and ethical values for the betterment of humankind. Even the spiritual practices they promote possess more similarities than differences. Aldous Huxley, observing the high level of similarity between the core teachings of all the world's great spiritual geniuses, coined the term "perennial philosophy" to describe this phenomenon. There does, indeed, seem to exist a universality that runs through all the world's religious traditions. Again, using historical analysis and literary tools, we are beginning to separate this universal teaching from the cultural and dogmatic overlays added by followers of the original leaders. This development is freeing us to enter an exciting new world of religion and spirituality.

People have understood rightly that a Christianity that has lost touch with its spiritual roots lacks the power to transform life, or to access the peace and serenity, the clarity and vision that was so apparent in the life of Jesus. But a new vision of Christianity is emerging today, a vision of a religious path and community deeply in touch with its spiritual roots and that possesses the ability to profoundly transform people's lives. While it has 2000 years of theological, moral, and community development behind it, this emerging Christianity can also openly accept, honor, and even learn from other religious traditions without experiencing fear or the need to claim superiority or exclusive access to truth. As such, it can become a wonderful agent of renewal and healing.

This book, then, is addressed to Christians – to those within the church, and to those who may have left the church because they have felt that Christianity has lost it way. It is for people looking to reclaim the ancient spiritual wisdom of the Christian heritage, while framing it in a new way that addresses the contemporary world and its challenges.

However, this book is also addressed to people who may come from other religious or spiritual traditions, or from a background of no religious tradition at all. It is my hope that these readers, too, will find here much food for thought.

I invite you, then, to join me on a journey of discovery and transformation!

THE VISION

Chapter 1

God

Then Job answered the Lord. I know, Lord, that you are all-powerful; that you can do everything you want. You ask how I dare question your wisdom… I talked about things I did not understand… You told me to listen while you spoke… In the past I knew only what others had told me, but now I have seen you with my own eyes. So I am ashamed of all I have said and repent in dust and ashes.

Job 42:1–6

Two little boys were always getting into trouble, so much so that their parents were at their wits' end.

One day, the mother heard that a local minister had been successful in disciplining children, so she suggested to her husband that they send the boys to him. Not knowing what else to do, the husband agreed.

The minister consented to speak with the boys, but asked to see them individually. The youngest went first. The clergyman sat the boy down and asked him sternly, "Where is God?" The boy made no response, so the clergyman repeated the question in an even sterner tone: "Where is God!?" Again, the boy made no attempt to answer, so the clergyman raised his voice even more and shook his finger in the boy's face: "WHERE IS GOD!?"

At that the boy bolted from the room, ran home, and hid in the closet, slamming the door behind him. The older brother looked in and asked, "What happened?" The younger brother replied, "We're in big trouble this time. God's missing and they think we did it!"

God has been missing from many people's lives for a long time and we do not have to look far to find the reason. For the past two centuries, our culture has increasingly placed more faith in the ability of science and technology to improve human life, than in God. At the end of the 19th century, Friedrich Nietzsche defiantly declared, "God is dead! God remains dead! And we have killed him!"

For Nietzsche and for many of his contemporaries, religion had become empty; it no longer possessed credibility or the power to change people's lives in positive ways. For Nietzsche, the future belonged to human beings, who would ascend to the throne of God, take full responsibility for their own existence, and create and judge their own world.[1]

Experience has shown, however, that human beings do not play the role of God very well. To name just one example, the world is on the brink of ecological and climatic disaster as a direct result of the presumption that we can play God with our environment.

In ever increasing numbers, people are discovering that we *do*, indeed, need God. But the understanding of God that proved so shallow and unconvincing to Nietzsche and his contemporaries has become even less convincing today. This has left many of us in a Catch-22 situation. We want to believe in God. Even more, we want to experience the reality of God in our lives. But raised in a scientific age and impressed by the necessity for critical reasoning, many of us have not found a convincing, new understanding of God to replace the old one.

It is time, then, to rediscover God. Fortunately, an understanding of God is emerging today that does not require us to park our brains at the door, or to leave our hearts in the lobby.

The Old Understanding of God

Bertrand Russell, a famous British philosopher, was sentenced to prison for opposing World War I. While filling out an admission form, the entry clerk for the jail asked Russell what his religion was. Russell replied that he was an agnostic. After asking him to spell "agnostic," the clerk, who wasn't too bright, said with a tolerant sigh, "Well there are very many religions, but I suppose we all worship the same God." Russell later wrote that this remark kept him cheerful for a week.

To fully appreciate the new vision of God that is emerging today, it is helpful first to describe the old understanding. In the process, we discover that we do not have to throw out the baby with the bathwater. There are dimensions of our previous understanding of God that we can carry into the new perspective. Thus, we can move forward with a sense of comforting familiarity. But we will discover some fundamental differences too.

The old understanding of God took two forms, one or the other holding a stronger attraction, depending on whether you were more rational in nature, or more piously religious. In both forms, however, God was imaged as an all-powerful, all-knowing person, who lived up in the sky in heaven. This "person" was most commonly depicted in art as a grandfatherly old man, with a long beard.

Deism

One form of the old understanding of God suggested that God created the world with a built-in set of laws, some of which determined the functioning of the natural world, and some of which governed human behavior. Natural laws, such as gravity, ensured that trees didn't float off into space and that the planets stayed in proper alignment with each other and with the sun. Moral and ethical laws ensured that sinful human beings would eventually suffer the consequences of their behavior. Goodness would ultimately prevail. Once God had established the functioning of the world according to these laws and principles, God withdrew to allow things to unfold in their own way. This was called the deist understanding of God.

Theism

The other form of the earlier understanding of God, and by far the more popular one, also suggested that God created the universe according to natural and moral laws. In this understanding, however, God did not withdraw from creation. God continued to take a very keen interest in the unfolding of the universe, and especially in human affairs. This meant that people could talk to God, pray about their problems, and ask for things. If God was in the mood, and if what you asked for was pleasing to God, then God might pull strings to make it happen – something like a kindly Santa Claus: magical, powerful, and loving at the same time. If God needed to intervene from time to time in the life of the world, to set things back on course, then God would do so, especially if asked sincerely in prayer. This was called the theist understanding of God.

Mind you, there was a dark side to this theist God. If God didn't like what was happening on earth, or if God didn't like the way you were behaving in your life, God might dish out severe punishment. Illness, loss of a job, even the death of a loved one might be the result of God's punishment for sins committed in your life.

To be sure, this is a simplified statement of the theist understanding of God. Nonetheless, it represents the beliefs most people have learned and many continue to live with. It is also the understanding of God that most people take away from the Christian Bible, though, as we shall see, it is by no means the only understanding of God found in the Bible.

As popular as the theist understanding of God has been, it is fraught with problems. For instance, it attributes a somewhat arbitrary nature to God's moods and favors. Why are some people born into loving, fortunate circumstances while others are born into terrible situations? Why is it that God seems to answer the prayers of some people, but not others? Why is it that truly wonderful people, like Job, sometimes suffer such horrible things? Yes, God created the world, but apparently not in a very just way. God's moral laws seem to break down pretty often. In fact, God's seemingly arbitrary manner of involvement in our lives appears to be cruel, and at times even sadistic. No wonder Job had a hard time figuring out this God. So has everyone else.

Experiences of God

The second thing we should do before naming the new understanding of God is look at how we *learn* about God. This is because new conceptions of God do not arise merely from intellectual speculation on the part of great theologians. You do not have to be a brilliant academic to understand God. Rather, our understanding of God derives from our lived experience.

Nature

For many of us, our understanding of God is shaped by our experiences of and interactions with nature. In nature, we find a beauty, an order, and often a sense of peace and well-being uncommon in our everyday lives. Our experience of nature gives rise to the intuition that there is an awesome reality permeating and sustaining the world, instilling it with design, filling it with beauty, and fashioning it for the preservation of life. It is this experience that led the Hebrew psalmist to write,

> O Lord, my God, how great you are!
> You are clothed with majesty and glory;…
> You have spread out the heavens like a tent,…
> You have set the earth firmly on its foundations,…
> You make springs flow in the valleys,…
> In the trees nearby, the birds make their nests and sing.
> From the sky you send rain on the hills,
> and the earth is filled with your blessings…
> You created the moon to make the months;
> the sun knows the time to set.
> Lord, you have made so many things!
> How wisely you made them all!
> Psalm 104:1–24, selected verses

God at work in human life

Reflection on our unfolding life experience and the sense that there is another, hidden dimension or factor influencing that experience, also shapes our understanding of God.

When I was a child, I used to giggle at my mom, who, prior to going on vacation, would always pray for good weather. Of course, most of the time, we *had* good weather. But, even at my young age, I understood that since it was summer the odds of having good weather were fairly high. I could not see how God figured into the picture.

As I grew older, however, I developed an affectionate appreciation for my mom's simple faith. I recognized that she prayed about *everything*, be it large or small. She prayed for help to find just the right house on a house-hunting expedition. She prayed for the neighbor experiencing a tough time out of work. She prayed for strength to combat her emotional despair after the drowning of my two brothers. And she prayed about the weather. But, most of all, she prayed for me every single day. Her prayer life was simple and maybe naïve, but over the years I came to see that much of what she prayed for came to pass.

The ancient Israelites, the people of the Bible, also prayed to God for everything and anything. They prayed for good weather for their crops, for physical health and healing, for prosperity, for liberation from political oppression. They even prayed to God to destroy their enemies. Like my mother, they believed that when they resorted to the awesome power and intelligence of the universe, the one they called Yahweh, Yahweh would respond.

Again the psalmist says,

> Praise the Holy One,
> who is so wonderful,
> whose faithful love endures forever.
> In their distress, [the people] screamed to the Holy One,
> who rescued them from their torments,
> leading them in the right way
> to a city where they could make their home.
> Psalm 107:1, 6–8 [2]

There are many possible objections to understanding God in this way. But the experience of people from time immemorial has been that when we call upon God, God responds in some way. The response may be mysterious and may not always occur in the way we ask. But, somehow, prayers get answered. It is the experience expressed in the words of Jesus: "Ask, and you will receive; seek, and you will find; knock, and the door will be opened to you" (Matthew 7:7).

Though it can be explained in many ways, for many of us, this experience shapes our belief in God.

Love

The most powerful experience to shape our belief in God is that of love. Today we tend to think of love as simply an emotion, a force of attraction structured into human beings for the preservation of the species. But love is much more than this.

The ancient Greeks, and the early church, used several words for love, the two most notable being *eros* and *agape*. *Eros* refers to romantic, sexual love that draws partners together for the pleasure of lovemaking and for procreation. *Agape* refers to a different type of love. It speaks to the profound depths of caring and compassion that humans feel for each other and for life as a whole.

It is *agape* love that inspired Mother Teresa to work with the hungry, homeless, and dying people of Calcutta. It is *agape* love that inspired martyrs like Oscar Romero and Steve Biko to stand up for the rights of the dispossessed in racist cultures, and to give their lives in the struggle. And it *is agape* love that inspires many environmental activists to work endlessly for the preservation of the planet.

Where does this love come from, if not from the very source of life, the one we call God? Jesus demonstrated such a love and was quite explicit that his ability to love in this way came from the God who first loved him. Speaking to his disciples he said, "I love you, just as God loves me… [therefore], love one another, just as I love you" (John 15:9, 12).

Our experience of love suggests that God has a vested interest in life. It suggests that God has established not just *eros*, a force of attraction for pleasure and procreation, but *agape*, a love that works to build up, care for, and sustain life as a whole.

Dreams and sixth-sense experience

For many of us, dreams and sixth-sense experiences also play a role in shaping our understanding of God. These types of experiences suggest that we live in a reality that is much vaster, and somehow less "solid" than we typically believe. Dreams sometimes contain within them premonitions of future events. They can also reveal solutions to struggles and questions that we have not been able to resolve with our conscious mind. Then there are experiences like the following one, told to me by a member of my congregation, which had for him a life changing impact.

> It was during World War II and I was stationed in France. I was returning to my unit after visiting a buddy recuperating in a field hospital. I was speeding along on a country road, late at night, alone on a motorcycle. Suddenly I heard a voice shout in my ear, as clearly as if someone had been sitting behind me on that bike: "Stop!" I slammed on the brakes just in time to come face to face with a taut, black wire strung across the road. Either enemy forces or vandals had hung it to create havoc. I would have been killed instantly had it not been for that voice that shouted at me from nowhere.

I could recount many similar experiences, from many different sources. But I think it is sufficient to say that dreams and sixth-sense experiences suggest that reality is much more characterized by mind than by matter. More and more, people are coming to identify this mysterious "mind" as the reality of God.

Mystical or unitive experiences

In my own life, it was the hunger to *know* God – not to talk about God or to discuss theology, but to *experience* God for myself – that led me to read the works of the early Christian mystics. As a young seminarian, I learned that the Christian tradition includes many centuries of incredible wisdom and experience about God, from profoundly wise women and men who experienced and came to know God in very direct and immediate ways: women and men such as the desert fathers and mothers; St. John of the Cross and Teresa of Avila, who were great saints and mystics of medieval Spain; the writers of the *Philokalia* and *The Way of a Pilgrim*, saints and mystics of the Eastern Orthodox Church; Julian of Norwich and the English author of *The Cloud of Unknowing*. Though it may have been ancient, their understanding of God, gleaned from direct experience, was fresh and new to me. It was definitely *not* what I had learned growing up in my local church.

Mystical experiences have been described by and are a part of every religious tradition the world over. In fact, they lie at the root and have given rise to every enduring world religion through the direct experience of the founder of those religions. The Buddha, Lao Tzu, Moses, the Hebrew prophets, Jesus, and Mohammed, all had mystical experiences.

For those unsure of what I mean by the term "mystical experience," "unitive experience" might actually be a better, more descriptive term. Generally preceded by a life of active prayer and searching for God, the unitive experience can assume a wide variety of expressions. But the single, most common element running through it is a sense or feeling of "at-one-ness" with all of life. Individuality seems to disappear. The feeling of separation between self and everything else softens and dissolves. Generally, this sensation is accompanied by euphoric emotional states of bliss and ecstasy, and by a deep serenity that may last for many days.

A simple type of this experience happened to me some years ago, around the time my first marriage ended. My wife at that time had gone to California to study with Matthew Fox at the Institute for Creation Centered Spirituality. Because I was serving a small rural pastoral charge, I had time available and often spent three to four hours a day in prayer and meditation. At the end of that year, my wife decided to leave our relationship. I carried on alone, taking on a new administrative job with the national church. As part of the job, I traveled extensively and continued to spend a great deal of time in solitude, prayer, and meditation. When I wasn't traveling, I enjoyed the daily walk to my office, during which I engaged in a form of walking meditation that involved chanting the name of Jesus in sync with my steps and my breathing. One day, while absorbed in this form of meditation, I suddenly perceived that the entire world was shining with a dazzling light. Everything I looked at – buildings, people, trees, and plants – seemed to be surrounded by and infused with an intensely bright light, like that of an aura. At the same time, I felt a sense of complete peacefulness and joy, a sense of oneness with all that is. Although in the weeks that followed life returned more or less to normal, the experience was a taste of life from a much deeper and more meaningful perspective that has never completely left me.

Sophy Burnham, in her book *The Ecstatic Journey*, gives an account of a more extraordinary and remarkable type of mystical experience. Sophy, a mother and writer, tells of being in Peru on a writing assignment. It was an intensely spiritual time in her life that included long periods of fasting and meditation. At one point, while alone at Machu Picchu, she had the following experience.

> I felt a pressure on my neck, as if a dark hand were pressing me down. Terrible and majestic it was. Nothing sweet and pretty in it, but frightening, full of force. From the midst of the black roaring, came a voice: "You belong to me or you are mine." Not in words, but rather as a form of knowledge, resounding in blackness... For a moment I fought it, terrified. Then: "If you are God, yes," I surrendered with my last coherent thoughts. "I belong only to God..." With that, I was immersed in a sweetness words cannot express. I could hear the singing of the planets, and wave after wave of light washed over me. But this is wrong, because I was the light as well, without distinction of self or of being washed. It is hard to speak of what happened at this point. At one level I ceased to exist, was swallowed into light. How long that lasted I do not know. At another level, although I no longer existed as a separate "I," nonetheless I saw things, thus indicating the duality of "I" and "other"... I saw into the structure of the universe... I saw the perfection of all things that had ever happened or ever will, and how the destruction didn't matter, for energy goes on, transmuted, so that even destruction is an expression of pure God-ness, love

and creativity... I saw that everything was perfect, and all was composed of love. I saw there is no death.

Slowly, slowly I came out of it, climbing like a deep sea turtle up toward the air. I opened my eyes – and closed them instantly. Blinded by daylight. Gradually the sound of silence faded. The black ringing stopped. My senses still enraptured, I was humbled by the indulgent love of the Absolute, and by a joy beyond description... I felt myself spring down the mountain full of power and joy, to meet my group.[3]

Sophy's description recalls to mind the experience of Jesus and of the early Christian church. Prior to beginning his public ministry, Jesus went to the Jordan River to be baptized by John the Baptist. Upon being baptized, he experienced the "heavens opening up and the Power of God descending upon him in the form of a dove." He also heard a voice proclaim, "You are my own dear son. I am pleased with you" (Mark 1:9–11). The story says that the Spirit then led him out into the wilderness for 40 days of additional prayer and fasting. Obviously, the entire experience was one of great power, because it was after this that Jesus began his formal teaching and healing ministry. Later in his ministry, Jesus' disciples had a similar experience in his presence. Alone on a high mountain, during a time of prayer, they saw Jesus surrounded by a field of bright, white light, and a voice spoke to them saying, "This is my own dear son, listen to him" (Mark 9:2–13). Then, after the death of Jesus, the disciples had been praying and fasting once again, yearning to experience God's spirit, which Jesus said he would send to them after his death. The writer of the Book of Acts tells us what happened next.

Suddenly there was a noise from the sky which sounded like a strong wind blowing, and it filled the whole house where they were sitting. Then they saw what looked like tongues of fire which spread out and touched each person there. They were all filled with the Holy Spirit and began to talk in other languages, as the Spirit enabled them to speak.

Acts 2:2–4

29

In the early life of Christianity, we clearly see this kind of mystical or unitive experience at work, giving great power and impetus to the first works of the disciples, and to the formation of the Christian tradition.

I want to share one other contemporary account of a much quieter, but equally profound mystical or unitive experience. This one comes from Irina Tweedie, a contemporary spiritual teacher who spent a number of years working with a Sufi master. In her journal, she describes her experience following the death of her master.

> I have been here [the Himalayas] for three months. Almost sixteen weeks have passed since Guruji's death. So much has happened within me; slowly, gradually, by degrees the world begins to look differently, to change imperceptibly. The sunrise, the sunset, the garden, the people, the whole daily life seem outwardly the same. But the values have changed. The meaning underlying it all is not the same as before. Something that seemed intangible, unattainable, slowly, very slowly becomes a permanent reality. There is nothing but Him. At the beginning it was sporadic: later of shorter or longer duration, when I was acutely conscious of it. But now... the infinite, endless Him... Nothing else is there. And all the beauty of nature which surrounds me is as if only on the edge of my consciousness. Deep within, I am resting in the peace of His Heart. The body feels so light at times. As if it were made of the pure, thin air of the snow peaks. This constant vision of the One is deepening and increasing in the mind, giving eternal peace.[4]

Irina Tweedie is one of those rare people in whom a temporary mystical experience eventually gave way to a more permanent experience of unity with all that is. Her awareness was conditioned by the discipline of spiritual practice, to see beneath or behind the multiplicity of life forms – different shapes, sizes, colors, and so on – to the eternal oneness or unity which permeates and binds everything together.

In photography there exists the concept of foreground and background. The unitive mystic sees the everyday world we all see as the foreground of their lives. But in addition, as the background to their everyday experience, they see a light that permeates and surrounds everything. What's more, they recognize this light as the force or energy that binds everything together, including one's own self. The "seeing" of this light or force consists of the vision of oneness or unity that is found in all of the world's mystical traditions. It is an experience that points powerfully to the new vision of God emerging today.

A New Vision and Understanding of God

There once was a little fish who swam up to its mother and asked, "What is this water that I hear so much about?" The little fish's mother laughed and said, "You silly little fish. Water is all around you and within you. It's what gives you life. Swim to the top of the pond and lie there for a moment. Then you'll know what water is." So too, a little fawn walked up to her mother and asked, "What is this air I hear so much about?" The little fawn's mother smiled and said, "Why, air is within you and around you. Air is what gives you life. If you want to know what air is, stick your head in the stream for a while. Then you'll know what air is." Once there was a young man beginning his spiritual journey in life, who asked a holy woman, "What is this God I hear so much about?"

Many of the writings in the Bible, and much of the sacred literature from other religious traditions, have arisen from the kinds of experiences I have just described. So, too, have many great works of theology, both ancient and modern. It is nothing more complicated than that. Experience precedes reflection. We have an experience of something larger than ourselves, something great and mysterious. Then we engage in a process of reflection and abstract thinking to make sense of that experience.

"The Genius of the AND"

In order to fully appreciate and comprehend the new vision of God emerging today, we must first develop a certain mental capacity, a specialized form of thinking and reflection not typically found in religious circles. Jim Collins and Jerry Porras, in their popular book *Built to Last, Successful Habits of Visionary Companies*, call this ability by a clumsy but descriptive name: No Tyranny of the OR (Embrace the Genius of the AND). In referring to modern, visionary companies they say,

> You'll notice... that we use the yin/yang symbol from Chinese dualistic philosophy. We've consciously selected this symbol to represent a key aspect of highly visionary companies. They do not oppress themselves with what we call the "Tyranny of the OR" – the seemingly rational view that cannot easily accept paradox, which cannot live with two seemingly contradictory forces or ideas at the same time. The "Tyranny of the OR" pushes people to believe that things must be either A OR B, but not both... Instead of being oppressed by the "Tyranny of the OR," highly visionary companies liberate themselves with the "Genius of the AND" – the ability to embrace both extremes of a number of dimensions at the same time. Instead of choosing between A OR B, they figure out a way to have both A AND B... Irrational? Perhaps. Rare? Yes. Difficult? Absolutely. But as F. Scott Fitzgerald pointed out, "The test of a first-rate intelligence is the ability to hold two opposed ideas in the mind at the same time, and still retain the ability to function. This is exactly what the visionary companies are able to do.[5]

This is also what religious people must be able to do if they are truly to appreciate the wonderful new vision of God emerging today. Collins and Porras list some of the seemingly contradictory ideas that companies must learn to embrace, such as "You can have change OR stability" but not both; you can have low cost OR high quality, but not both. They suggest to companies that, indeed, they *can* have both and *must* have both in order not just to survive, but also to thrive. Some of the seemingly contradictory ideas that religious people often hold are

- God can be loving OR disinterested
- God can be personal OR impersonal
- God can be everywhere OR somewhere
- God can create goodness OR evil
- The universe can be separate from God OR part of God
- We can be part of God OR separate from God
- After death we go to heaven OR to hell
- The universe is material OR spiritual

We will see these apparent contradictions manifest throughout the rest of this book, but will embrace a vision of God that includes them all. To be comfortable with paradox and ambiguity, to rise above the "tyranny of the OR" and to embrace the "genius of the AND" lies at the heart of contemporary thinking. It must occur not just in the realms of physics and management theory, but within the realm of religion – perhaps *especially* within the realm of religion.

Today, human experience, often seemingly contradictory, is giving rise to a new and inspirational understanding and image of God. And the very first concept requires that we embrace the "genius of the AND."

God as Visible *and* Invisible

God is both invisible *and* visible at one and same time. There is an infinite, invisible dimension to God. The force of gravity is invisible, but we know it is real. Today, scientists speculate that another invisible force, one predicted by Einstein, also exists. While gravity draws objects together, this force fills all of space and pushes objects apart. It cannot be seen, but scientists have observed effects pointing to its reality.

The same is true of God. God can be described as an infinite, invisible force. And although we can't see God, numerous experiences, and most of all the very fact of existence itself, point to God's reality. Today, we often use such terms or names as Divine Source, Great Spirit, and Ultimate Reality to refer to this infinite, invisible dimension of God. This aspect of God is what human beings have traditionally referred to as the "sacred dimension of life."

But the new vision suggests that there is another dimension to God that is visible. The entire creation, indeed all of life, is a part of God and an expression of the very being of God. When God created the universe, God did not make it out of some energy or substance that God had on hand, then toss it out into space and time, to exist separate and apart from God. Rather, God constructed the universe out of God's own being and power. Consequently, the visible universe can be likened much more to a mental construct, an idea or image held eternally within the mind of God, than to a material reality created by God and existing outside of and apart from God.

In other words, the universe is created as something distinct *by* God yet lives *within* God at the same time. The visible universe constitutes a physical manifestation of God's infinite spirit-energy and power, and is held within space and time by that spirit-energy and power.

You can see examples of this principle at play in everyday life. Children create sandcastles by shaping the sand on a beach into a space-time object, which, when a wave comes, will be washed back into the formless, timeless beach sand from which it came. Other children create snow people from the snow spread across winter fields. Eventually, the sun and the winds disintegrate them and they merge back into the snow from which they came. Just as sandcastles or snow people take their shape and form from the endless sand or snow around them, every single bit of life is created out of the invisible, unending spirit-energy of God that permeates all of existence. Each blade of grass, drop of rain, fish and bird and animal, and each and every human being is nothing other than a construct, an expression of the very being and power of God, sustained by the life of God.

I shall consider later why some of these life constructs appear so flawed. But for the time being it is important to grasp this notion. The visible universe, all that we can see, is as much a part of God as is the invisible, spirit-energy dimensions of God. And because both constitute different parts of God, both are sacred!

The old vision of God was more "dualist" in this respect, in that it separated the universe into two, distinct realities. In this earlier framework, the invisible, infinite spirit dimension of God existed separately and apart from the visible, created, finite universe of space and time.

The new vision of God is often referred to as being "non-dualist" or "unitary." It suggests that the invisible, infinite spirit dimension of God, and the visible but limited created universe, although distinct from each other, are really just two different aspects of one larger reality.

To embrace this concept, we need to let go of the "tyranny of the OR" and live with the "genius of the AND." We need to see that every single expression of life is fundamentally one with God, is made out of the very being and power of God, and is, indeed, sustained by God. At the same time, each expression of life has its own separate and distinct existence. While participating in the reality of God, we nonetheless live distinct and individual lives.

It is important to grasp this understanding of God because it affects and shapes all further considerations of the spiritual life, including prayer, healing, the question of suffering and evil, and so on. Before we move on to such topics, however, there are other aspects of the new vision of God to consider.

The spatial infinity of God

The new "non-dualist" vision of God builds upon and is in harmony with Einstein's theory of the relativity of space and time. The old understanding envisioned God as a person living in a specific place called heaven. The new understanding envisions the invisible, infinite God as a context, field, domain, or "sea" of infinitely expansive spirit-energy, present and alive everywhere throughout space and beyond. God is a field or domain of sheer light, of spirit-energy surrounding and permeating not just the entire earth and every single life form in it, but indeed the whole cosmos, including the solar system, the star fields, and the outer reaches of intergalactic space and beyond. God is here and everywhere at one and the same time. God is the invisible force that permeates and holds everything together. God is the ultimate "connecting tissue" of life that binds everything together into a single, seamless whole.

The temporal infinity of God

Likewise, the new model of God takes a different approach to time. Contemporary cosmology replaces the biblical story of creation in seven days with a story of creation via the "big bang." The ancient biblical tale of creation places God, the creator, at the beginning of time. The new vision of God, again building on Einstein's theory of the relativity of space and time, positions God entirely outside of space and time. God, or Ultimate Reality, has simply always existed.

This is a very difficult concept for our minds to grasp because we are so conditioned by the experience of time. But the fundamental nature both of God and of the manifest universe is timeless. God did not begin in time and God will not end in time. Time is not fundamental to life or to reality. According to the ancient Greek philosophers, God is the "alpha and the omega," the beginning and the end. In fact, God is neither. Beginnings and endings have no relevance to God whatsoever, or for that matter to the life of the universe.

To appreciate this concept is to wrestle with the equivalent of a Zen koan, an unsolvable riddle for the intellect that can only be penetrated or understood by direct intuitive insight. Time, like space, has only a relative reality for manifest existence. God totally transcends space and time, but God is also totally present throughout space and time.

The origins of God

If God exists totally outside the categories of space and time, then the question of "who created God" is no longer relevant. Indeed, no one created God. We, as human beings created in time and space, have an extremely difficult time conceptualizing an *uncreated* reality. But God, or that which is most real, has simply always existed beyond space and time. Again, this is like a Zen koan or paradox. It is only in a moment of non-conceptual, intuitive insight that we can grasp any sense of the true nature of this reality.

God as self-sustaining power

God as Ultimate Reality is also self-sustaining. As human beings, we depend on food, shelter, heat, and a variety of other things to sustain us. But the very life and power of God requires nothing. God simply exists, independently and perpetually, in eternity.

God as supreme intelligence

Scientists are beginning to think that just as energy is a fundamental substratum of the material universe, so too is information. If the entire universe is sustained not just by energy, but by information and intelligence too, then God, its source, must include intelligence. However, God's intelligence so transcends our human intellect and mind that we can never fully comprehend it.

God as sheer bliss and power

God as Ultimate Reality exists in a state of sheer bliss and power. This is the experience of the great mystics throughout time. In ecstatic states of contemplation, which transcend the limitations of individual self-awareness, they experience God as God experiences God's own self. And that experience is one of incredible power and bliss.

God as personal reality

Finally, thinking of God as an infinite, invisible, spirit-energy domain, in which all of life arises, unfolds, and into which life eventually disappears, does not mean that we cannot think of God in personal terms. Here we come again to the "genius of the AND." The new vision allows us to conceive of God as both personal and transpersonal at the same time. It is true that God is not a person and looks nothing like a human being. But since God creates human life, God understands it totally. Human personality comes to birth and lives within the very being of God. So although God is transpersonal, that is to say far beyond the functioning of human personality, still, God understands and comprehends human personality.

Since we are shaped and conditioned by personality, it is entirely appropriate and understandable that we relate to God in personal terms. Huston Smith, in his wonderful book *The World's Religions*, says,

It is easy to smile at the anthropomorphism of the early Hebrews, who could imagine ultimate reality as a person walking in the Garden of Eden in the cool of the morning. But when we make our way through the poetic concreteness of the perspective to its underlying claim – that in the final analysis ultimate reality is more like a person than like a thing, more like a mind than like a machine – [we must ask]…is the concept intrinsically less exalted than its alternative? The Jews were reaching out for the most exalted concept of the "Other" that they could conceive, an Other that embodied such inexhaustible worth that human beings would never begin to fathom its fullness.[6]

On the one hand, God is a vast domain or sea of self-sustaining power, existing beyond the limitations of space and time as sheer bliss and spirit-energy, totally incomprehensible and unknowable to our limited human intellect and mind. On the other hand, God is capable of responding to human beings and of being approached by human beings in a personal way, because God is the very source and sustainer of our lives.

To summarize, then, in the old vision, God, the Great Spirit, looked and acted suspiciously like a human being, with all of our human foibles. In the emerging new vision, God is also a Great Spirit, but one not styled after any human form. Rather, God as Ultimate Reality gives rise to all of life out of God's own being. God creates, permeates, surrounds, and sustains all of life. At the same time, life has its own independent functioning within God. God has given all of life, including human life, the freedom to live a unique, self-chosen destiny. And finally, God as Great Spirit, as Ultimate Reality, exists beyond space and time, was not created, and requires nothing beyond God's own self to exist, living as sheer intelligence, bliss, and power.

It is this vision of God that the Bible points to when the Hebrew psalmist says,

Lord, you have examined me and you know me.
You know everything I do.
You see me, whether I am working or resting;
    you know all my actions.
You are all round me on every side;
    you protect me with your power.
Your knowledge of me is too deep;
    it is beyond my understanding.
Where could I escape from you?
Where could I get away from your presence?
If I went up to heaven, you would be there;
If I lay down in the world of the dead, you would be there.
If I flew away beyond the east or
    lived in the farthest place in the west,
You would be there to lead me;
    you would be there to help me.
I could ask the darkness to hide me or
    the light round me to turn into night,
But even darkness is not dark for you,
    and the night is as bright as the day.

                    Psalm 139, selected verses

The implications of this old yet new understanding of God for how we live are enormous!

Chapter 2

Life

In the beginning, when God created the universe, the earth was formless and desolate. The raging ocean that covered everything was engulfed in total darkness, and the Power of God was moving over the water. By the seventh day, God finished what God had been doing and stopped working. God looked at everything God had made, and was very pleased.

Genesis 1:1 – 2:2, selected verses

There once was a monk named Bruno. He would often rise in the quiet of the night to pray and to chant the psalms. One night, while at prayer, he found himself disturbed by the sound of croaking bullfrogs. He tried to ignore the sound by concentrating on his chanting, but it simply did not work. Finally, he shouted from his window, "Quiet. I'm praying." Immediately his command was obeyed. Every living creature in the swamp nearby held its voice so Brother Bruno could pray in silence. The only problem was that when Bruno went back to praying, another voice, this time the inner voice of his conscience, intruded into his prayer. It said, "Bruno, maybe God is just as pleased with the croaking of the bullfrogs as with your chanting." Bruno scornfully replied, "What can please the ears of God about a frog's croaking?" But the voice persisted. "Bruno, God created the bullfrogs too. Surely God appreciates their singing." Bruno decided to find out why. Leaning out his window he shouted, "Sing!" Immediately the bullfrogs, the birds, the crickets and all the other creatures of the night commenced singing once again. As Bruno listened, eagerly trying to discover what God might appreciate in this cacophony of sound, he started to sense in the noise a beautiful texture, a harmony and a unity, of which his prayers and chants were simply another part. And Bruno went back to chanting the psalms filled with a new sense of the beauty, the wonder, and the sacredness of all of life.

Life is sacred! *All* of life is sacred! Why? Because it arises out of and participates in the very *being* of God. The visible, material world is simply an expression of the invisible, divine spirit-energy that is God. And that makes it holy!

Although the aboriginal people of North America have taught this truth for generations, I learned it from Da Free John. Born as Franklin Jones on Long Island, New York, in 1939, Da Free John was one of the most influential spiritual teachers of my early adult years. During the same period I was learning about the great Christian mystics of the past, I was blessed to encounter a living spiritual genius.

I was browsing in the Bob Miller Bookroom, a popular bookstore close to Toronto's fashionable Yorkville district, when I quite randomly picked up a work called *Easy Death*. I opened the book and began reading the introduction. Never before had I experienced a reaction like I did in that moment. It was as though bolts of lightning illuminated an inner space that prior to that moment had been filled only with murky darkness and confusion. Waves of emotion swept over me and tears filled my eyes. With incisive clarity, Da Free John spoke about the sense of sorrow and separation that lay within the ground of every human psyche, in my case made so pronounced by the death of my brothers. Here at last was someone, a living person, who had plumbed the utmost depths of the human heart. It was clear beyond all doubt that he knew, really knew, what he was describing. It was also clear that, as a result of his experience, he had come to know God. As with Moses on the mountain, as with Jesus in the wilderness, as with the great Christian mystics in their desert cells, this man had come face to face with God and had returned to share his story and his wisdom.

Da Free John's spiritual autobiography, *The Knee of Listening*, provides one of the most fascinating and illuminating accounts ever written of a human being's successful search to know God. As a child, Da Free John had been remarkably aware that he lived within a field of continuous light and bliss that he later named "the bright" and that we would call Spirit. He knew himself to be happy and at one with all that is. As he grew older, however, that early awareness gradually dissipated and instead he was left with a pervasive feeling of sorrow and angst. In his early adulthood, the sense of contradiction between his experience as a child and his present experience became overwhelming. He says, "If God existed, I knew I must find him or die in the process." Thus began his spiritual adventure, unmatched in the annals of contemporary literature.

Da Free John worked first with an American spiritual teacher, Rudi. After several years of disciplined spiritual work, Rudi instructed him to enter into a Lutheran seminary to study Christian theology. Upon finishing his theological studies, Da Free John traveled to India where he engaged in spiritual exercises and intense meditation with the renowned spiritual teacher Baba Muktananda. In the process, he had mystical experiences of many great saints, including the Virgin Mary who instructed him to undertake a pilgrimage to the major Christian holy sites in Europe and the Middle East. Along the way, he experienced additional visions of Jesus and the Virgin Mary. He then returned to America, where he spent close to a year in solitude in the coastal caves of southern California engaged in a radical discipline of meditative introspection. Finally, in a Vedanta Temple in Los Angeles, the absolute experience and truth of God was revealed to him and he went on to write and to teach.

Da Free John's final and great insight, which he achieved by direct intuitive insight rather than through intellectual consideration, was that of radical non-separation. After close to a decade of intense spiritual searching, he discovered himself not just to be made by God, but also to be one with God. Indeed, there is only one true reality and that is God. The entire universe, and all that is in it, is simply an expression of this power and being in space and time and form. All of our searching to discover God leads in the end to a radical discovery about ourselves. We are never separate from God because we are made of God and held in existence by the very power of God.

Throughout history, however, there has existed a sense of dichotomy between the material world and the spiritual world. Many religious people, in particular, have viewed the material world as something base, inferior to the spiritual world, and even evil. As a result, they have judged such things as eating, drinking, engaging in sexual love, and caring for the body, as negative, worldly activities that divert attention from the spiritual realities, the things that truly matter in life. However, when we view the invisible, spiritual dimension of God and the visible, material manifestation of God, as simply two aspects of God's single all-encompassing reality, this changes our entire relationship to the world and to each other.

The Purpose of Life Is Life

When we look at life stripped of the religious dogmas and meaning systems that we have overlaid upon it, we are confronted with this simple reality. Life exists. It is. It has emerged out of an incredible mystery that transcends both space and time. It comes to birth, grows, decays, dies, and then returns to that great mystery from whence it has come.

When Daniele and I were married, we designed a quilt to symbolize these features of life. The quilt is bordered on all sides by a yellow strip of material about two inches wide. The yellow symbolizes the light of God, the great mysterious source from which we have come. The quilted background inside the yellow borders is a rich blue, symbolizing the waters of life, out of which the story of Genesis says God brought forth dry land and the earth. In the middle of the blue background is a circle representing the earth and all life on it. The circle is made from four different types of material representing the four seasons: spring, summer, fall, and winter, both in the natural world and in the lifespan of human beings. The material for spring reveals a lovely pattern of blue and green flowers representing the emergence of new life. The cloth for summer is bright yellow, with multi-colored parrots and monkeys hanging from branches, celebrating the joy of life. The material for fall is a rich, deep orange, reflecting the changing colors of the leaves in the Northern Hemisphere. And the material for winter is a dark abstract (blue, white, and black) symbolizing this cold and fallow time. From the right lower corner of the quilt's yellow border emerge two green vines, separate but intertwining across the waters of life, across the circle of the earth, and eventually leading back into the opposite, upper corner, the yellow representing the great mystery of God. From the lower left corner of the quilt, emerges a red rose symbolizing the love of God pervading the entire universe. For Daniele and me, it is a symbol of our lives embedded in the larger tapestry of life as a whole.

Human beings emerge out of the mystery of life. Yes, we know all about the logistics of sexual intercourse, conception, gestation in the womb, and birth. Yet there is a greater mystery to all of it than this. How do we happen to exist in this moment in time at all? How does anything come to be? How does life itself exist? *Why* does life emerge out of God, the great mystery? We really have no idea. We simply know that it does.

Yet the very fact of our existence suggests that God is predisposed towards life. The Genesis story, in the Hebrew Bible, offers a very simple notion of an anthropomorphic God who, like a human being creating a work of art or like a couple wishing to create a child, intends to create, and then does so. Really, we don't know that God thinks or intends or processes desire as we do. But probably it is not such a bad notion. Fundamentally, what the Genesis story of creation tries to tell us is that God has given rise to life. This suggests that God considers life to be good and worthy of expression. As the Genesis story says, "And God saw that it was good." If that's the case, the most fundamental purpose of life is simply life. This statement has enormous moral and ethical implications, as we shall uncover later.

Life to the Fullest

If the purpose of life is simply life, then God surely intends life to be expressed to its very fullest potential. In the realms of physics and biology, we see some of the processes and principles that God has structured into life to ensure that this happens. As noted earlier, life is structured to emerge out of chaos, to take form, to break down, and then to re-enter the fundamental mix so as to re-emerge in new forms once again. The greater the variety of species, the greater the cross-fertilization, the more mixed up things become, the more exciting, new, and creative possibilities emerge. Darwin's theory of evolution is based on precisely these observations. Jim Collins and Jerry Porras state it this way:

> The central concept of evolutionary theory – and Charles Darwin's great insight – is that species evolve by a process of undirected *variation* ("random genetic mutation") and natural *selection*. Through genetic variation, a species attains "good chances" that some of its members will be well suited to the demands of the environment. As the environment shifts, the genetic variations that best fit the environment tend to get "selected" (that is, the well-suited variations tend to survive and the poorly suited tend to perish – that's what Darwin meant by "survival of the fittest"). The selected (surviving) variations then have greater representation in the gene pool and the species will evolve in that direction. In Darwin's own words: "Multiply, vary, let the strongest survive, and the weakest die."[1]

The theory of evolution does not contradict the role of an underlying God, but simply points out the dynamics this incredible divine reality has designed to achieve its supreme purpose of sustaining and enhancing life to the fullest.

Love

Just as evolutionary processes not only determine and shape life, but also help to enhance and sustain life, so does another key principle assist in sustaining and enhancing all of life, and human life in particular. That principle is love. The Hebrew and Greek Bibles, otherwise known as the Old and New Testaments, describe many different kinds of love. But each contributes in its own way to the creation, sustaining, and enhancement of life.

I have already spoken of two ancient Greek terms – *eros* and *agape* – used to describe two different kinds of love. *Eros*, found in the Greek New Testament, refers to passionate, sexual love. It is essentially egocentric, seeking its object for the sake of its own satisfaction and self-fulfillment. But it does contribute to the creation of life. In addition, I spoke of *agape*, which can best be described by the English word "compassion," and which refers to a deep, generalized sense of empathy for other people. It is a term that was frequently used by the early Christian church and refers less to emotion and more to the exercise of will, of showing love by actions of caring.[2] As such, *agape* love helps to sustain human life.

In the Hebrew Bible, we find another type of love defined by the Hebrew term *hesed*. *Hesed* describes a type of kindness, caring, and commitment that people in relationship are called to exercise towards each other. It also often refers to God's love for humankind.

In the New Testament, we find other kinds of love. *Phileo* and *philia* refer to social love, the affection between friends that serves to enhance and make life so much more enjoyable and meaningful. *Stergo* and *storge* refer to family affection. *Philadelphia* refers to the love between brothers and sisters. *Philanthropia* refers to love for humanity, to general kindness and courtesy.

In all its different manifestations and expressions, love functions to create, sustain, and enhance human life.

Narcissism

Love is absolutely essential for creating, sustaining, and enhancing human life because there is another principle – that works in the opposite manner, to actively promote death. The word narcissism comes from an ancient story told by the Greek writer Ovid, in his well-known work *Metamorphoses*.

The story is about Narcissus, the most beautiful young man imaginable, with whom many young maidens and men fell head-over-heals in love. But such was Narcissus' pride that he spurned them all. One young woman in particular, Echo, eventually withered away from her love for Narcissus, as did many other nymphs who sought to have him return their love. Finally, one spurned nymph issued a prayer to the gods: "So may he himself fall in love, so may he not be able to possess his beloved." The prayer was just, and the god Nemesis heard it.

One day, tired out by the midday heat and from his hunting for game, Narcissus lay down by a beautiful spring, its clear waters glistening like silver, untouched by shepherds, mountain goats, or other animals. Grass grew round about, nourished by the water nearby, and the woods protected the spot from the heat of the sun. While trying to quench his thirst, Narcissus became captivated by the beauty of his own image, which he saw reflected in the pool. Believing the image to be real, he marveled at all the things others saw in him: the deep, lovely eyes; the smooth white skin; the waving locks of hair… Unwise and unheeding, he desired his very self, bestowing kisses upon himself, reaching into the water to embrace himself, all of it in vain. Eventually, he died in a state of unrequited, passionate yearning to embrace the reflection in the pool.[3]

Derived from this story, the word narcissism has come to mean an unhealthy preoccupation with oneself to the exclusion of other people and the needs of the world. Narcissus' downfall was not that he was an evil person, but that he would not *give* himself to other people and their concerns. He would not express care and love for other people because of an overly inflated self-pride. After once too often spurning the love offered to him, he was condemned to his own form of unrequited love.

We all know people who are overly self-centered, vain, and preoccupied with themselves. They seek constantly to be the center of attention and to be in control of everything and everyone. They have difficulty separating their own needs and desires from those of other people. They are psychologically and morally deficient in their ability to see and embrace the larger picture and realities of life. As such, they are forever condemned to admiring their own self-image in the pool of self-absorption.

Although this describes an extreme form of narcissism, one not found in the majority of people, all of us are to a greater or lesser degree afflicted by narcissism. For the majority of us, narcissism takes a much more benign but still potentially damaging form – self-preoccupation with the everyday concerns of life. We are so busy making a living; so preoccupied with our jobs, families, and leisure pursuits; that we have very little free energy or attention to give to the larger picture and issues of life. This includes the needs of other people, the needs of the planet, and the sacred dimension of life, which we call God. Again, it is not that we are bad or evil. Rather, we are just so preoccupied with self-related concerns and issues that we neither see nor give ourselves over to the larger picture of life and its needs. This preoccupation, this myopic self-concern, is detrimental not only to human life, but to life as a whole. In many ways, it has led humankind to the brink of political and ecological disaster.

Ultimately, narcissism is a failure to love, both on a personal level and in the larger circles of life. Thus, the solution to narcissism is not fundamentally political, sociological, or economic, but a resort to love. As suggested by the word *agape*, love needs to be an act of will. It needs to be an intentional act of serving and caring for the well-being of all of life. But in order for this to take place, we must be able to see how we fit into the larger picture and can contribute to the well-being of the whole. The new vision of God contributes to this "seeing."

The Interconnectedness of Life

In the new vision of God, every single aspect of the visible, material world, including every human being, is connected to everything and everyone else by the invisible, all-pervasive, spirit-energy dimension of God. Remember in the last chapter the story of the little fish that asked its mother, "What is this water I hear so much about?" Mom responded, "You silly little fish. It's all around you and within you. Water is what gives you life." It's a good analogy. We all live within an ocean of divine, spirit-energy that connects us together. A Hindu greeting, *namaste*, which means "The God in me greets the God in you," or "The Spirit in me meets the same Spirit in you," expresses something of this idea. When we truly recognize that every living thing is created out of and is sustained by the very same source and power, namely God, we come to see that at the deepest level we are one with everyone and everything else.

The apostle Paul used the analogy of the body to describe this truth.

> Christ is like a single body, which has many parts; it is still one body, even though it is made up of different parts. In the same way, all of us, whether Jews or Gentiles, whether slaves or free, have been baptized into the one body by the same Spirit, and we have all been given the one Spirit to drink.
>
> For the body itself is not made up of only one part, but of many parts. If the foot were to say, "Because I am not a hand, I don't belong to the body," that would not keep it from being a part of the body. And if the ear were to say, "Because I am not an eye, I don't belong to the body," that would not keep it from being a part of the body. If the whole body were just an eye, how could it hear? And if it were only an ear, how could it smell? As it is, however, God put every different part in the body just as God wanted it to be. There would not be a body if it were all only one part! As it is, there are many parts but one body.
>
> 1 Corinthians 12:12–20

Continuing with the analogy of the body, the eyes are connected to the feet by the blood flowing through the veins, and by the nerves and skin and connecting tissue that link the entire body. The well-being of the eyes depends upon the feet being able to move the body to acquire food and resources for the good of the whole body. Likewise, the feet require the eyes to locate food and resources for exactly the same reason. From one perspective, the eyes are quite separate from the feet, but from another perspective they are intimately interconnected by one shared body. Indeed, their life and well-being depend upon each other.

This interdependence of life is illustrated by the story of the blind man and the lame man who came across each other in the forest. The lame man said to the blind man, "Carry me on your back and be my legs and I will be your eyes." Separate but together, they shared one life. Human beings arise out of, are created from, participate in, and share the one life of the invisible Spirit we call God.

This profound spiritual view of life's interconnectedness in God is also mirrored in the natural world around us. Ecologists, for example, describe the interconnectedness of the entire ecosystem. Environmentalist Ian Lowe of Griffiths University, in Australia, relates the following example of this.

> In a study of truffles, an edible underground fungus not to be mistaken for the delicious chocolate truffles, that grow in the dry eucalyptus forest of New South Wales, it was found that the truffles perform a service for the trees near which they are found. Because both truffles and trees extract water and minerals from the soil, trees with truffles in their roots obtain more water and minerals and grow better than those without. The truffles are a favourite food of the long-footed poteroo, an animal related to the kangaroo and now classified as rare. After eating the truffles, the poteroo then excretes the spores of the truffles and thereby enhances the health of the forest. Poteroo, truffle, eucalypt – are all bound together in a remarkable web of interdependence.[4]

Mind you, we do not need an exotic example from Australia to recognize the truth of the interdependence of life on this planet. Trees depend on soil, water, and sunlight to live. Human beings depend on trees to process carbon dioxide in the air and to provide fuel and raw materials for building. Literally everything in the natural world is connected to and depends upon everything else.

In the quilt that Daniele and I designed, there are no words suggesting how it came into being or why. There is no explanation for the richness of color, shape, and movement found within its yellow borders. There is no signature to say who created it. The quilt is silent. But its beauty is captivating, its logic and symmetry entrancing. Layer upon layer of shapes and colors fit together exquisitely. Everything suggests that regardless of who made it and for what reason, a great deal of thought, care, and love went into it.

The purpose of life is simply life. God is predisposed towards life and intends it to be lived or expressed to its fullest potential. In order for this to occur, God has structured into life principles and forces that contribute towards its creation, sustenance, and enhancement. In human life, love is the principle force driving us towards the achievement of God's aim. Although love develops and is expressed in many different ways, its foundation lies in the capacity to see the unity or oneness that links all of life together, the invisible spirit-energy dimension we call God.

And so the spiritual life is about learning to love. It is about learning to see, to feel, and to intuit our connectedness to and within ever-expanding circles of existence: from family, to neighborhood, to community, to country, to the planet and its ecological systems, to the cosmos, and ultimately to the sacred reality of God. When we see those connections profoundly, then our desire to live differently and to serve the world compassionately grows and deepens. This is ultimately what God, the sacred source behind life, is seeking to accomplish in human beings. It is in this spiritual process of learning to love that we achieve our fullest potential and find our deepest happiness.

Chapter 3

Human Destiny, Self-Transcendence & God-Realization

Whoever wants to come with me, must forget himself, carry his cross and follow me.

Whoever tries to save his own life will lose it; but whoever loses his life will save it.

Mark 8:34–35 and Luke 17:33, paraphrased

With the drawing of God's Love and the voice of God's calling,
We shall not cease from exploration
And the end of all our exploring
Will be to arrive where we started
And know the place for the first time.

T. S. Eliot

After the drowning death of my two brothers, I still appeared on the outside to be a fairly normal, happy-go-lucky little boy. I went to school, played with my friends, and did the kinds of things most kids do. But inside, a deep anxiety had settled upon my heart and my mind. Each night before falling asleep, I would call out "good night" to my parents, sometimes a dozen times or more. They sensed something was wrong, but lacked the psychological understanding to help me. They were dealing with their own grief and did not recognize the voice of grief in their child. My goodnight calls were actually a cry for reassurance that Mom and Dad were still there, were still alive. I was developing what today would be called an acute case of "separation anxiety," the fear of being left alone in the world.

At the same time, I was being raised in a deeply religious, Pentecostal household. My dad was a lay preacher for the local Pentecostal church and I attended services on Sunday morning and prayer meetings at night. My parents were not dogmatic fundamentalists. What drew them to the Pentecostal church was its emphasis on knowing the Holy Spirit. One summer, my mom experienced the "in filling" of the Holy Spirit while worshipping at a Pentecostal camp meeting. Walking down the aisle, in a state of ecstasy and completely oblivious to the hundreds of people around her, she praised God while speaking in tongues. I, too, can remember, shortly after the death of my brothers, rolling on the floor of our local Pentecostal church, praising God and speaking in tongues. But it was more an imitation of others than true experience. I remember that my self-consciousness was still quite intact during those seemingly ecstatic moments. Still, within this religious setting, I was learning an important message. It was possible to know God. It was possible to experience the Spirit of God so deeply that you could entirely forget about yourself in God. All this was possible, because the Spirit of God was always with us. For a little boy whose two brothers had just died, this was a highly charged message.

From the beginning of this book, I have suggested that we need a new understanding of God. In this chapter, I suggest that we need something else, too. That "something" is an entirely new understanding of our human destiny or evolution in God.

Jesus clearly names that destiny in the words that begin this chapter. He says, in effect, "To follow me you must learn to leave your self behind." In other places he expands on this comment, suggesting that if we learn to leave the self behind, we will be ushered into the realm of God, not in some far off heaven, but here and now. To live with love and compassion, to live with courage and joy, we must learn to let go of our limited selves to find our true identity in God. I can state it no more succinctly than this. In the process of letting go of self, we find life in all its fullness.

This is the central message of every major world religion, including that started by Jesus. This is the quest of all spiritual practice, the destiny that spiritual seekers the world over attempt to fulfill. This is the quest that became my destiny upon the death of my two brothers.

The Traditional Understanding of the Purpose of Christianity

Salvation through Jesus

Jesus taught a spiritual path of self-transcending love for God and humankind. "Love the Lord your God with all your heart and soul and mind, and your neighbor as yourself. Thereby, fulfill the law and the prophets" (Matthew 22:34–40, paraphrased). Jesus understood this to be the core message of Judaism, his religion of birth. However, Jesus experienced the Judaism of his day as having been distorted by a spirit of legalism and dogmatism that had very little to do with its core message. He sought to correct that situation. If he came today, he would address the same situation in Christianity.

For 2000 years, the Christian church has proclaimed that the central message and significance of Jesus' life was to save human beings from their sins. This saving act would allow us to go to a glorious realm called heaven after we die. Entire books have been written on how and why the church got snared in this dogma. Suffice it to say here that much of this understanding is based on the New Testament theology of Paul, which, in turn, was based on the Orthodox Judaism of Paul's day. Although Paul was a committed Christian convert, he never actually left his orthodox Jewish roots. In some very significant ways, he fundamentally misunderstood what Jesus taught and what Jesus' ministry was all about.

Paul and the early church desperately needed to find a reason for the death of Jesus, their spiritual leader. They needed to be able to make sense of his execution by the Romans. In this, they were no different than anyone else. Everyone tries to make sense of suffering in life, to find a reason for our suffering. The early Jesus movement proclaimed Jesus as their risen Lord, not just to Gentiles, but also to Jews. No doubt the people on the receiving end of this proclamation will have asked skeptically, "If Jesus was so special and so powerful, why did he end up being tried and killed as a common criminal by the Romans?" The answer that Paul and the early church developed was one their Jewish listeners, accustomed as they were to the ancient practice of animal sacrifice, would have found familiar. Jesus' death was not an accident, but an intentional act by God, who required an eternal sacrifice for human sin. It was a requirement demanded by God's justice, and a redemption offered in God's love.

With this doctrine, often referred to as the atonement, the early church transformed the death of Jesus from a horrible, confusing loss, into a profound and uplifting act of redemption for the entire world! Today, however, anyone who views this doctrine of the atonement with even a little objectivity sees a very different picture. It is an interpretation developed by the early church desperate to put a positive spin on the death of their spiritual leader. It is simply an idea, a conceptual belief, which no longer makes sense to the majority of women and men outside the church, and to fewer and fewer men and women inside the church.

There is, however, another reason why the church fixed its attention on the theme of Jesus as an eternal sacrifice for human sin – a much darker and more sinister reason. Specifically, this belief provided the church with a very powerful and convenient means of control over people's lives. Over time, the Christian church constructed a progressively more restrictive theology. It proclaimed that the only way to enter heaven, to enter into eternal life after we died, was through belief and vicarious participation in the death and sacrifice of Jesus for human sin. This sacrifice became effective through participation in the Eucharist, or the Lord's Supper, whereby the whole death and resurrection of Jesus was relived over and over again. Of course, the administrator of the sacrament of the Lord's Supper was the church. You could only be granted permission to partake of the Lord's Supper by the church. And if you were not given that permission, or had that permission removed by a process known as excommunication, you would be damned to hell for all eternity.

For many Protestant churches, participation in the Lord's Supper was not required for salvation. All that was required to go to heaven after death was to publicly profess acceptance of Jesus as your personal savior, and as the sacrifice for your sins. If this confession was not made, however, you would still be condemned to eternal hellfire.

As I've said, this doctrine of salvation originally developed from the need of the early church to understand and make sense of the death of Jesus. But over time, it developed into a powerful methodology of control over people's lives by a church that increasingly sought to hold power over society at large. No wonder so many churches, still today, seek to propagate this belief system, even as it has become less and less credible to more and more people the world over. It is time for the Christian church to acknowledge this horrible past, to let go of this "crazy-making" doctrine, and to embrace a much more profound understanding of the significance of Jesus' life and ministry.

The "social gospel"

Many churches today have begun to see the emptiness of the doctrine of vicarious salvation. However, few have rejected it outright for fear of alienating people. Instead, mainline churches have quietly begun to replace this doctrine with a new theological emphasis. This new focus consists of caring for the world as Jesus cared for the world in his life and ministry. Many Christian churches are becoming a religious counterpart to the secular and humanist groups struggling for every conceivable cause under the sun. These causes range from the call to ecological stewardship, to pacifism, to feminism, to abolition of the death penalty, and so on. Indeed, many Christians work at the forefront of these movements to create a more decent and caring, a more just and equitable earth. The situation calls to mind people such as Dr. Martin Luther King Jr., who led the civil rights movement in the United States; Nelson Mandela and Desmond Tutu, who led the struggle against apartheid in South Africa; and Mother Teresa, who took care of the outcasts and who fought poverty in India. The list of Christian women and men who have helped to make the world a significantly better place is endless.

But despite this, people have discovered that while caring for the planet is a wonderful thing to do, it does not necessarily answer the deepest longings and yearnings of the human heart and mind.

Furthermore, the church is discovering that people can be profoundly moral, ethical, and principled in their lives, without reference to religion. The human race is slowly maturing and large groups of people are starting to assume moral and ethical responsibility for the planet as a fundamental human duty. Thus, the Christian church has tried to remake itself as the moral champion of society only to find that many people no longer feel a need for the church to fulfill that role.

The traditional *raison d'être* of the church, as the mediator of the death of Jesus as salvation for human sin, no longer persuades thinking men and women. Yet neither does the newer social gospel, and the attempt of the church to be society's moral and ethical champion. This brings us, then, to the true purpose of religion and spirituality, and to the most important role that the church and organized religion can play in the life of contemporary society.

A New Reason for Being

The famous spiritual director Anthony de Mello tells a story about a lion taken into captivity. This lion was thrown into a concentration camp where, to his amazement, he found all sorts of other lions, many of whom had been there for years, and some for all of their lives. The lions had created a society for themselves. Some were business lions; others were social conveners; still others the maintainers of lion culture, who kept alive the lion traditions and memories of times before life in the concentration camp. Some were religious lions, who met primarily to sing songs and to talk about a future jungle, in which there would be no more fences. From time to time there would be uprisings; the lions would plot against their captors and some of the guards, or other lions, would be killed.

As he looked around, the newcomer noticed one lion who always seemed deep in thought, a loner who mostly kept away from the other lions. There was something about him that commanded the other lions' admiration and hostility, for his presence aroused fear and self-doubt. When approached by the newcomer this lion said to him, "Join no group. These poor sods are busy with everything, except that which is essential." "And what is that," asked the newcomer. "Studying the fence," replied the wise lion.

I suggested at the beginning of this chapter that the true purpose of religion has been revealed to us by Jesus. That purpose is to facilitate our letting go of "self" so that we might enter into the realm of heaven, not as some future place after we die, but as an awareness here and now of our oneness with God, and of God's Spirit presence pervading all of life. This awareness gives birth to joy, courage, peace, and compassion. I now want to consider this thing called "self," also named "ego" in the spiritual traditions and by psychologists – the fence in de Mello's story of the lions. To examine the self is to examine the fences that lock us out from the experience of bliss and joy God intends for our lives, both individually and collectively.

The Formation of Human Identity

The New Yorker once ran a cartoon in which a little boy sits on his father's knee. The father is looking at a report card the little boy has just brought home from school and has a dark scowl on his face. The little boy, with a rather impish expression, asks his father the following question: "What do you think it is, Dad, heredity or environment?"

In order to discuss the self or the ego, we need first to look at the formation of human identity. This is because the two are inextricably connected;

in fact, we often interchange the terms. We say, for example, that a person with a strong identity possesses a strong ego or sense of self, and that a person with a weak identity possesses a weak ego or sense of self. If we ask what *Jesus* meant when he encouraged us to let go of self, we discover that he wanted us to let go of many of the self-definitions that determine our sense of identity, who we think we are. We define our identity in so many ways; according to sex, culture, roles, and so on. But the spiritual traditions, and what Jesus seems to suggest, is that our true identity is far greater than anything these definitions imply. All of our self-definitions place limits on our capacity for freedom and joy and therefore we must find ways to transcend them. Before discussing how we can do this, however, it will be helpful to consider how we develop our sense of identity in the first place.

Body image

First and foremost, the development of human identity is strongly linked to our physical representation in the world, also referred to as body image. Each of us represents a unique physical expression of life, as unique and distinct as our fingerprints. Except in the case of identical twins, no two "bodies" are alike. Different in time and space from every other "body" around us, our bodies give us a sense of being separate and distinct. Our sense of ego or identity is strongly linked with the characteristics of our bodies, be they male or female, strong or weak, athletic or sedentary, healthy and whole or disabled in some way. Our sense of identity is also shaped by how our society values our body characteristics. For example, if a society values males over females, this will strongly influence our sense of self-esteem and well-being. Our physical attributes, and society's response to those attributes, determine much of our emotional, mental, and psychological functioning. Our identity is inextricably wrapped up in our physical nature.

Character and personality

In addition to developing a sense of identity that is linked to our body, from early childhood on each person begins to establish a unique character and personality. This character or personality is based on and defined by a set of likes and dislikes, interests and inclinations, motivations and patterns of relating to other people and to the world. Some of these are genetically "hardwired" into our human makeup. Others are established as a result of socialization processes. For instance, introversion and extroversion may be inherited or "hardwired" character traits, whereas the preference for drama over sport, or for history over literature may be a result of socialization processes, such as the influence of family, peers, and teachers. Over time, then, we become identified with a variety of specific interests and characteristics, some of which are built-in and some of which are acquired. Today, studies in genetics reveal a very complex interplay between inherited traits and sociological forces such as race, culture, religion, education, and family dynamics, all of which combine to establish human personality.

Language and the "I" construct

The above factors, illustrated in very broad strokes, are the commonly understood ingredients that contribute to the formation of human identity or ego. But there is another very significant factor that makes its own contribution – language. All languages possess the personal pronouns "I" and "me," "you" and "we." Language is based on the assumption that we exist as separate, discrete entities in the world. As we use the words "I" or "me," consciously or unconsciously, day after day, every day of our lives, our psyches generate an unassailable image of ourselves as independent, separate, physically discrete entities.

The spiritual dimension of human identity

The self or ego consists of all those factors that shape and determine our sense of identity, as outlined above. However, the spiritual traditions of the world suggest that these things comprise only part of the puzzle that in its totality makes up the human identity or person. This is where the spiritual journey becomes truly fascinating!

It is true that we exist as discrete biological entities. At the same time, we are also expressions of the single, underlying power and force that pervades all of existence, which we call God. A field can have numerous flowers of different type, shape, size, and color growing out of the soil. Yet it is one and the same field, one and the same soil giving rise to them all. Thus, the underlying soil is also a part of the identity and being of the flowers.

The spiritual traditions suggest that the fundamental source of suffering in human life comes from the fixation of our attention upon the qualities that define our sense of identity as separate and unique, namely the ego or self. Because we are so fixated upon our individuality, we do not see the underlying power from which we receive life and in which we live. This is the source of our undoing. If we could see and experience ourselves with the "genius of the AND" – as both separate and distinct and, at the same time, as "one with" the universal source of life – everything would change. If, as mentioned in the previous chapter, we could see our individual lives as the foreground of our existence and the ever-present Spirit of God as the background (a capacity possessed by the great mystics), we would know the peace and bliss of living consciously in God. In such lives, love emerges as we recognize everyone and all of life to be expressions of the one, shared life that is God. When we recognize our sisters and brothers around the world as literally expressions of the one life of God, as being the same as ourselves, then our social, political, and economic structures would all change.

When Jesus calls us to forget our selves, to leave our selves behind, he is not calling us to deny that we are discrete, flesh-and-blood human beings with unique personalities. Jesus himself was a unique, physical, human being with a remarkably distinctive personality. Rather, he is calling us to stop identifying ourselves solely by the characteristics that define our separateness and uniqueness, and instead to recognize our oneness and identity with God and with him. Jesus says, "I am in God, and you are in me, and I in you" (John 14:20, paraphrase). We are all bound up in each other, in God, and in Jesus.

This is how we need to see our larger identity. But instead, we live in a form of spiritual and psychological bondage by identifying solely with human characteristics and qualities that define us as limited and mortal, and that destine us only for decay and death. Shortly, we shall consider what our lives would be like if we were free from this bondage. But first we need to consider how this fixation on our limiting self-definitions occurs and why we do not see the other dimension to our human existence – the divine, God dimension in which we live.

Mind, awareness, and attention

In order to understand this spiritual bondage, we need to speak about three central components of human life: mind, awareness, and attention. To date, neuro-scientists have gained very little understanding of how any of these three dynamics emerge or function. Some believe that mind, awareness, and attention are by-products of purely physiological processes. Others believe them to be the result of physiological and psycho-spiritual processes that transcend the body and brain. But how they arise really does not matter. What matters is the role they play in our lives.

For our present purpose, "mind" can be understood as the human apparatus that produces thoughts, images, emotional states, memories, dreams, desires, and so on.

The second concept we need to understand is "awareness." Awareness or consciousness can be described as the inner light that enables human beings to experience themselves as alive. By virtue of awareness or consciousness, we know ourselves to exist; we are conscious of ourselves as human beings.

Finally, "attention" is the mechanism that directs or focuses awareness on various objects arising both in our mind and in the world around us. Attention is the selection and focusing process that we use to choose what we will look at, think about, or consider in any moment of time. In other words, attention chooses what we will become aware of.

To illustrate the relationship between these three processes, we can use the analogy of a spotlight in a live theater or concert hall. On the stage, a play is taking place. Actors come and go, express lines and emotional states, engage in relationships with one another, and move off stage. However, the audience can see none of this unless light shines on the stage. The light is what enables the audience to be aware that a play is going on and to see what is taking place. This scenario parallels the functioning of our minds and of our lives. We think and talk, work and play, and experience a variety of emotional states in relationship with other people. The light symbolizes awareness or consciousness in our own lives. We could not be conscious of what goes on in our lives, either of our inner thoughts and feelings, or of our activities in the world, were it not for the light of awareness or consciousness. Returning to the metaphor, in the theater, the spotlight operator can choose where to shine the light. The audience can only see the action under the spotlight. One side of the stage may be brightly lit; the other side may be left in the dark. *Attention* functions as the spotlight apparatus, directing awareness to various things within ourselves, such as thoughts, feelings and memories; as well as to various objects and activities outside ourselves in the world, such as a television set, a tree, or a conversation with someone.

The bondage of attention

Our dilemma, the conundrum that keeps us from growing spiritually, is that in most cases, our attention is not free to move where we wish it to move. Our attention becomes bound or fixated in life to those things that constitute our human limitations and that define us as separate. These consist of a whole host of inner objects – thoughts, memories, feelings, and desires, as well as a whole range of objects in the outer world – our bodies, other people, events, and all manner of things from which it cannot freely move away.

Unfortunately, this is particularly true of painful thoughts, feelings, events, and people. A relationship that has come to an end either through separation or death has a way of absorbing and attracting our attention so that it is not free. We cannot stop thinking about what went wrong, or about memories of life with the other person. We keep thinking "what if," and may mercilessly berate ourselves or the other person in our own minds. A medical situation or a workplace circumstance may absorb our attention much more than is necessary or healthy for us. Certainly, we need to think about and work to resolve problems. But the amount of thinking and obsessing we apply to our problems is generally much greater than is warranted or necessary. Yet we cannot help ourselves.

Attention also has a tendency to become fixated upon or bound to objects of attraction or stimulation that, in excess, may be totally unhealthy for us. Sex, food, and recreational drugs of various sorts, can all absorb our attention and become addictions in our lives. Or we may become fixated on the acquisition of material objects, such as houses, cars, clothing, and recreational objects like boats, televisions, computers, and the like. We become obsessed with such things far beyond what is healthy either for us or for the planet.

But the most common thing to which our attention becomes fixated or bound is our work. Our work can be enormously interesting and important, and it is certainly a principal source of security in life. Work can be a very healthy place to put our attention, but when we are not free to leave it behind we become bound to it, often to the detriment of our families and our own physical health.

When attention lacks the freedom to move when and where we wish to move it, then we are not free as human beings. The thoughts, feelings, people, activities, and objects to which our attention becomes bound govern our lives. Even more significantly, when attention is bound to the ego or self, it continues to reinforce and define our sense of self and identity as separate, material beings.

The spiritual calling in life is to free attention so that it can gravitate towards and focus upon the infinite, spiritual reality of human life, and identify it as a key component of our identity and existence. In the process of becoming ever freer, attention does not just open for us the possibility of discovering an entirely new, unbounded, blissful, and divine dimension of life. It also leads to some very wonderful and practical consequences along the way. We shall consider these first, and finally look at the ultimate consequence of freeing our attention.

Consequences of Free Attention

When attention is not free, it contributes to a host of problems that lead to suffering in life. The less bound to thought patterns, people, objects, and defined activities attention becomes, the more relaxed and enjoyable life becomes.

Freedom from inwardness

When I was working for my denomination as the Conference Minister for Personnel and Global Justice in North Bay, Ontario, I met a couple who were moving to our region from Toronto. They were part of the Catholic worker movement. He was a carpenter and she was a social worker. For the previous ten years in Toronto, they had opened their house to needy people from the streets: psychiatric patients, drug addicts, and runaways, all of whom had fallen through the cracks in the social safety net. Over supper in my home one evening, they told me of their experiences. Frequently they would come home to find the police parked in front of the house, called there by a neighbor; or they would find the front picture window smashed because two of their guests got into a fight and threw furniture through it. But they continued to invite such people into their lives and home because they held deeply to the commitment to serve the poorest amongst us with the love and care of Christ. When I met them, they had moved to a small, economically depressed town in the area, to open a Catholic worker house there. At the end of the evening, I asked the woman, "How have you grown spiritually through this whole ten year process?" Her answer surprised me with its simplicity. She said, "You know, it's no big deal. All I can say is that today I'm inwardly a quieter and more relaxed person. I simply don't get as uptight about stuff anymore."

One symptom of bound attention is an excessive sense of inwardness that leads to a feeling of separation from other people and from life in the world. We all know people who are obsessive thinkers. Often, they are so fixated in their own minds, in their own inner thoughts, images and feelings, that they have poor listening skills and consequently lack the ability to respond and relate effectively to other people. Such people also see very little of the world around them. Although they live in the world, their constant, inner verbalization and thinking creates a screen through which everything gets filtered – usually in a way that only serves to reinforce their sense of separateness from the world.

As our attention becomes increasingly free of such inwardness and excessive absorption in states of mind, we become less self-preoccupied and self-concerned. In addition, we begin to see the world and other people more clearly and realistically. Rather than observing the world through all of our thoughts and feelings, rather than trying to force the world to fit into our mental image of how it should be, we become gentler and more accepting of the ways things and people are. Over time, my dinner guest had developed the capacity for free attention. The headaches and hassles of ordinary life no longer possessed the same power to attract and fixate her attention. She could let go of "stuff" more easily and became much more relaxed and accepting in the process.

Freedom to be spontaneous

When our attention is not free to move easily and at will, we lack spontaneity in our lives. Spontaneity consists of the ability to shift our attention easily and at will to new people, circumstances, and opportunities that are constantly emerging. However, if our attention is fixated on present thought patterns, activities, objects, and people, we have a hard time shifting gears to the new circumstance.

People with free attention are less defined by established patterns of thinking and being. Therefore, they are more willing to take risks and to engage in creative endeavors even though there may be no guarantee of success. In relationships they are more sexually demonstrative, expressive of care and joy, and are less governed by the need to act within socially established roles and expectations. Parents are less concerned about playing specific roles, such as nurturer and disciplinarian, and can simply respond freely to their children as the moment and circumstance dictate, either with joy and caring, or with appropriate discipline as they understand it.

Freedom from attachment to results and desires

For several years, I was involved with a local chapter of Da Free John's spiritual community in Toronto, helping members of the community renovate an ashram and bookstore. However, I had very little carpentry experience and was basically a gofer. One day, Jack, one of the ministers in the community, asked me to attach some drywall to a section of wall framing. He gave me a quick lesson, then moved on to another task with some other helpers. I don't remember exactly how, but I thoroughly botched my first effort to hang the drywall. Either it didn't hang straight, or didn't line up with some other drywall already in place. But what I do remember most clearly was Jack's response to my dismal efforts. I called him over and we both agreed I had to rip the whole thing down. Yet no flicker of annoyance or aggravation crossed his face, nor did he disparage the job I had done. With a quiet and calm awareness, he simply accepted what was. I observed that same characteristic about him through my entire time in the community. He wasn't flat, or dull. Like the woman I mentioned earlier, he simply appeared centered and serene in the midst of life's ups and downs.

Jack demonstrated the potential of free attention in the workplace. At work, people with free attention will be active and productive, but not obsessed with a particular result. This requires some reflection on the nature of desire. Despite the Buddha's notion that desire lies at the root of all suffering and must be extinguished, desire can be, in fact, a very strong and positive motivating force. The desires to be sexually active, to have children, to engage in work that is meaningful, to participate in certain forms of play and artistic endeavor are all healthy and valuable. Desires arise naturally within us. But when our attention is free to move where we choose, we no longer need to cling to our desires. We experience greater freedom to allow them to be, to hang on to them if we choose, but also to let them go. What this means for work, and for any kind of action, is that we may desire to achieve a result, but if the result is not achieved in the manner expected we can shift gears or turn in another direction. We can accept what life brings and move on.

Freedom to choose how we respond

Generally, we remain largely unaware of how and when thoughts, images, and feelings arise within ourselves. Likewise, we are often unaware of how and when our actions occur in response to these arising thoughts and feelings. Somebody insults us and we automatically lash out with a sarcastic remark. A feeling of sorrow overwhelms us and we withdraw from our partner or friends into a self-imposed isolation. As attention becomes freer, we become more aware of how emotional states and thought patterns dictate our behavior.

Stephen Covey speaks about the word "responsible." He notes that we can break the word down into its two roots to discover its deeper meaning. "Responsible" becomes "response able." As we become more aware, as our attention becomes freer to look at emerging thoughts and emotions and is not so bound by them, we become more "response able," or able to respond as we choose. Between any stimulus and its response there is a gap, a brief amount of time during which we can choose how to respond, if we are aware of it. As attention becomes freer and self-awareness increases, we develop a greater freedom to respond as we choose. We become less robotic and automated in our functioning.

Emotional freedom

Free attention also leads to a much deeper and richer emotional life. Emotions still arise. Anger, sadness, joy, and exuberant laughter all continue to occur quite spontaneously. But we no longer hang on to our emotional states. We can let them go and can move on with the flow of life.

It is quite evident that Jesus had this ability. People may think that a spiritual genius or master never gets angry or sad. But this is not true. Jesus could get quite angry, as demonstrated when he threw the moneychangers out of the temple. But his anger passed when the circumstance had ended. He could also be deeply sad and filled with grief, as when his friend Lazarus died. But his sadness and grief likewise passed spontaneously as the circumstance changed. From an emotional perspective, free attention allows us to live richer and more varied lives. This is because we no longer try to shut down painful emotions or attempt to rein in joyous and exuberant ones. We can allow ourselves to experience and to express the full range of our emotions.

The expansion of awareness

I noted above that as attention moves more easily across the range of inner and outer objects, we become less fixated upon and identified with certain ideas, objects, and even self-concepts. In the process, we become more self-aware. That is to say that awareness itself, rather than the *contents* of awareness, becomes much more our moment-to-moment experience. We become more conscious and present in the world as simple awareness.

The objects to which our attention is bound usually govern our sense of self. If my attention is fixed upon my children, I think of myself primarily as a parent. If my attention is fixed upon my work, I think of myself primarily as a worker; for example, as a carpenter, executive, or lawyer. But as our attention becomes freed from attachment to objects, in our minds or in the outer world, we become less identified with those objects. We still work and we still play with our children; we still consider them, but we no longer identify ourselves with them. In the process, a profound shift in our sense of identity begins to occur. We begin to understand and experience ourselves as the light of awareness, the light that enables us to experience both the inner world of our psyche and the outer world in which we live, move, work, and play.

Freedom from defensiveness

A member of my congregation has often commented on my capacity not to respond in anger or defensiveness to people's put-downs or negativity in the life of our community. He sometimes says to me, "David, you are the least defensive person I know." This capacity, in my case, is partly the result of a deep awareness of how unhealthy a defensive posture can be in life. But it is also a result of free attention. As we begin to identify with the quality of pure awareness and free attention, rather than with defining roles or positions, we can relate to people more freely and playfully. The opinions of others no longer determine our sense of self. We can receive and hear criticism, but then let it go. We learn from it, but do not dwell on it. Attention constantly moves on. We also feel freer to share creative criticism with others because we no longer are so worried about receiving it in return. Criticism does not define who we are. All of this leads to much greater honesty and openness in our relationships. Someone once said, "Until the age of 40, whenever I walked into a room, I used to worry about what people thought of me. Now that I've turned 40, I have resolved to focus instead on what I think about other people." I like that. Regardless of the age, achieving this maturity is something we all recognize as valuable to our lives.

Freedom from the need for control

A bus driver in New York City once approached a spiritual master with the following complaint. "Master," he said, "I am going mad driving a bus. People are crazy. Everyone is out to get me. They're cutting me off, yelling and swearing at me, giving rude hand signals, speeding through red lights. I think I'm going to have to quit. I come home at night and get upset with my wife and kids. My meditation practice has gone down the drain. What should I do?" The master simply said, "My son, when you start your shift tomorrow morning, think of your day as a spiritual game. You and all the other drivers on the streets are simply players. The object of the game is to see who can throw the other person off their equilibrium. The driver who passes out the most love throughout the day, and who manages to stay the most centered, wins the game." A few weeks later, the bus driver came back to the spiritual master and said, "Master, your advice was amazing. I started to watch for all the different ways people were trying to throw me off kilter and became very adept at sidestepping them. I started smiling and blowing kisses to nasty drivers and yelling to them out the window, 'God bless you.' And it's working. I'm not as tired anymore, and I'm much more relaxed at the end of my shift."

The need for control drives us to distraction and can cause all sorts of severe health issues, including high levels of stress. This need stems from an excessive sense of being a separate "I." The more our attention is fixated on being a separate "I," the more we feel threatened by life's circumstances and relationships. We become obsessed with our mortality and life threatens to spin out of control destroying our sense of equilibrium. Therefore, we constantly need to order and control events and people to create for ourselves an illusion of security and immortality. As attention becomes less fixated on our sense of being a separate "I," as we begin to identify more with the unchanging, underlying awareness flowing through life, we can give ourselves over to life with abandon. As we come to appreciate the random and chaotic nature of life, we are not so concerned with trying to control the way circumstances unfold. Yes, disappointments and losses occur, but we can give our being over to life, with a continuous and delightful sense of anticipation for the surprises to be revealed, surprises that are good and joyous, but also surprises that can bring pain and sorrow.

When the bus driver began to view life as a spiritual game, he stopped taking it so personally. No longer was he the center of the universe and the object of everyone's animosity. Rather, he became simply a player in the larger flow of life. The result was a profound sense of liberation.

God Realization and Enlightenment

The righteous will then answer him, "When, Lord, did we ever see you hungry and feed you, or thirsty and give you a drink? When did we ever see you a stranger and welcome you in our homes, or naked and clothe you? When did we ever see you sick or in prison, and visit you?" The King will reply, "I tell you, whenever you did this for one of the least important of these children of mine, you did it for me!"

Matthew 25:37–40

A little boy was walking home from Sunday school one day. He couldn't get the teacher's remark out of his head: "When you give something to another person, you are really giving it to Jesus." Walking through a park, he noticed an old woman on a bench. She looked lonely and hungry so he sat down beside her, took out a chocolate bar he had been saving, and offered some to her. She accepted with a smile. He liked her smile so much he gave her some more. They sat in silence exchanging gentle smiles. Finally, the little boy got up to leave. As he began to walk away, he turned, ran back, and gave the woman a big hug. And she gave him her very best smile. When he arrived home, his mother saw a big smile on his face and asked, "What makes you so happy today?" He said, "I shared my chocolate bar with Jesus and she has a great big smile." Meanwhile, the old woman returned to her little apartment where she lived with her sister. "You're all smiles," said the sister. "What makes you so happy today?" To which she replied, "I was sitting in the park, eating a chocolate bar with Jesus. And you know, he's a lot younger than I expected."

It is a nice sentiment to suggest that we need to learn to see the face of Christ, or the face of God, in everyone we meet; that when we do something for somebody else, we are really doing it for Jesus. But this idea has a radical and literal basis in the deepest dimensions of the spiritual life. And the capacity to truly see the face of God in everyone we meet represents the very deepest and highest attainment of the spiritual life.

When attention is freed of fixation, of addiction and bondage to the various objects of the mind and of the external world around us, including painful and angst ridden thoughts and emotional states, fascinations with sex or violence and the many entertainments provided by the media, desires for money, different relationships, and so on; when attention becomes free to move where we wish it to move, then an enormously wonderful possibility opens up for us. We are ready to discover what Jesus called "the realm of heaven," or "kingdom of heaven," located here and now on earth and in our lives.

> The kingdom of heaven is like this. A man happens to find a treasure hidden in a field. He covers it up again, and is so happy that he goes and sells everything he has, and then goes back and buys the field. Also, the kingdom is like this. A man is looking for fine pearls, and when he finds one that is unusually fine, he goes and sells everything he has, and buys that pearl.
>
> Matthew 13:44–45

When attention is no longer bound, then the spiritual person is free to focus upon the infinite being and reality of God. And when we place our attention ever more permanently upon the Ultimate Source, something quite amazing occurs within our psyche. A transformation of awareness and consciousness occurs, and we literally begin to see God everywhere and in everyone. We begin to see God as the ultimate reality, as the sacred oneness that gives rise to and connects all of life together. God is present in the world and in our lives all the time, underlying and supporting all of existence in each and every moment.

By the time we enter fully into this awareness, it does not come as something strange or new, but as something that has been progressively dawning upon us. We recognize it as the reality that has been there all along.

> And the end of all our exploring
> Will be to arrive where we started
> And know the place for the first time.
> T. S. Eliot

Of course, our attention is still free to move to various objects within the mind and within the world around us, but at the same time we remain constantly aware of the oneness, the sacred dimension of life, the ultimate connecting reality. This state or condition has been referred to in some of the world's spiritual traditions as God-realization or enlightenment.

When God-realization or enlightenment occurs, a paradoxical but wonderful transformation takes place in regard to our sense of identity. Whereas previously we defined or identified ourselves in terms of our ego, our sense of separateness or distinctness, we now become identified with the very being and power of God. We still understand that we are limited, mortal, biological life forms. But we also recognize ourselves and others to be expressions of God. We live out of the paradoxical, "genius of the AND" realization that we are divine and human at the same time. As human beings, we recognize our dependence upon God. This gives rise to a deep sense of humility and gratitude for the gift of life. At the same time, we live with a tremendous sense of freedom and power, because we recognize that we do not simply exist as limited, biological life forms, but as the reality of God, too, which continues to exist after we die.

What I am speaking about probably borders on the unimaginable for most people, so unaccustomed are we to this possibility. To their great discredit, the world's religions have not revealed the true depths of their spiritual traditions; have not helped people to understand the incredible potential for joy, bliss, and freedom inherent within life. But it is precisely to this life that Jesus calls us when he asks us to leave self behind, to renounce the ego, and to follow him. This is the treasure of great value that a person finds buried in a field, and sells everything he or she has in order to acquire. This is the realm of heaven, lived here on earth today. This is the eternally old and new task, the grand purpose of the religious endeavor and quest in today's world. Religion is not about providing or ensuring salvation in some future life, but about leading us into the life God intended here and now, in this world – a life beyond self, a life beyond the limiting definitions of the ego, a life without narcissism.

Because of the difficulty of the path of self-transcending love taught by Jesus, the church succumbed to teaching an easy path of intellectual belief in, and assent to doctrine: specifically, the doctrine of the atonement, that the death of Jesus was a sacrifice for human sin. Jesus' life was indeed a sacrifice, but it was a sacrifice of the human self or ego; the same sacrifice he calls each of us to make.

Developing free attention, transcending limiting "self" definitions, and de-conditioning and disengaging the ego is incredibly difficult work. It is difficult because the bondage of attention to the self-limiting objects of mind and world is so ingrained into our individual and collective lives. In addition, our society and our religious institutions are uninformed, and lack the structure and resources to support those who have given themselves over to this grand venture. Most of all, there are very few coaches and spiritual masters truly experienced in this way of life who can help people on this journey. But this is the true role of religious institutions. Religious institutions and churches need to be places that train people in the psychological and spiritual processes of self or ego-transcendence and they need to possess the resources, teachers, wise techniques, and methodologies to do so.

In the next section, we shall look at the methodologies and practices of the spiritual life that work to break down the fences that keep us in bondage to a sense of self that is governed so much by limitation and sorrow, and that lead to an expanded awareness and understanding of our human identity, one rooted in the very being of God.

REALIZING
THE VISION

Chapter 4

Faith

"I assure you that if you have faith as big as a mustard seed, you
can say to this hill, 'Go from here to there!' and it will go. You
could do anything!"

Matthew 17:20

*A tourist was peering over the edge of Niagara Falls when in his zeal he lost
his footing and plunged over the side. While falling, he managed to grab hold
of a little scrubby bush growing out of the side of the cliff. Filled with terror, he
called out, "Is there anyone up there? Can anyone help me?" Suddenly, he heard a
reassuring voice say, "I'm here, the Lord your God." The man said, "Dear God,
I'm so glad you came along. I can't hold on much longer." The Lord said, "Before I
can help you, I want to know if you have faith in me." The man answered, "Lord,
I do have faith. I go to church every Sunday, sometimes even on Wednesdays. I
read my Bible, pray every day, even put a few dollars on the collection plate."
The Lord replied, "Yes, yes, but do you really have faith in me?" By this time the
man was getting desperate. "Lord, you can't possibly know just how much faith I
have in you." The Lord then said, "Well, good. Now let go of the bush." The man
stammered, "But, but Lord." The voice of the Lord came back, "If you really have
faith in me, let go of that bush." The man was silent for a long time and then called
out, "Is there anyone else up there?"*

Faith is a critical ingredient of life! Organized religious traditions have long proclaimed this fact, but people also recognize it intuitively.

When my brothers drowned, my parents' faith in God was seriously challenged. Years later, my mother told me about a dream she had had at the time, in which the devil appeared to her complete with tail and pitchfork. "This is what you get for believing in God," he sneered at her. There were many days when she felt herself tottering on the edge of a long black tunnel leading to insanity. Two things helped her to maintain a hold on reality. The first was her love for me and the need to care for me. The second was her faith in God. At the core of her being, she believed that God was just and loving, and that the universe was a good and loving place despite its horrors and losses. In the deepest recesses of her heart and mind, she possessed a conviction that the death of my brothers had a meaning and that it served some kind of purpose in the larger mystery and unfolding of God's creation. Like Job, she didn't understand *why* she had to suffer this loss, every parent's worst nightmare, but she continued to trust in the mysterious ways and love of God.

Over the years, I have worked with people with cancer, heart disease, and other life-threatening ailments. Statistically, many of them should have died. Instead, they overcame their illnesses to carry on with happy and full lives. Many of these people claim what medical scientists today are beginning to acknowledge – that faith provided them with a hopeful, optimistic attitude that contributed to their healing.

I also have known many people who have faced other serious challenges to do with raising children, starting new careers, or engaging in the difficult work of bringing about social change. They all acknowledge that they could never have achieved the things they did had it not been for faith carrying them through some of the most difficult and stressful moments. Jesus seems to have been right when he said to his disciples, "If you had faith as big as a mustard seed, you could say to this mulberry tree, 'Pull yourself up by the roots and plant yourself in the sea!' and it would obey you" (Luke 17:6). With faith, nothing is beyond us; nothing is too big to tackle, or too scary to face. Faith lies at the very core of the spiritual and religious life. Indeed, faith is the first step on the journey of the spiritual life.

The Need for Faith

Despite the fact that we are created out of the being and power of God, despite our participation in the life of God; in our visible, material forms, we are bound and defined by limitation. This means that we are not born spiritually mature; we are still subject to a spiritual maturation process during which we become increasingly aware of God's Spirit as an ever-present reality and as the ground of all being. Developing this awareness involves spiritual disciplines and practices of many types, which ultimately help us to increase our capacity for free attention, a prerequisite for awareness. Eventually, we transcend the notion that we are separate beings – separate from each other and separate from God – and recognize the fundamental unity of all existence in God.

Because this experiential awareness of God is the result of a process of spiritual maturation, because it is not something most of us inherently possess, at the beginning of our spiritual journeys we need to rely primarily on faith.

The Search for Certainty

There's a story about an elderly farmer who suffered dreadfully from asthma. Many doctors had examined him over the years and had prescribed all sorts of medicines, but nothing ever worked. Then, one day, the farmer's wife noticed that his wheezing and shortness of breath seemed to come on whenever he saw the weather vane on the barn pointing east. So that night, she climbed up the barn roof, pointed the weather vane to the west, and nailed it there. The husband never had asthma again.

Just as the farmer's health depended on his seeing the weather vane pointed to the west, so does happiness for many of us depend on our feeling a sense of certainty in life. We yearn for certainty about the future, for certainty about God, for certainty about many things, both in this life and the next. But absolute certainty does not exist in life. Karl Marx was partly correct in his stinging critique of religion when he said that often it did little more than provide an "opiate for the masses." Like the farmer's wife, religion has tried to nail the weather vane permanently in one direction. Often, it has attempted to provide certainty in order to help us feel more secure in life. But the demand for certainty represents a rejection of faith. When religion stoops to providing guarantees, it betrays its own wisdom and understanding that we meet the great mystery of life, God, in the humility of faith.

Religious beliefs

The most common way in which religion tries to offer us certainty is with the promise of absolutely true beliefs. When I was a young minister, I knew Eileen, a woman who struggled with some of my early attempts to articulate a thoughtful theology for postmodern, post-scientific people. She was a lovely, caring woman, but she so clearly demonstrated for me the difference between faith and belief. One Sunday, after I had attempted to explain why it was not necessary for a Christian to believe that the virgin birth of Jesus was a literal, historic event, she said to me, "David, my faith is grounded in the virgin birth. If that event didn't happen, my faith cannot exist." I felt so sad. Faith is not the same as belief! Belief has to do with intellectual ideas, with conceptual knowledge. Faith is something much deeper and more profound.

One of the reasons many people have become disillusioned with the Christian church is because they have acquired in their church the understanding that to be "faithful" means to believe all sorts of things, which as postmodern, scientifically educated people, they can no longer believe – things such as that the earth was created in seven days, or that Jesus had to die on a cross for the salvation of the world, or that women today must play the same roles that women were required to play in ancient, patriarchal biblical society. When I started ministry at my present congregation, time and time again people would come up to me and say, "Thank you for telling me I can still be a Christian and a person of faith, even if I don't believe all these things."

Religious beliefs are ideas; they are abstract, conceptual approximations of reality. They are constantly changing human constructs, not absolute, divine dictates. Contemporary scientific ideas are no different. The theory of the Big Bang is just that – a theory. We treat these ideas seriously as road maps, but recognize that the map is not the reality. A map of New York City is not the same as New York City itself. The same is true of all belief systems, religious and otherwise. Often they can help to make sense of our lives and of reality, but we must not mistake them as being absolute in themselves.

Religious fundamentalism, however, constitutes precisely the effort to make religious beliefs and ideas absolute. In fundamentalist churches and organizations, people are required to hold to the same "fundamental ideas" as absolute truth. These fundamental ideas constitute what can be called a "consensus view of reality." Because no one is allowed to challenge this "consensus view," it breeds an illusion of certainty. But, of course, someone always, eventually, proclaims a disagreement with the consensus view, creating the proverbial "crack in the egg." Schisms and separations then occur on the basis of the disagreement over the conceptual beliefs and dogmas. This process has repeated itself time and time again throughout the history of the Christian church and explains why there are so many different denominations to this day. In the end, just because everyone agrees to believe a certain idea does not mean that it is true!

Spiritual experience

Another way we seek certainty in life is through religious experience. Across North America and around the world, thousands of religious organizations are springing up in response to people's desire to know God experientially. In one of these groups, the Vineyard movement, people speak in tongues, are slain in the spirit, growl like animals, and can engage in incredibly intense laughter and a variety of other experiences interpreted to be signs of the presence of God's Holy Spirit. Other groups offer chanting, sacred dancing and drumming, sweat lodges, and different forms of meditation. These things can often lead to the experience of energies and powers that are unusual and blissful. For many people, these experiences become reassuring signs of God's presence in their lives and in the world. And, indeed, they are. Life and reality, which arise in God, contain many subtle and psychic dimensions. Certain forms of prayer and religious expression can enable people to experience all sorts of energies and aspects associated with these other dimensions of reality.

None of these religious experiences is bad. Indeed, they can be very valuable because they reveal to us that life consists of something much larger and more mysterious than first meets the eye. They put us in touch with different dimensions of life in God and can be very encouraging to our spiritual journey. But these experiences can still be subject to doubt and questioning. We have the experience, but after the initial effects have worn off we start to wonder if they were real, if we were hallucinating, or we simply question their significance. We find we are no more certain about life and God than before.

Thus, until we reach full spiritual maturity, and that involves much more than having these types of spiritual experiences, we will require faith to relate to God.

Qualities of Faith

Faith as primal feeling and intuition

First and foremost, faith is a feeling or an intuition that we are immersed in something so grand, so powerful, and so incomprehensible that our minds collapse in the effort to understand it. The experience of watching the sun rise over the horizon in a blaze of light, or set in the evening as a fiery ball of red and gold, may elicit this feeling and intuition. An experience like the one I had as a child, of gazing up at the endless stars, may do the same. The mind becomes quiet and one simply participates in the moment with a sense of reverent appreciation and awe. In those moments, we may sense the sacred dimension that permeates all of life. We may feel or intuit that something wonderful and gracious is at play in all of this, and, for want of a better word, we may call this God. Faith refers to this first, primal feeling or intuition. It occurs prior to the activity of the thinking mind, which later develops all sorts of abstract, conceptual ideas and theories about life and creation.

Faith as perspective on the world

A samurai warrior came to a Zen master and commanded him, "Teach me about heaven and hell." The master looked at the warrior and laughed: "Why would you think I would waste may time teaching an ignoramus like you? You are an uneducated buffoon!" The samurai, severely insulted, began to breathe heavily and grew red in the face. Furious, he drew his sword and lifted it to chop off the master's head. "That sir," the master interrupted, "is hell." Immediately the warrior was overcome with humility. In deference to the profundity of the lesson, he fell at the master's feet and began to thank him profusely. "And that sir," continued the master, "is heaven."

Whether we live in heaven or in hell depends very little on any external reality, but on the perspective we bring to life. Faith is about the quality of that perspective.

Richard Niebuhr wrote that there are three ways of looking at life.[1] The first way sees the whole of life as hostile and threatening. All of us probably know someone who lives with a "gut feeling" that the universe is out to get them, so they'd better look out. This perspective puts us into a very defensive mode and elicits an effort to make life as secure and as safe as possible – often through the acquisition of material wealth. Or, if we are of a particular religious bent, we may see God as a threatening power inclined towards judgment and punishment. If this is the case, the religious strategy to achieve security may be to placate God by living a life of moral perfection and purity. It is a demanding life, ultimately governed by fear.

According to Niebuhr, the second perspective views the universe as just a swirling mass of matter and energy, totally indifferent to the life forms emerging within it. From this viewpoint, human beings are just another species that has evolved in the unfolding of time, and that possesses no more value, relevance, or meaning that anything else in the universe. Our loss, or extinction as a species, would mean nothing in the larger picture. Once again, this perspective may elicit various attempts to achieve security and protection as a hedge against a vast, cold, indifferent world. If we hold this outlook, we may also engage in an endless variety of distracting pursuits to alleviate the sense of meaninglessness that such a viewpoint engenders.

The third perspective we can bring to life represents the truly religious path. This is the perspective of faith. People who have observed geese know that they have been designed by the universe to depend upon each other. In their flying "V-formation," the lead goose does most of the work, setting the direction and pace, and breaking the air ahead of the rest of the flock. Whenever it is tired, however, the lead goose falls back and another takes its place. Furthermore, when geese fly in the wake of each other's wings, they literally get a lift from one another.

The perspective of faith sees that the whole of life is giving and gracious. God, the source of life, has designed life to be self-sustaining and mutually supportive. Indeed, the universe, like the geese, is structured this way. Yes, the universe contains randomness, suffering, and even evil. Nonetheless, it is structured to create and to sustain life, including human life. When we see the universe and God from this perspective, trust and courage become possible.

Faith as trust

An old tale tells how Adam came home in the wee hours one morning to find a very jealous Eve. "Where were you?" Eve demands. "Checking on the animals," replies Adam. "A likely story," says Eve accusingly. "Come on, you know that in all of creation there's no one but you and me," says Adam. Reassured and mollified, Eve snuggles up to Adam in bed. Still, when Adam falls asleep, she very carefully counts his ribs.

Trust is perhaps the most commonly understood quality of faith. Trust depends, however, on our ability to view life from Niebuhr's third perspective, as noted above.

This kind of trust is very difficult for many people. It is a well-known fact that children who grow up in loving families have a much easier time believing in a loving God than children who grow up without a healthy experience of being loved. The same is true for trust. Children who grow up in families in which trust is warranted find themselves able to trust that the universe and God are trustworthy. Likewise, children who grow up in families where trust is not warranted often find themselves unable, as adults, to trust in life or in God. In addition, experiences of randomness, suffering, and evil make trust difficult for many people. Later in this book I will speak about an understanding of suffering and evil that does not negate the reality of trust and love. But for now, I simply want to say that, despite these realities in the world, trust is warranted and is a vital component of faith. Trusting in life and in God to support and sustain us gives us courage to follow dreams and to live in ways we believe to be life-giving. Trust enables us to believe in and to work for change from a perspective of hope and optimism, enabling things to happen that otherwise might not happen. More times than I can count, I have seen healing happen in the lives of people who trusted deeply in the prayers and desires of other people for their healing; who believed strongly in God's own desire for their healing. Some people view such healing as miraculous. But what we realize today is that an attitude of trust probably has as much to do with healing as anything else. What we envision and believe in, and what we have faith in and trust, so often come about. This, too, is a principle of life. In the end, trust is a key component of faith and of the religious life.

Faith as relationship

Less common to our understanding of faith is the dynamic of relationship. Specifically, faith consists of a relationship to life and to God. Marcus Borg speaks about faith as fidelity, not to a set of ideas, but to a relationship with God.[2] The word fidelity stems from the word faithfulness, and refers to being loyal and committed. If you have fidelity in your relationship to your spouse or partner, you are true to that relationship. You come back to your beloved daily, expressing your love and keeping your promises. You support your beloved and receive support in return. You are constant, committed, trustworthy, and loyal – in a word, you are faithful. Most importantly, there is no hiding, cheating, or lying between the partners. You open your life to your beloved and together you become intimate. This intimacy is characterized by openness and transparency in all things.

I like the story about Tom, who went fishing but didn't catch a single fish. On the way home he stopped at a local fish market. The salesperson asked him what he wanted and Tom said, "Just stand over there and throw me five of the biggest trout you've got." "Throw em?" asked the bewildered salesperson. "What for?" "So I can tell my wife I caught them," snapped Tom. "I may be a lousy fisherman, but I'm not a liar." Obviously, Tom had not "caught" the true meaning of faithfulness.

To be a person of faith is to have fidelity in your relationship with God. In the Bible, the opposite of fidelity in a husband/wife relationship is called adultery. However, the opposite of fidelity in our relationship with God is described as idolatry. When we are not true to God, when we are not open and transparent to God, when we are not centered in God but instead place other objects at the center of our lives and attention, we are being "idolatrous."

When adultery takes place, it almost always happens because there are problems in the relationship between the partners. People run from their troubles to the delight of a new fantasy, but invariably come to the point of having to face the depths and darkness of their problems. The same is true of idolatry in our relationship with God. We seek happiness, meaning, and identity in all sorts of places other than in God. But there is no real happiness to be found apart from God. Placing anything other than God at the center of our lives will result in pain and suffering of some sort.

In a marriage, we can live our whole life with our spouse and still there will be depths to that person that we don't fully understand. Most people don't fully understand themselves, so it stands to reason that others, even a beloved spouse or partner, will never fully comprehend us. But that does not prevent us from remaining faithful in the relationship. That does not prevent us from loving and caring for our beloved, or from making our relationship with the beloved the single most important relationship in our life.

The same is true with God. We may have all sorts of intellectual questions about God. Indeed, we are incapable of understanding the fullness of God no matter how long we think, no matter how many questions we consider. But in the end, the spiritual journey doesn't lead to perfect answers; it leads instead to our being comfortable and relaxed with the questions and the mystery. Faithfulness to God does not require perfect understanding of God. Faithfulness to God means keeping God at the center of our life, despite the limitations of our understanding. It means keeping God at the center of our hearts and minds.

If you understand God in the personal way more common to Christianity and to the life of Jesus, to be faithful to God involves giving your life over to God in the same way that Jesus did. It means coming to God daily in prayer. It means inviting God's love, wisdom, and strength into your life consistently. It means exercising the muscles of conscience and the quality of compassion in all of life. It means following through on your Christian commitment to support the work of Jesus' church and the ministry of that church in the world.

If you understand God in the more transpersonal, non-dualist fashion suggested in this book, to be faithful to God means to be true and accountable to your own deepest spiritual insights and to your practice of the spiritual life, including service to others and to the earth.

Faith and Doubt

We cannot leave the topic of faith before considering briefly the matter of religious doubt. For many of us, doubt poses a serious obstacle on the spiritual and religious journey. It has not helped that traditional religious teaching has condemned doubt as a sign of insufficient faith. However, the roots of doubt must be understood before we can deal with it appropriately.

Doubt as intellectual skepticism

Doubt is most commonly understood to be an expression of intellectual skepticism about certain religious ideas and beliefs. For example, as I've already said, many contemporary Christians find the belief in the virgin birth of Jesus, or the belief that Jesus had to be killed on a Roman cross to redeem humanity from its sins, simply untenable. Such beliefs no longer make any sense to these people. The first does not wash with our knowledge of how human life is created. The second makes no sense given that Jesus himself understood that he served a God of love and compassion.

Intellectual skepticism is a natural consequence of the recognition that certain ideas are flawed or insufficient for explaining ultimate reality, or even one's experience in life. This kind of doubt or skepticism, far from being a hindrance to spiritual growth, is in fact *critical* to spiritual growth. It encourages us to seek deeper and more profound understandings of our experience and of our questions about life and God. It leads to maturity and greater wholeness.

Doubt as emotional recoil from life

There is another type of doubt, however, which can best be described as a form of emotional recoil from life. This kind of doubt exists as a subtle feeling of anxiety, emptiness, and meaninglessness lying beneath the surface of our awareness and daily activity. It may consist of feelings of aloneness or separateness even in the midst of an extended network of family and friends. As a form of disengagement or recoil from life, it often manifests in the belief that life is a meaningless, materialistic phenomenon with no inherent significance. In other words, it leads to the belief that there is no God and no sacred dimension to life.

This form of emotional doubt, of emotional recoil, is a symptom of narcissism and results from an exaggerated sense of psychological inwardness. Each of us is involved in a subjective inner drama that is based on the circumstances of a life script that tends to reinforce our subjective feelings of isolation, of being a separate "I." If this perspective grows to an extreme, we can become wholly absorbed within our own issues and concerns, and may grow to feel very separate and cut off from other people, life, and God.

However, the truth of our existence is that we are always immersed in life and within the great mystery we call God. Like the little fish swimming in the ocean, we reside in an ocean of divine, spirit-energy – existence itself. The feeling of being cut off from life, other people, and God, does not reflect the truth of our existence. Rather, it reflects our own inner psychology.

Much of the spiritual life involves learning to understand and let go of this feeling of emotional doubt or emotional recoil. Indeed, we will spend considerable time later in this book considering different forms of spiritual practice to facilitate precisely this endeavor.

Thoughtful, intellectual understanding of our religious tradition and of life in general is an important ingredient of the spiritual path. We should never need to "park our brains" when we enter a church or join a religious group. If intellectual doubt and questioning is not permitted, we should take it as a warning flag concerning the integrity of the organization. At the same time, learning to observe our personal psychology, our own life scripts and sense of inwardness, is also a critical to the spiritual life.

In summary, then, faith is a necessary ingredient of a spiritual life. It recognizes that God or the universe has structured the world for life, and for the sustaining of life. Faith grants us the feeling or the intuition that despite the suffering and even evil inherent in life, life can be trusted. Faith involves a conscious commitment to a relationship with God, the source of life. If we discover that we are lacking in such faith, we need to observe our own personal psychology and inwardness.

Faith is not primarily a process of searching for more and more elaborate proofs of God's existence, or for more and more exotic experiences of God. Rather, faith consists of a vibrant and alive intuition, perspective, and awareness of the great mystery surrounding and permeating life, which we celebrate as God. And faith involves letting go of the blocks in our lives that prevent us from growing into that feeling and perspective. Faith is intended to lead us to the observation that Rumi, the famous Persian poet, stated in this way:

> Something opens our wings. Something makes boredom and
> hurt disappear.
> Someone fills the cup in front of us. We taste only sacredness.
> We are so weak. We need more help than we know.
> So give up to grace. The ocean takes care of each wave till it
> gets to shore.[3]

Chapter 5

Prayer & Meditation

No one lights a lamp and then hides it or puts it under a bowl; instead, he puts it on the lampstand, so that people may see the light as they come in. Your eyes are like a lamp for the body. When your eyes are sound, your whole body is full of light; but when your eyes are no good, your whole body will be in darkness. Make certain, then, that the light in you is not darkness. If your whole body is full of light, with no part of it in darkness, it will be bright all over, as when a lamp shines on you with its brightness.

Luke 11:33–36

Two men were walking through a field when they saw an angry bull. Instantly, they made for the nearest fence with the bull in hot pursuit. It soon became evident to them that they were not going to make it, so one man shouted to the other, "We've had it! Nothing can save us. Say a prayer. Quick!" The other shouted back, "I've never prayed in my life and I don't have a prayer for this occasion." "Never mind," said the other. "The bull is catching up with us. Any prayer will do." So the friend said, "Well, I'll say the one I remember my father used to say before meals: 'Lord, for what we are about to receive make us truly thankful.'"

Prayer is the engine of the spiritual life. Going to church is good. Reading is helpful. Attending retreats and various events dedicated to spiritual renewal is important. But a disciplined, systematic, ongoing habit of prayer is what drives real spiritual growth and enables it to move forward. Prayer is the fundamental, practical tool that brings freedom to the movement of attention, leads to greater awareness, helps us feel beyond the limitations of the egoic self, and ultimately results in the awareness of God's presence everywhere. In addition, prayer has some remarkable and mysterious healing and transformational abilities. It is quite simply the most important tool available to the spiritual aspirant. Prayer takes place in many different ways, but all prayer is an intentional, conscious opening up and connecting of the human psyche and personality to God. Prayer is what makes the religious life work.

Prayer has been part of my life from the very beginning. In my family, grace at mealtimes represented a daily expression of thankfulness to God for the gift of life and all its blessings, even when we had very little in the way of material resources. As noted earlier, my parents prayed in tongues, both at church prayer meetings and in our home. Praying in tongues is a form of prayer utilized by the early Christian church and is still common in some evangelical churches. In an ecstatic mood, with one's heart and mind focused on God, the person praying spontaneously generates and utters a series of sounds that have no basis in common language. To observers it appears that the person is simply uttering a lot of gibberish in a highly excited emotional state. But for the person praying, this is a profound experience of unity with God and they believe that the sounds are generated by the Holy Spirit. I had free rein to experiment with this type of prayer in my early childhood years. In addition, using more traditional prayer forms, my family prayed for people, for health, for assistance with problems, and for the Holy Spirit to ever more fully enter their lives.

As I grew older, I began to experiment with my own forms of prayer. As a student of the Rosicrucian movement, I meditated on candles and attempted to see auras. For many years, I engaged in a form of sitting Zen meditation that involved utilizing the breath and mantras to clear and silence my mind. I engaged in devotional meditation on Jesus, sitting for hours in front of a picture of Jesus, praying to him and meditating upon him. I used affirmations and walking meditation. Throughout the entire process, an ever-deeper self-awareness grew within me, which culminated, one day, in an experience of what Da Free John calls the "thumbs," and what some Christians would refer to as the in-filling of the Holy Spirit. I experienced a force descending upon my head and body, a power so great and so phenomenal I have no words adequate to describe it. One thing was crystal clear, though. This force had nothing to do with my daily experience. It was an expression of the power of the universe itself, the very being of God. In that moment an insight of enormous profundity arose within me and has never left: "I am contained within and am part of the very being and power of God." Nothing else could have been clearer. It was a simple observation, but it burned itself into the core of my psyche.

Prayer, then, happens in many different ways and has many different results. But the overarching purpose of prayer is to connect us with God, the mysterious reality that gives birth to all of creation.

A good way to think about prayer is to use the analogy of a deep-sea diver connected to a supply boat by a tether and air line. While diving deep in the darkness of the ocean, the diver depends absolutely upon that tether and air line. If it is cut off, the diver quickly loses all bearing and may die. Likewise, prayer is our lifeline to God. It gives us the energy and wisdom we need to live, and helps us to maintain our bearings in life. Not praying, in effect, cuts off that lifeline.

As with many things in life, however, the process of prayer is a little more complex than first meets the eye. And most people, like the men being chased by the bull in the story above, have never been taught how to pray, beyond saying the Lord's Prayer, or some equivalent in other world traditions.

Historically, within the Christian spiritual tradition, there have been three broad categories of prayer: discursive or talk prayer, meditative prayer, and contemplative prayer. In addition, we find a form of prayer known as "mindfulness," which has been popularized by contemporary Buddhism. But mindfulness prayer has been part of the Christian tradition, too. Each type of prayer has its own unique purpose and methodology and contributes in a particular way to our spiritual growth.

Dualist and Non-Dualist Prayer

Before we look at the different types of prayer, it is important to consider briefly the overall movement or direction that prayer takes in the spiritual life.

The vast majority of people the world over live with a "dualist" consciousness and experience of life and God. I have spoken about this in an in-depth way in previous chapters, so I won't repeat the argument in full here. Suffice it to say that if we operate from a "dualist" perspective, we understand ourselves to be separate and distinct beings or subjects, within a world composed of billions of objects separate from ourselves. As a consequence, we also experience God as a being or object separate from ourselves. In terms of prayer, the principal way we relate to another person or being we believe to be separate from ourselves, including God, is by talking with them. Obviously, we connect with each other in a variety of other ways, too, such as with eye contact, touch, and smell. But the easiest way to connect with God, the invisible source of life, is by using what I call "talk prayer." Yet the important point right now is that this notion of two separate beings attempting to connect and to communicate with each other is called "dualist prayer."

As with the dualist perspective, I have discussed the "non-dualist" or "unitive" perspective in previous chapters, so again I won't repeat a full description of it here. In essence, if we operate from a non-dualist or unitive perspective, we understand and experience ourselves to be part of the much larger oneness and unity of the great mystery of God. On the one hand, we still experience ourselves as distinct and separate physical beings. On the other hand, we experience ourselves as participating in and being a part of a larger life, which we call God.

In this circumstance, prayer changes from being a process of talking to a God we feel to be separate from ourselves, to a simple resting in the awareness of the God who is our own true self. This form of prayer, this simple resting in God and being aware of and attentive to God as the deepest dimension of our own lives, leads to progressively deeper levels of inner silence and is called contemplative prayer – the highest form of "non-dualist" prayer.

This brings us to the overall movement, direction, or development of prayer within the spiritual journey. Simply stated, as our awareness moves from a dualist to a non-dualist or unitive outlook, the forms of prayer we use tend to change. To be clear, the fundamental nature of God never changes; it is *we* who change. And for each stage of change, we need different tools and resources for the spiritual journey. One set of tools is not inferior to another set. Rather, different needs and stages in the spiritual journey require different approaches and resources.

As I discuss in greater detail these different forms of prayer, it will be helpful to keep this insight in mind. For some people, talk prayer will be a very important part of their spiritual practice. For other people, meditation, mindfulness, or contemplative prayer will be the required tool. For many people, using all the different forms of prayer will still be appropriate. People who practice advanced forms of contemplative prayer may still talk to God. Such people recognize the paradoxical nature of existence and express the "genius of the AND" in their thinking and praying. Such people also recognize that in some ways, we will always be separate and apart from each other by virtue of the physical bodies we possess. But they recognize, too, that we are moving towards a form of consciousness in which we see and feel our ultimate unity within the deeper dimensions of life. Engaging in forms of prayer that recognize this paradoxical nature of our existence is entirely appropriate. Let us now look more specifically at the different forms of prayer.

Discursive or Talk Prayer

The word discursive derives from the word discourse and means simply "to talk." This is the most commonly known form of prayer and is used by millions of people the world over. When I was in high school, I played the lead role of Tevye, in the well-known musical *Fiddler on the Roof*. *Fiddler on the Roof* is the story of a Jewish dairyman, his wife Golde, and the trials and tribulations they experience as their five daughters grow up and wish to become married. Tevye, a very pious man, talks to God almost every moment of the day. He talks to God about his business, about his community, about his wife Golde, and most of all about his daughters. It is mostly a one-way conversation, a continuous natter that goes on throughout his daily life. But Tevye's talking to God provides a wonderful illustration of some of the different types of talk prayer.

Sometimes, Tevye growls and complains to God.

> Today I am a horse. Dear God, did you have to make my poor old horse lose his shoe just before the Sabbath? That wasn't nice. It's enough you pick on me, Tevye, bless me with five daughters, a life of poverty. What have you got against my horse? Sometimes I think when things are too quiet up there, you say to yourself: "Let's see, what kind of mischief can I play on my friend Tevye?"

At other times, Tevye asks God for protection and blessing on his family, as with this family prayer that he and Golde sing together.

> May the Lord protect and defend you. May the Lord preserve you from pain. Favor them, O Lord, with happiness and peace. O hear our Sabbath prayer. Amen.

Sometimes, Tevye asks God to intervene in the life of his family, to provide them with things they need. After the wedding of his daughter Tzeitel to a poor tailor named Motel, Tevye says to God,

> Tzeitel and Motel have been married almost two months now. They work very hard; they are as poor as squirrels in winter. But they are both so happy they don't know how miserable they are. Motel keeps talking about a sewing machine. I know You're very busy – wars and revolutions, floods, plagues, all

those little things that bring people to you – couldn't you take a second away from Your catastrophes and get it for him? How much trouble would it be? Oh, and while You're in the neighborhood, my horse's left leg – Am I bothering you too much? I'm sorry. As the Good Book says – come to think of it, why should I tell you what the Good Books says?

It goes on and on. Sometimes complaining to God, sometimes thanking God, sometimes asking God for a variety of things, Tevye constantly talks to God about his daily life. And this is why it is called "talk prayer."

Most people with a religious background talk to God. Before going to bed at night, we might be feeling happy and thankful for the day, and spontaneously tell God how thankful we are to be alive and for all the good gifts God has given us in and through life. Or just before getting up in the morning, we might ask God to be with us during what we know is going to be a tough day at work. On the way to work in the car, we might be listening to the news and hear about a flood or earthquake in some part of the world, and we may feel moved to pray for the people affected by that situation. Or we might see someone on the bus that looks depressed, and silently ask God to be with that person that day. We might be in a hospital room beside a loved one who is suffering, and ask God for healing for that person. Throughout the day, thinking about our spouse or our children, we might ask God to be with them, and to protect and keep them. Some of us pray about these things each and every day. Others of us pray only in times of personal emergency and then don't pray again for years.

Within the worship life of churches, we see these different kinds of talk prayers given different names, such as prayers of approach, prayers of confession, prayers of adoration, prayers of supplication, and prayers of thanksgiving. But regardless of the type of prayer, whether we are thanking God, or complaining to God, or confessing to God, or asking God for something, it's all basically the same kind of prayer. It all amounts to talking to God about whatever is on our minds. An outside observer might conclude that we are just talking to ourselves, or carrying on a purely imaginary conversation. But from our own perspective, as the person who is praying, we understand in a profound way that we are directing our thoughts and words to a force or presence vastly beyond ourselves, but real nonetheless.

How talk prayer works

A man decided to shed some excess pounds. He took his new diet seriously, even changing his route to work to avoid passing his favorite bakery. One morning, however, he arrived at work carrying a gigantic coffee cake. His colleagues scolded him, but his smile remained cherubic. "This is a very special coffee cake," he explained. "I accidentally drove by the bakery this morning and there, in the window, was a host of cakes and cookies. I felt this was no accident, so I prayed, 'Lord, if you want me to have one of these delicious coffee cakes, let me have a parking place directly in front of the bakery.' And sure enough," he continued, "the eighth time around the block, there it was!"

It's a funny story, but it reflects a problem many spiritual seekers have discerned with talk prayer. So much of talk prayer is geared towards asking God to fix our lives, to change things in our lives, and to bless our lives with all sorts of wonderful things. People growing in the spiritual life recognize the inherent egocentricity of this kind of prayer, this practice of always asking God for "stuff." Wisely, they recognize that we can delude ourselves and justify getting whatever it is we want in life by saying, "I prayed to God and God gave it to me." Anything can be used unwisely, including prayer.

Still, despite some of its inherent limitations, talk prayer *does* have value, both for beginners and for long-time journeyers on the road of spiritual growth. But it needs to be understood from a new perspective. Let's look, then, at some of the practical ways in which talk prayer works and can advance our spiritual growth.

Talk prayer can be likened to a patient speaking to the greatest, wisest, most loving psychotherapist in the whole world. With God, and often only with God, can we feel truly secure to open up our inner lives, with all the fears, darkness, and ugliness they sometimes possess. We may not be able to talk about a certain fear or anxiety or grief with anyone else, because it feels too painful and we will feel too exposed. But we know that God can handle it all. We trust God to be unconditionally loving and accepting. That is why we can be absolutely honest with God.

In this process of talking honestly to God, we begin to become more honest with ourselves. Most people are seldom completely honest with themselves. We live in denial and delusion about many aspects of our personalities and lives that we don't want to face. But in prayer we become more honest and self-aware. In this process, we also become more aware of what needs healing in our lives.

The healing sciences have made an important observation. It is not primarily doctors and drugs that heal people. Rather, doctors and drugs empower the body's own defenses to facilitate healing. In a psychotherapeutic situation, the counselor enables the client to become aware of his or her issues. In the process, the therapist helps the person to find his or her own solutions and answers in life. God has built healing power into our lives. What people need is to be honest and open about where the healing needs to take place, and to invite the body and the psyche to work for that healing. When we do so, it often occurs.

Frequently, people tell me about having prayed for something and shortly afterwards finding a book or meeting a person who can help them with that issue. This is not so mysterious as we might first think. In sharing the problem with God, we allow ourselves to look at it. This is turn heightens our awareness of potential sources of help and inspiration. These sources of help are always present, but if we hadn't opened our lives to God in prayer, we might not have been aware of what we needed or of the resources available to us. Prayer, then, is a very practical technique that helps us to get in touch with our issues, and to find solutions for them.

Another way in which talk prayer nurtures our spiritual growth is by encouraging us to reflect on the deepest principles and values that guide our lives. Ralph Waldo Emerson once said, "Prayer is the contemplation of the facts of life from the highest point of view." When we communicate with God, we naturally begin to reflect on our life from God's perspective and to think about what is truly important. The universe functions according to principles. In the process of talking to God, we reflect on these principles and become inspired to live by them. When we live by our principles, life is not always easier, but it is always healthier and more meaningful.

Not all the effects of talk prayer can be explained by the above rational means. There is always a mysterious dimension to prayer. Prayer often results in the experience of profoundly healing synchronicities or meaningful coincidences in our lives. Understanding God from the new perspective described in this book helps to explain this mysterious dimension of prayer.

Most churches have what are called healing circles or prayer groups. People gather together to pray to God for healing, or for other concerns, on behalf of various members of the congregation. Sometimes, they may not physically gather together, but instead pick a common time to pray to God about specific people. Many people I have known, who have been recipients of this type of prayer, have said they could feel an inner sense of well-being and renewed confidence when people were praying for them. They have attributed much of their healing directly to this power of prayer. Is this merely subjective, wishful thinking or is there some reality to this process and experience?

The earlier understanding of God, which has created much skepticism about discursive prayer, looks like this. When we pray to God about something, our prayers go up to heaven. In heaven, God hears these prayers, pulls some strings, and rearranges circumstances down on earth to effect a certain positive change. Of course, this leads one person to complain that God may have pulled strings on behalf of someone else's wife who had cancer, but didn't pull strings on behalf of his own wife who died. What kind of God is that? The whole notion of God responding to some people's prayers and not to other people's prayers is highly disturbing and doesn't make sense to a great many people these days.

However, in the newer vision of God emerging today, God doesn't exist as a being somewhere up in the sky or in outer space. Rather, God is the ultimate Spirit reality, in whom all life emerges and lives. God is like the ocean in which plants, fish, and all sorts of life come into being and live.

When we pray to God for someone, although our words suggest that we are asking God to fix things for the other person, what we are really doing is directing loving intention, energy, and care to the other person. To a great degree, we live under the illusion that as separate, distinct individuals, we cannot effect change in other people. Only God can do so, we think. The truth is that we live in an invisible ocean of Spirit, one that connects us all together, and so our energy expressed as intention, as loving thought and emotion, as care and empathy, actually travels across or through the invisible spirit reality of God, to surround the other person. All of that loving energy does, indeed, effect positive change, even if at only a very subtle level. Praying for other people, then, is a very powerful way to effect change.

A good example of this comes from Francene, a nurse and former political leader in my region, who engages in a ministry of healing touch. Healing touch involves laying hands either just above or physically on an ailing part of the body. Often, the healing touch practitioner will engage in a stroking motion over a person, as a way of "smoothing out" a rough or damaged energy field. Smoothing out the energy field around a person is understood to facilitate healing at the physical level. Today, a similar modality called therapeutic touch is used widely in the nursing profession. Francene recounted to me the following event in her life.

> My mother, who lives in New Brunswick, broke her leg and was in the hospital, in a cast from heel to thigh. Infection set in and, because she is a diabetic, we were all worried. There was a fair bit of swelling. Then, with the appearance of gangrene, the doctors were worried that she might lose her leg. I was in Halifax and unable to get to her during the first four, most critical days, and so I chose to do healing touch from a distance. I used the technique of sweeping her energy down over the cast and off the foot, visualizing the swelling and infection draining away. The third night I called her at the hospital and she said, "Dear, I think I am having hallucinations! At night I feel a ghost in my bed, running its hand down over my broken

leg!" I nearly dropped the phone! When I explained it was no ghost, but rather me visualizing and sending healing energy into her leg and into the infection, she was thrilled. The swelling and the infection went away and when I finally did get to New Brunswick to visit, the nurses met me at Mom's bedside and asked for a demonstration of healing touch. She fully recovered from this close call.

This is not airy-fairy stuff. Francene normally engages in healing touch with clients in her presence, in a special room at our church or in the hospital. But because of her strong emotional attachment to her mother, she intuitively sensed that this process might work from a distance. And it did! The reason the process worked is because energy can be transmitted across the invisible, web-like, spiritual body of God, which connects us all together.

I often encourage people to pray not just for each other, but also for the planet as a whole. Our prayer may take the form of words, of talking to God and asking God to bless and help heal the planet. But what is actually happening in that moment is that our energized, loving intentions, thoughts, and emotions, are literally spreading out, in and through the body of God, to surround the planet and to help it heal, once again, even if only in very subtle ways. And don't forget: saying those prayers also makes us more aware of the needs of the planet, raises our awareness, and helps us to change how we live in relationship with the planet.

There is one other very practical dimension to talk prayer. Talk prayer moves us beyond self-centeredness and leads to a greater sense of peacefulness. People often ask when they should pray. When it comes to talk prayer, I always say, "Pray every day." Discursive or talk prayer doesn't need to have a great deal of discipline associated with it. Pray in the car, pray on the bus, and pray at work. Like Tevye, the more we do it, the closer we will feel to God. As we develop an increasing sense of closeness to God, we tend to open our lives more fully to God. Along the way, we develop increased patience and understanding, an ever-greater inner quietness, and we discover that solutions for life's problems appear more quickly and easefully.

Because we live our lives "flat out" so much of the time, I particularly encourage people to pray in bed, either in the morning before getting up, or in the evening before going to sleep. Evening prayer is particularly wonderful and relaxing, because we often fall asleep having turned everything over to God.

Different Forms of Meditative Prayer

The term meditation is used differently within the various religious and spiritual traditions. Within the Christian tradition, it refers to a mixed bag of practices that people can use. But the difference, in meditative prayer, is that we begin to relate to God less as an outside source and more as an inner presence working in and through our lives. In meditative prayer, although we still feel separate from God, there is a growing sense that God is a part of us, that God is the deepest and truest part of our lives and that we are part of God. Meditation consists of the first, preliminary effort to begin to contact the deeper dimensions of our lives where our identity merges with that of God.

Creative engagement with scripture

Historically, the most popular form of Christian meditation has involved taking a passage from the Bible and reflecting deeply upon it. Very often people do this when they are looking for some specific kind of help or inspiration regarding a problem or question. In such a situation, it is important to begin the meditation with a sincere talk prayer to God asking for guidance or help. Holding the concern or question clearly in mind, try flipping through the Bible at random until it opens to a passage. Read the passage and see if it speaks to the concern or question in some way. In this process, the Bible almost never gives a yes/no answer, but the passage may spark insight and cause us to look at the problem from a new angle or helpful perspective. This form of meditation is part of the "oracular" tradition, in which the divine wisdom within us makes a mysterious connection with some source of help upon which we rely, in this case the Bible.

Another form of biblical meditation involves taking a pre-assigned or chosen passage from the Bible, or simply one that you think might speak to your situation. If you are sick, you might take a passage from the gospels where Jesus heals someone. In this situation, you would read the passage and imagine deeply the whole scene in your mind, including how Jesus felt and how the person being healed felt. Then you would imagine yourself in that situation asking Jesus to heal you, and listening to what he would say to you, what advice he would give.

In another situation, you may be wondering what direction to take in your life. You might then take the passage of the rich young man who came to Jesus and asked, "Master, what must I do to be saved?" You would read the passage several times. You might imagine who the young man was, what his life was all about and why he was coming to Jesus. You might ponder what Jesus was feeling and thinking in that situation about what the young man needed. You would then read the passage again, this time putting yourself in the scene asking Jesus that question and listening for what he would say to you.

In this kind of meditation, we creatively enter into and engage with scripture using visualization, imagination, and our rational mind to try to connect it to our daily lives. In the process, we believe that the deep wisdom of God within us will speak through the Bible reading. Very often, we start to feel a connection or sense of unity with God as the deepest part of our lives. We start to feel that God is guiding us from within, which in turn provides a strong sense of peacefulness and strength.

Guided imagery

Other forms of meditation can be used to heal painful psychic and emotional states. Guided imagery meditations are often used this way.

In this type of meditation, you sit comfortably, shut your eyes, and relax your breath and body, while a leader or meditation tape takes you on an imaginary, visual journey in your mind. For example, you might be invited to travel through a dark forest, filled with difficulties and fearful anxieties, up and over a mountain into light, then into a beautiful clearing with a waterfall, where you immerse yourself in a pool of healing, soothing water. The images used represent inner difficulties and emotional states, as well as places of healing and wholeness; inner sources of healing and love that derive from God.

Affirmations

Affirmations are another form of meditative prayer. Many people use affirmations with great benefit. My mom's favorite affirmation, one she uses every day, goes like this:

> The light of God surrounds me.
> The love of God enfolds me.
> The power of God protects me.
> The presence of God watches over me.
> Wherever I am, God is.

Over the years, I have developed my own affirmation.

> I am the radiant divine heart,
> the very force and ground of being,
> undifferentiated love and bliss,
> ultimate reality itself.

The two most important things about an affirmation are that it should be simple, and it should reflect our deepest beliefs and values. Repeat the affirmation in the morning when you get up and before you go to bed at night. Repeat it regularly throughout the day, either out loud, or in your mind. Repeating it over and over throughout the course of days, weeks, months, and years, enables the meaning of the affirmation to take hold as a reality in our life. We become what we meditate upon.

Mindfulness practice

Joe walked into work on Monday morning with both ears bandaged. "What happened to you?" a colleague exclaimed. "I was watching the ball game on TV and ironing my shirts at the same time," Joe replied. "Some idiot got the wrong number and called me on the phone. I reached for the receiver and accidentally picked up the iron." "Tough break," said Joe's friend. "But what happened to the other ear?" "Well," said Joe, "the fool called back!"

Mindfulness is a very common practice in the Buddhist tradition, but is also well known in the Christian tradition. The practice of mindfulness involves exactly what the word suggests – being mindful from moment to moment of what is going on in the world around us. So often, we engage in one activity, but our attention is focused somewhere else, far away. We are ironing a shirt, but our attention is on the television. Or we are mowing the lawn, but our mind is absorbed in the fight we just had with our wife or husband. Mindfulness meditation invites us to bring our full attention to whatever it is we are presently doing. It is based in the understanding that God exists not in far-off space and not in some other time, but here and now as the background of our lives. As we become more and more attentive to what is going on in our immediate life and circumstance, we develop awareness and inner stillness, which are the prerequisites for encountering God in the here and now.

Breath relaxation

Another classic form of meditative prayer involves focusing attention on the breath. On the in-breath, we visualize or imagine the spirit of God flowing into our body and as we exhale we visualize all darkness and negative thoughts and stress leaving our body. As with mindfulness meditation, this process also stills the mind, develops awareness, and creates the inner conditions to enable us to be more aware of God.

The important thing about all these different forms of meditative prayer is that they aim to help us contact a deeper dimension of our selves. In the process of meditative prayer, we go down into what Jesus called the "well of living water." In meditative prayer, we cut through the stress and anxieties of daily preoccupations and enter into a more aware part of our lives, where healing energy resides..As we become more aware of God within, the sense of separateness that we feel from God and from the world starts to dissolve. We feel more peaceful and more alive. There is a lovely Arab saying that states, "The nature of the rain is the same, yet it produces thorns in the marsh and flowers in the garden." The reality of God is the same at the core of each of our lives. Whether we turn to that reality, and how we utilize that reality is up to us. But doing so makes all the difference.

Contemplative Prayer and Silence

Contemplative prayer attracts people who are growing into maturity in the spiritual life. It is the most demanding and challenging form of prayer because it requires that we progressively slow the thought generating process of the mind. It requires that we learn to enter and stay within a highly unusual condition of deep mental silence and alertness.

Contemplative prayer functions without imagination or visualization, and without thought or words. Often, it has been described as "sheer emptiness," because it involves a total letting go of the inner content of our lives, content that gives us our sense of identity. However, "emptiness" is far too negative a description for what becomes a very special and rewarding condition once we become accustomed to it. It should rather be called "fullness": fullness of awareness, fullness of being, and fullness of desire for God.

In contemplative prayer, we don't talk to God, we don't visualize God, and we certainly do not reflect on questions about God or on concerns about life. Rather, we silently gaze into the great unknown with a feeling of openness, receptiveness, and desire to know God. We sit quietly, but with incredible alertness to any indication of God's presence. In the process, a great silence descends or emerges within our psyche.

Emotional states also gradually subside like a strong wind slowly blowing out. A paradoxical state then develops. In this state, there is neither joy nor sorrow, neither hope nor despair, neither anger nor happiness, just a quintessential peacefulness and serenity. The psyche becomes like a pond of water completely free of ripples, both on the surface and underneath. But burning within the center of this absolutely serene condition continues this naked desire for God, totally uncluttered by anything else.

What I have described thus far is really just the beginning of the contemplative process. However, it is as far as many people ever get. In fact, the desire to know God that permeates contemplative prayer does not begin as a red-hot flame or passion. It actually begins as a small spark that flickers on and off. As we develop a greater level of familiarity with the contemplative "gazing into infinity," as we become more able to separate awareness from the contents of mind, as we develop a deeper capacity to concentrate, this tiny spark or flicker begins to grow. Eventually it builds into a continuous yearning or longing, a continuous passionate desire to know God that never wanes.

Along the way, our sense of distance and separation from God progressively dissolves. It is as though the desire to know God links us ever more deeply with God. And eventually we enter into a sense of union with God that overshadows everything else in our lives.

The practice of contemplative prayer

Anthony de Mello tells a story about a talkative lover. The lover pressed his suit unsuccessfully for many months, suffering the atrocious pains of rejection. Finally his sweetheart yielded. "Meet me under the palm trees on the shore as the sun rises," she said to him. At that time and place, the lover finally found himself seated beside his beloved. He then reached into his pocket and pulled out a sheaf of love letters that he had written to her over the past months. They were passionate letters, expressing the pain he felt and his burning desire to experience the delights of love and union. He began to read them to his beloved. The hours went by and still he read on and on. Finally the woman said, "What kind of a fool are you? These letters are all about me and your longing for me. Well, here I am sitting with you at last and you are lost in your stupid letters."[1]

There comes a time when we have to stop reading and talking about God, thinking and reflecting about spiritual life, and simply enter into appreciation for and the presence of the beloved, of God. The reason we do all the other things is because we are scared of what might happen in the actual relationship with God, or simply don't know how to start. This section will provide a short primer on how to begin and engage in contemplative prayer, also called the prayer of silence.

A time to pray

Because contemplative prayer is based on inner silence and the emptying of the contents of the psyche, it can easily lead to sleep. Most people never realize how tired they are much of the time. When our minds and emotional states relax and the body becomes still, sleep is a natural result. However, the goal of contemplative prayer is not sleep, but rather a highly alert desire for and attentiveness to the great mystery of God.

First, you need to consider the time for prayer. Although many books encourage people into this form of prayer by suggesting they can pray in this way for as little as ten to 20 minutes, the optimal time is actually from half an hour to a full hour. As you progress in this form of prayer, the time span can increase from one to three hours. It is important, therefore, to choose, first, a time when you will be the least preoccupied by other concerns of the day, and, second, a time when you are the most fully alert and awake. For myself, this time is the very early morning. Sometimes I get up at 3:30 a.m., pray for an hour or two, then go back to bed for another hour before getting up. The middle of the night is the quietest time both in the surrounding environment and in my own mind. Other times, I will get up between 5:30 a.m. and 6:00 a.m. and pray for an hour before the rest of the household awakens. People with a different biorhythm may find the time at the end of the day the most conducive to the quiet alertness required for this form of prayer.

A place to pray

The place for contemplative prayer can also be quite important. Two important characteristics come into play here. First and foremost, it needs to be a place where you can feel relaxed and know that you will not be disturbed. It needs also to be a place free from noise and other distractions either from within the house or from the outside. Second, it should be a place that holds a special, worshipful ambience. Many people create a small shrine or worship space somewhere in the house where they will place flowers, a special picture of a spiritual hero, or some incense to help them focus.

Using stimulants

People sometimes ask whether they may use a mild stimulant, such as a green tea or herbal tea prior to engaging in this form of prayer. These may be helpful, however, using stimulants such as coffee may make the body and mind edgy, which is not conducive to relaxation. You can experiment with all these suggestions, but the general rule of thumb is to stay away from stimulants as an aid to wakefulness and alertness.

Posture

Next to the time of day and place chosen for prayer, posture is the most important factor contributing to alert and wakeful prayer. Forget all the fancy yoga positions you may have seen in books, such as the half lotus or the full lotus. These are not necessary and we can waste a lot of time trying to become used to them. What we are striving for is a relaxed but very alert, upright position. The very best position in which to engage in contemplative prayer is with the feet placed flat on the floor, the spine erect, as though held up straight by a string attached from the ceiling to the top of the head, and the hands placed in a relaxed position interlinked and resting in your lap or simply lying flat on your thighs. A simple chair will do. I use an ottoman that has a slightly tilted seat. I face the downward tilt to the back and rest my back against a cushion on the wall. This keeps my back very straight, yet also provides it with support.

Three Stages of Contemplative Prayer

Recollection

The reason contemplative prayer takes more time than other forms of prayer, particularly talk prayer, is because it consists of three quite distinct stages: recollection, the prayer of quiet, and spiritual ecstasy.[2] When you first sit down to pray, you will discover that the mind is never quiet and it never seems to stop. Thoughts and emotions constantly swirl around in the psyche. Recollection is the process of gathering the attention from thinking and feeling, imagining and daydreaming, in order to focus on only one thing – the desire for God. This is not easy and doesn't happen instantly. A good way to rein in the attention from its normally distracted state is to pay attention to one's breathing. Do not think about breathing. Simply observe the breath coming in and going out.

Another aid to recollection is to engage for a short while in talk prayer. Take a few moments to talk with God about whatever is on your mind, or about whatever it is that you generally share with God each day. Pray for your family, your friends, your work situation, the well-being of the planet, and for your own spiritual growth. Although talk prayer utilizes the mind, it also focuses the attention on God where you want it to be. After observing the breath or after simply talking to God for a short while, the mind will begin to slow down. You will become a little more peaceful and quiet. This is what the stage of recollection is all about. It also is called centering, a form of psychological relaxation. In this case, we are relaxing into the presence of the divine.

The prayer of quiet

The second phase of contemplative prayer is called the "prayer of quiet." This stage requires the majority of our time. In order to engage in this stage of prayer, we must learn to be comfortable with doing nothing, and with apparently accomplishing nothing. This is another reason contemplative prayer is so difficult for contemporary people. We are so used to constant doing and accomplishing that we berate ourselves whenever we are not engaged in some form of useful activity. Even talk prayer feels like a useful activity. But this prayer of quiet will, for many people, at first feel useless. We need to let go of this feeling and thought.

For the prayer of quiet to be successful, we may still require a focal point. Some spiritual traditions use one of the various energy centers of the body, in Eastern philosophy known as the chakras. The two most common energy centers utilized for the focusing of attention are the heart center located in the center of the breastbone at the level of the heart – often considered the physical centre for the divine/human interface in the body – and the brow center, located between the eyebrows at the center of the brow and known in some spiritual literature as the "third eye." Simply focus your attention, your desire for God, on this point of the body. Whenever thoughts or images arise, simply observe them and let them go.

Another time honored method for focusing attention involves repeating a name for God. Choose a name for God that appeals to you: Father, Abba, Mother, Ma, Yahweh, Jehovah, or the name of a spiritual master whom you understand to be a clear window to God, such as Jesus. Simply repeat the name over and over, directing both attention and desire to the presence indicated by the name. Repetition of the name helps to clear all other thoughts from the mind. The process eventually leads to a deep inner silence, in which even the repetition of the name may cease and silent desire for God alone remains. If thoughts intrude into the silence, you should simply return to repeating the name. The repetition of the name can also be linked with the focus on a physical energy center in the body. You can focus the attention both on the energy center and the repetition of the name at the same time.

It is important to point out that the prayer of silence is not about simply sitting in a vacuous silence. Rather, it consists of directing attention and desire to God, or to a human expression of God, such as Jesus. Our entire being is poised and alert, listening for the sound of the divine lover about to come into our midst.

As you deepen into the prayer of quiet, a variety of things may happen. You may feel tremors and tingling sensations throughout the body. You may see lights and visions. You may hear sounds. Often, you may be inclined to make sounds, or to lift your hands in an attitude of adoration or supplication to God. These are all very common experiences. As you become quieter and your attention becomes more focused, there is a growing concentration of energy in the nervous system that produces these various experiences. They are not important in themselves, but are just indicators of a deepening progress. It is best to simply notice them, and to let them go.

However, one experience is particularly important to note. Very often, as we enter more deeply into an inner quiet, a tremendous fear can suddenly arise within us. This fear is a natural consequence of the contemplative process. As we become quieter, our sense of inner identity based in memory and the verbal thought processes of the mind begins to dissolve. There is a sensation of ceasing to exist. When this happens, it is important to observe the fear and then let it go. If the fear is too intense, it will disrupt the contemplative prayer and make it difficult to proceed. Simply conclude the session for the day and return to prayer the next day. Deep silence takes some getting used to and as we become more accustomed to it, the fear will dissolve on its own.

Spiritual ecstasy

The final stage of contemplative prayer is referred to as spiritual ecstasy. There are different dimensions to ecstasy, but this is such a subjective experience that I will touch on it here only briefly. Ecstasy occurs when the prayer of quiet has become very familiar and very deep. It can never be controlled or predetermined. It comes unexpectedly as a gift and generally stays only very fleetingly. It consists of an experience of profound peace and joy, which floods your entire being. Although it may last only a brief moment, the memory and the effect of it can last for days, infusing you with a sense of peace and well-being, and an assurance of God's love that passes beyond any conceptual knowledge. But even the experience of ecstasy is not an end in itself. You should not feel at this point that you have arrived and that the need for contemplative prayer is over. It is just a gift to signal growth and God's grace.

The final goal of contemplative prayer is to bring the attentiveness and the desire for God that we experience in prayer into our daily lives. Eventually the silence leads to an ongoing awareness of oneness with God. The famous contemplative, Irina Tweedie, whom I quoted earlier, says that eventually all we see is oneness. Seeing that oneness gives rise to profound compassion and love, and we become the fullest expressions of God's Spirit and life possible here on earth.

Chapter 6

Jesus

One day when Jesus was praying alone, the disciples came to him. "Who do the crowds say I am?" he asked them. "Some say that you are John the Baptist," they answered. "Others say that you are Elijah, while others say that one of the prophets of long ago has come back to life." "What about you?" he asked them. "Who do you say I am?" Peter answered, "You are God's Messiah."

Luke 9:18–20

The story is told about actor John Drew who was widely recognized by his very distinctive mustache. At one point in his career he shaved it off to play a particular role. Running into the British comedian Max Beerbohm, Drew was unable to recall who Beerbohm was. But Beerbohm still recognized Drew even without his mustache. Beerbohm was overheard to say, "Mr. Drew, I'm afraid you don't recognize me, without your mustache."

"Jesus is hot. He is being silk-screened on gowns from Gaultier and Dolce & Gabbana. He has a board game. He is setting the publishing industry on fire. Jesus is the icon of choice on T-shirts and tote bags sold in trendy shops on Toronto's Queen Street West, and he pops up in the lyrics of some of rap music's biggest acts." So began a front-page article entitled, "Give them Jesus, but hold the theology," from the national Canadian newspaper, *The Globe and Mail*.[1]

In this chapter I want to speak about Jesus. I don't have to tell you who Jesus is, because his is the most widely recognized name the world over. In North America, after a religious malaise of several decades, a Jesus phenomenon has emerged that has taken society by storm. Jesus is indeed hot. But although everyone knows who we are referring to when we mention the name of Jesus, most people know next to nothing about who this remarkable being really was. In this chapter, I want to talk about who Jesus really was.

I do this for various reasons: first, because I am a Christian and because I love this man who has been part of my life from its very beginning. Jesus has been in my heart and mind since my parents first told me Bible stories about him. In recent years, I have related to him as a spiritual presence guiding my life. He has been my spiritual master and my mentor.

Second, I want to speak about Jesus because many people – not just churchgoing Christians, but people everywhere – have a hunger to know who he was and what he represents. People recognize that Jesus is important as a guide and a mentor to the spiritual life, but they're just not sure how. People today continue to ask the same question Jesus himself asked his disciples: "Who do you say that I am?" We ask it because, intuitively, we know that when we answer that question we will also discover who *we* really are. We sense that when we answer that question we will learn what our hearts ultimately require to be happy and fulfilled. Learning about Jesus will teach us about ourselves.

Third, I need to speak about who Jesus really was because – and I say this with some personal sorrow – the church that developed in Jesus' name, and of which I am a part, has got it so badly wrong for so long now. Jesus, himself, would be appalled at so much the church has said about him and done in his name. Jesus recognized that, much of the time, his own disciples didn't understand what he was really all about. And this caused him great distress. This lack of understanding has been present in the church from the very beginning. For Jesus' sake, it's time to put the record straight.

Finally, I need to speak about who Jesus really was because he continues to be one of the most powerful agents for spiritual growth and transformation available to people. People are attracted to Jesus because he demonstrated in his life a connection to God and an experience of God's transforming grace and power. People want an experience of God in their own lives; they want to feel touched by the transcendent power of the divine; they want to know that their lives are significant and that they are cared for by God. Jesus, perhaps more than any other figure in the history of religion, demonstrates this profound connection with God. He is a window through whom the Spirit of God can shine and be revealed.

New Views of Jesus

Jesus according to contemporary scholarship

He comes as yet unknown into a hamlet of Lower Galilee. He is watched by the cold, hard eyes of peasants living long enough at subsistence level to know exactly where the line is drawn between poverty and destitution. He looks like a beggar, yet his eyes lack the proper cringe, his voice the proper whine, his walk the proper shuffle. He speaks about the rule of God and they listen as much from curiosity as anything else. They know all about rule and power, about kingdom and empire, but they know it in terms of tax and debt, malnutrition and sickness, agrarian oppression and demonic possession. What, they really want to know, can this Kingdom of God do for a lame child, a blind parent, a demented soul screaming its tortured isolation among the graves that mark the village fringes? Jesus walks with them to the tombs, and in the silence after he has exorcised the woman they brought him to see, the villagers listen once more, but now with curiosity giving way to cupidity, fear, and embarrassment. He is invited, as honor demands, to the home of the village leader. He goes, instead, to stay in the home of the dispossessed woman. Not quite proper, to be sure, but it would be unwise to censure an exorcist, to criticize a magician... The next day he leaves them, and now they wonder aloud about a divine kingdom with no respect for proper protocols – a kingdom as he said, not just for the poor, like themselves, but for the destitute.[2]

According to biblical scholars, Jesus was born, possibly just before 4 BCE, to Joseph and Mary, not at Bethlehem but at Nazareth,[3] a tiny hamlet whose population has been estimated at anything between 200 and 1200 people. He was born into, but not necessarily as the first of, a large family of six siblings.[4] His father was a carpenter and it is likely that Jesus learned the trade as well. The biblical scholar John Dominic Crossan cautions us, however, to avoid interpreting the term carpenter in modern terms, as a skilled, well-paid, and respected member of the middle class. In Jesus' world, a carpenter would have been from the "lower class" in a society in which the great divide lay between those who had to work with their hands and those who did not.[5] This has led to the insight that Jesus was a peasant, maybe even an illiterate peasant, contrary to what some of the biblical stories would have us believe. This may explain his love for and work with the poor and needy people of his society. He did not come from a wealthy, educated family. But this only tells us a very tiny part of the story.

Jesus was Jewish. It may seem obvious, but it's a point that always bears repeating. I love the following story.

Rabbi Joshua, having lived an exemplary life admired by all, died in the fullness of time and went to heaven. There he was greeted with hosannas of delight. Inexplicably, he shrank back, covered his face with his trembling old hands, and refused to participate in the festivities held in his honor. All persuasion having failed, he was ushered respectfully before the high judgment seat of God. The tender presence of God bathed the noble rabbi, and the divine voice filled his ears. "My child," said God, "it is on record that you have lived entirely in accord with my wishes, and yet you refuse the honors that have, most fittingly, been prepared for you. Why is this?" Rabbi Joshua, head bent low and voice meek, said, "O Holy One, I am not deserving. Somehow my life must have taken a wrong turn, for my son, heedless of my example and my precepts, turned Christian." "Alas," came the still voice, filled with infinite sympathy, "I understand and forgive entirely. After all, my son did the same."

It's a delightful tale, but not true. Jesus never became a Christian. Christianity emerged after he died – in fact, quite some time after.[6] He grew up in a Jewish household, and would have been raised with stories of the Jewish faith: the stories of Abraham and Sarah, and of Miriam and Moses. His Bible was the Jewish scriptures, the material many Christians refer to as the Old Testament. He celebrated the Jewish religious holidays, for example the Passover and Hanukkah. Contemporary scholars are certain that he never intended to start a new religion, but saw himself as reforming Judaism. He spoke as a Jew to other Jews and his first followers were all Jews. In the end, it was not the Jews who rejected him, for many were very sympathetic to his message. Rather, it was a small group of religious, political, and military leaders, Jewish and Roman, who decided they didn't want any problems during the feast of the Passover, who decided to do away with him as a potential troublemaker, a challenge to the status quo. His death was probably a very simple and barbaric act, not the highly dramatized version we find in the gospels. He died, very much still a Jew. This tells us a little more about Jesus. But we can go on.

Marcus Borg, another well-known biblical scholar, gives the following impressions of Jesus, which I will quote at length because they are so well-stated.

> His verbal gifts were remarkable. His language was most often metaphorical, poetic, and imaginative, filled with memorable short sayings and compelling stories. He was clearly exceptionally intelligent. Not only were his insights pointed and illuminating, but he was very clever in debate, often turning a question back on his interrogators so that they could not respond without discrediting themselves...
>
> He used dramatic public actions. He ate meals with untouchables, which not only generated criticism but also

symbolized his alternative vision of human community...
On one occasion he provocatively staged a demonstration in
the temple, overturning the tables of the money changers and
driving out the sellers of sacrificial animals.

There was a radical social and political edge to his message and activity. He challenged the social order of his day
and indicted the elites who dominated it... He must have
been remarkably courageous, willing to continue what he was
doing even when it was clear that it was putting him in lethal
danger...

He was a remarkable healer: more healing stories are told
about him than about anybody else in the Jewish tradition. He
attracted a following, including people who left their previous
lives behind, and any sketch of Jesus with a claim to historical
credibility must account for this fact. There must have been
something quite compelling about him...

And finally, he was young, his life was short, and his public
activity was brief. He lived only into his early thirties, and his
public activity lasted perhaps as little as a year (according to the
synoptic gospels) or as much as three or four years (according
to John). The founders of the world's other major religious
traditions lived long lives and were active for decades. It is
exceptional that so much came forth from such a brief life.[7]

Fleshing out these attributes even further, Borg describes Jesus in terms
of four positive roles he played. First, although Jesus was a Jew, and never
intended to start a new religion, he probably did have in mind to start
a religious revitalization movement within Judaism itself. As such, he
was a movement founder. Second, like the classical prophets of Israel,
he criticized the religious, economic, and political elites of his time and
advocated an alternative social vision that was based on compassion and the
breaking down of the traditional social boundaries that divided people into
socio-economic classes. As such, he was a social prophet. Third, he was a
teacher of wisdom who used stories, short parables, and sayings to instruct

people. And finally, he was a spirit person, one of those exceptional people in human history with a remarkable awareness and experience of God.[8]

The above understanding of Jesus, generated by contemporary biblical scholarship, points out what most people have always realized – Jesus was a truly remarkable being. What biblical scholars cannot tell us, however, because the data simply isn't available, is how Jesus got to be the way he was. It's that question I want to turn to now.

Jesus as spiritual genius

To really understand Jesus, we need to understand something about spiritual genius. Just as some people are born with musical genius, like Mozart, for example; or with athletic genius, like Tiger Woods or Wayne Gretzky; or with intellectual genius, like Einstein; some people are born with spiritual genius. Jesus was such a person.

We don't know why such people are born with this kind of genius. No doubt, genetic inheritance will be the primary factor. But family and socialization also contribute to the creation of such a person. Mozart's genius was encouraged and supported at a very young age by his father. Wayne Gretzky and Tiger Woods were nurtured in their athletic abilities by their parents. If the potential for genius is present, it will unfold when lovingly nurtured and supported. Tradition says that Mary and Joseph were religious and saintly people, and it's probably true. In all likelihood, Jesus grew up in a poor household, but one that was deeply devout and spiritual.

But the origin of spiritual genius remains mysterious, genetically based, and uniquely inherent to the person. We know today that the temporal lobe of the brain contributes to feelings of spiritual transcendence and mystical presence. It may be that people of spiritual genius have highly developed temporal lobes. Ancient peoples, who had no understanding of genetics or of personality development, came up with their own theories and stories to account for spiritual giftedness. In the case of Jesus, his later followers invented the story of the divine birth, to explain his amazing, mysterious presence in the world.

It's important to note that Jesus was not the only person in his day to be credited with divine origins. Gaius Octavius was born on September 23, 63 BCE, and became the adopted son and legal heir of Julius Caesar, who was assassinated on March 15, 44 BCE. After Caesar's deification by the Roman Senate on January 1, 42 BCE, Octavius immediately became *divi filius*, son of a divine one. Some 59 years later, after defeating all of his foes and bringing peace to the Roman Empire, the Roman Senate deified Octavius on September 17, 14 AD, a month after his death on August 19.[9] Crossan notes that it is amazing not that Octavius, supreme Roman emperor, was considered divine, but that Jesus, the poor, lowly carpenter from Nazareth was also considered divine. Stories of divinity represented the ancients' way of acknowledging that something amazing had been revealed in certain human beings. In the case of Jesus, that "something" was spiritual genius.

People of spiritual genius are found all over the world; from every different ethnic, cultural, and religious background; and from both sexes. However, they are not all born equal or the same. Some possess different kinds of spiritual genius and some are simply more gifted than others.

The brilliant American mystic and teacher Adi Da Samraj has suggested that spiritual development occurs according to a seven-stage process. According to this model, the first stage spans the first seven years of a child's life and is when simple biological competence is acquired. In the second stage, relational, or emotional-sexual competence is acquired. This should ideally be achieved during the period from seven to 14 years of age, but seldom is. The third stage, from 14 to 21 years, sees the acquisition of intellectual competence, which permits the integration of the biological and emotional-sexual aspects of one's being. Devotional competence is gained in the fourth stage, which marks the beginning of spiritual life. This coincides with the awakening of higher psychic sensitivity, and the capacity for heartfelt devotion, selfless service, compassion, and genuine love, involving a reorientation of one's entire life. The fifth stage is that of mystical competence, which entails the ability to focus attention on the inner psychic dimension of one's being, and which ultimately leads to the mind-shattering experience of formless ecstasy. The sixth and seventh stages, characterized as the stages of witnessing competence and enlightenment competence respectively, lead to a deeper and more permanent realization of total immersion and unity in and with ultimate reality, the divine source of life itself.[10]

People of spiritual genius often undergo mystical experiences without realizing that such experiences do not necessarily represent the highest goal of the spiritual life. Ultimately, as the New Testament claims, the highest achievements of the spiritual life have to do with selfless love and compassion for others, not with remarkable experiences. The medieval Spanish contemplative, John of the Cross, was the spiritual director for the mystic Teresa of Avila. John of the Cross constantly had to caution Teresa, who was prone to all sorts of remarkable mystical experiences, that these were not the point of it all. In Christian spirituality, a clear distinction is made between contemplatives and mystics. Mystics tend to have a wide variety of experiences, as they focus their attention on God in prayer and meditation. They may see visions, hear sounds, and feel various energies or moments of bliss. Contemplatives, on the other hand, simply become more and more immersed in a loving, silent, attention, which they focus on God.

People of spiritual genius often need to undergo an intense period of exploration and development of their spiritual abilities, before they begin to work with others. Typically, this work involves two components. One is functioning as an apprentice under another great spiritual leader. The second involves entering into solitude and utilizing intense spiritual discipline, including various forms of prayer, meditation, and contemplation. Very often, when spiritual geniuses emerge from their training with other teachers and from their work in solitude, they, too, become not only teachers, but also healers and channels of spiritual energy transmission, with the power to transform other people.

That Jesus fits into the category of highly evolved spiritual genius is undeniable. The entire New Testament makes this very clear. Likely, Jesus had John the Baptist as a spiritual mentor. Jesus had visions, including the vision at his baptism, when he "saw the heavens opened and the Spirit descending upon him like a dove." That experience prompted him to enter a period of prolonged solitude in the wilderness, where he experienced more visions and temptations, the familiar dark night of the soul known by all spiritual seekers. In the wilderness and throughout his ministry, he spent long periods in solitude, silent meditation, and prayer. Through this process of prayer, he developed a profound sense of intimacy and closeness with God, to the degree that he referred to God using the deeply personal term *Abba*, or Daddy.

Although scholars believe the gospel of John to be the farthest removed from the actual life and sayings of Jesus, it is fascinating to note how John presents Jesus' self-awareness. John describes Jesus as someone who is brilliantly capable of "the genius of And" thinking. In chapter 14 of John's gospel, Jesus says to his disciples, "Now that you have known me," he said to them, "you will know my Father also, and from now on you do know him and you have seen him... Whoever has seen me has seen the Father... I am in the Father and the Father is in me... The Father, who remains in me, does his own work" (John 14:7–10). Although the wording of these sayings may have more to do with the writer of John's gospel than with Jesus, the same sense of intimacy and closeness that they reveal between Jesus and God is also noted in the synoptic gospels (Matthew, Mark, and Luke) that scholars believe more accurately reflect Jesus' life, from a historical perspective.

In these sayings, Jesus demonstrates a paradoxical both/and awareness of his relationship with God. Although Jesus obviously relates to God as *Abba*, as "Father" – that is to say, as a reality separate from himself – he also expresses a profound sense of unity and oneness with God. "Anyone who has seen me has seen the Father." "I am in the Father and the Father is in me." "The Father who remains in me." These words express precisely the sentiments, and the actual awareness, that people of spiritual genius have expressed in all the world's different spiritual and religious traditions. The more you give yourself over to God, the more you become aware of your fundamental unity and oneness with God.

When Jesus returned from the wilderness, having established himself in his relationship with God and in the awareness of his unity with God, he began his public ministry with the tangible aura of authority of someone who knew from personal experience what he was speaking about.

And finally, Jesus became a healer. He conducted spiritual energies of such power, that he was able to promote healing in many people.

Obviously, Jesus was a remarkable spiritual being. He had a deep and continuous relationship with God that totally transformed his life and that enabled him to be an agent of transformation in the lives of others. It is to this dimension of Jesus that we now turn.

Jesus as agent of spiritual transformation

Notice that I have not used any of the traditional language about Jesus, which describes him as the Son of God. Nor have I referred to him as a means of salvation. Salvation, understood as going to heaven after we die, is not primarily what interests people about Jesus, at least not people outside the church. What interests people today is achieving a personal, spiritual transformation that will bring peace, happiness, and a sense of wholeness to their crazy and chaotic lives, and to the life of our society as a whole. This is what matters. And the question for Christians and non-Christians alike is, "How can Jesus do this for us?"

There are three principal ways in which Jesus serves as a powerful agent of transformation in human life today. Some 2000 years after his death, Jesus remains a spiritual hero and a role model, a teacher, and a spiritual presence to whom we can relate.

Jesus as spiritual hero

In 1992, my sister-in-law, Silken Laumann, was the unquestioned Canadian contender for the gold medal in the women's single rowing event at the Olympics, to be held in Barcelona, Spain, that summer. She had been the world champion several times over. During warm-up exercises at the world championship games held in Germany in May of that year, her boat was struck by another rowing shell. The metal cap of that boat slashed through the lightweight shell of her own boat and cut into her leg, tearing away a huge chunk of skin, muscle, and ligament. She was rushed by ambulance to emergency surgery at a German hospital. When she was stabilized a few days later, she was flown back to Canada for additional surgery and medical treatment. Doctors initially warned her that she might never walk on that leg again, and likely would never row again. Silken just wanted to know if she could compete in the Olympics, a short two and a half months later. It had been her lifelong dream. The doctors told her it was impossible to even contemplate. However, they didn't know Silken. Not only did she contemplate the impossible, she worked feverishly to achieve it. In August 1992, she not only competed at the Olympics in Barcelona, but won the bronze medal. It was a monumental, once-in-a-lifetime achievement. And it guaranteed Silken a permanent place as a Canadian hero and role model, who has since inspired many others, by her great act of courage and will power, to strive to achieve their own dreams.

We need heroes. We need role models. We need people to emulate, people who can inspire us to move beyond our limitations, beyond our discouragement and our despair, to achieve great things, our very fullest potential.

Throughout history, Jesus has served as a spiritual hero and role model of the very highest order. Jesus was the quintessential kid who came from the wrong side of the tracks, but who made good anyway. Born from poor and humble origins, he went on to transform the world with his vision of God's love and goodness. He was compassionate and loving, and defended the rights of the poor and oppressed. He confronted religious, economic, military, and political powers with the strength of his courage, integrity, passion, and spiritual insight. And although seemingly defeated at first, he was reborn in the lives and efforts of his followers to transform the world. Today, few remember Gaius Octavius, the Roman emperor of that time, but millions remember Jesus. He is truly a hero and an inspiration.

Jesus as teacher

We all need teachers. As a parent, I realize that love is the very first and principal ingredient needed to raise a happy and healthy child. But love alone is not enough. Children need to acquire information and skills that will enable them to become mature and independent. They can never achieve their full potential without doing so. For this to take place, they need teachers. They need teachers to train them in the arts and the humanities, in the skills of communication and interpersonal relationships. They need teachers to train them in mathematics and science, and in the technical skills required to function in the world. They need teachers to train them in basic life management, but also in the organizational skills required by today's highly complex society. And they need teachers who will train them in ethics and morality, and the deepest issues of life. Without this training, our children can never be truly happy and society cannot survive.

From time to time, often when civilizations seem to need it most, a spiritual genius of the highest order will be born, a person who is capable of reorienting and reestablishing the benchmarks of spiritual and religious training needed for that time and place. Jesus was one of these great teachers. He never wrote a book, but his moral and ethical teaching, and his demonstration of that teaching in his life and actions, left such a mark on his followers that they went on to transform the world.

Fundamentally, Jesus taught very simple yet profound lessons. He taught that the traditional values and indicators of success – namely wealth, prestige, and power – do not in the end bring happiness or well-being. He taught that lives lived with compassion, love, and in relationship to God are lives in which true happiness can be found. He conveyed this message using numerous stories and examples that continue to guide us. His teaching was simple, but living it out in daily life is not. His message carried over the centuries and continues to challenge and inspire us still today.

Jesus as spiritual presence and object of devotion

When I was seven, my parents bought me a children's story Bible that was filled with beautiful pictures. The creation of the earth, the animals walking into the ark, Joseph in his multicolored coat, the Israelites passing through the Red Sea, Samson pulling down the pillars of the temple, Ruth and Naomi picking sheaves of wheat in Boaz's field: all of these and many more etched themselves into my psyche and imagination. But the most powerful image for me was one of Jesus, not surrounded by sheep or children or disciples, as you might expect, but simply standing on the shore of the Sea of Galilee looking out across the water. Standing tall in his cloak and sandals, he wore an expression of perfect wisdom and utmost serenity upon his face. And at the age of seven, I knew I wanted to be like this man.

I've said it before and I'll say it again: "What you meditate upon is what you become." For years, I have meditated upon Jesus, sometimes more intentionally, sometimes less. I have learned everything there is to learn about this man. I have read all the essays and all the books produced by scholars. But in the end I have discovered that I have to place him in my heart. I need to situate him at the very center of my life, in terms of its prayer and feeling. I need to let go of intellectual enquiry, doubt included, and simply accept him as a living, spiritual presence in my life. Doing so has made all the difference in my life!

As I said earlier in this book, the spiritual journey is ultimately about learning how to love at ever-deeper levels. It can be likened to the growth experienced by a couple who, throughout years of marriage, have learned to love and appreciate each other ever more fully, not just in the romantic and exciting moments of life, but in the very simple and mundane times as well. Love is not just an emotional state or the desire to do good for others. Ultimately, love resides in the awareness of the interdependence of all life, in the recognition that all of life emerges out of and is contained within the sacred body of God. As you recognize that you are a part of God just as I am a part of God, the compassion and the grace of God flows through each of us for the other. To enter into this truth, not just as an intellectual observation, but also as an emotional, intuitive, and direct conscious awareness, is the great challenge of the spiritual life. The higher reaches and stages of the spiritual journey are all devoted to fostering this awareness and ability in people. And the role of the spiritual genius, the spiritual hero, plays a very critical function in this development.

Devotion to a spiritual hero is a path found in all of the world's religious traditions. Hindus worship Krishna with flowers and incense; Sufis worship Allah with ecstatic dancing; Buddhists worship the Buddha in silent meditation. Most religions have sacred times and places for devotional worship. For Christians, Jesus is the central being of faith and the object of worship and devotion.

The path of spiritual devotion is about becoming spiritually married to the central figure of your faith, to your spiritual hero, and then keeping that one in your heart and mind forever.

The path of spiritual devotion starts with a premise that cannot be proven any more than the existence of God can be proven. This premise has two parts. The first part most people simply take for granted. It is that Jesus lived as a flesh-and-blood human being, in Israel, 2000 years ago, and that he was the source of a small "Jesus movement" that arose around him.

The second part of the premise is a little more obscure and, as I say, not subject to any kind of objective verification. Rather, it requires a subjective transformation within each of us before we can see it. It is simply that, in some form or fashion, Jesus continues to live on in the vast power and being we call God.

The resurrection of Jesus has been an article of Christian dogma and faith for 2000 years. The New Testament is a witness to it. However, we know from contemporary biblical scholarship that what we find in the New Testament are storytellers' versions of events, and not literal historical descriptions. Still, in some mysterious and subjective way, the early disciples of Jesus and the followers of Jesus up to this day have sensed that Jesus is alive.

A parallel exists with people who have undergone near-death experiences. Science can provide a variety of plausible explanations for such experiences, attributing them to the brain chemistry and psychology of the dying person. But the person who has gone through such an experience knows beyond all shadow of a doubt that, regardless of the explanation, death is not an ending. As a result, they typically go on to live without fear of this critical passage.

Some esoteric spiritual traditions believe that in the vast being of God there exists a personal dimension of creative power. According to this belief, and from time to time as needed, this creative power literally comes to life or incarnates as a highly spiritualized hero, a God-transparent human being. In Christian terminology, this dimension of God has been referred to as the *logos*, the Word of God, which was spoken and gave birth in Jesus of Nazareth. Other world traditions speak of a whole hierarchy of lesser gods or divine beings, all of which are expressions of God and which manifest in human realms as great spiritual beings.

Upon death, the physical body of the historical figure is shed. But the true, transcendent identity and power that came to life as that person – for Christians, Jesus of Nazareth – lives on within the vast realms of God.

So when Buddhists worship the Buddha, or Hindus worship Krishna, or Christians worship Jesus, they are not just worshipping the historical human being that has long since died. In the spirit of the "genius of the AND," they are worshipping both the historical figure of the spiritual genius *and* the personal, transcendent power of God that came to life on earth as this person. For Christians this creative power is the Christ, often referred to as the Cosmic Christ, the personal energy or power of God that came to birth as Jesus of Nazareth long ago.

The path of spiritual devotion, then, is about developing and nurturing a feeling of love for the spiritual hero. It is about learning to fall deeply and passionately in love not solely with Jesus the historical figure who lived and died 2000 years ago, but with the Cosmic Christ, that power of God that became expressed as Jesus of Nazareth, and that continues to live in the transcendent realms of God today.

So how do we fall in love with Jesus? First, we need to give ourselves over to the belief and understanding that the historical Jesus of Nazareth continues to live on as a creative energy and power in God. Second, we need to meditate on the life of Jesus by reading the gospels and the stories they tell of him; by learning to worship him in church and services of worship, perhaps using pictures and other sacred objects to inspire our devotion; and by generally coming to understand what a tremendously beautiful and wondrous expression of God's love and power he was. Third, we need to learn to pray to Jesus, to relate to him as real and alive, "here and now." Fourth, that prayer and cultivation of the sense of his presence must become more and more continuous in our life.

The great spiritual traditions recommend that we keep the name of the beloved in our heart and mind always, repeating the name over and over until it becomes a permanent fixture in our consciousness. Whenever our mind is not being used for work or daily activities, it simply slips back into repeating the name of Jesus. With the name comes remembrance, and with remembrance comes the sense of presence. In the Eastern Orthodox tradition of Christianity, this practice is known as the Jesus Prayer.

Eventually, two things happen on this path of spiritual devotion. First, we fall more deeply and passionately in love with Jesus as a spiritual presence. Our human love is always limited and surrounded by the barriers of ego. But in this spiritual relationship with Jesus, our hearts truly begin to open up. We start to feel a continuous love for Jesus. That love then naturally flows outwards into our relationships with other people and with the world around us. We become transformed. We become more loving, more caring, more compassionate, and, paradoxically, more like Christ himself.

The second thing that happens is that our attention becomes more deeply absorbed in either the repetition of the name of Jesus, or in an actual sense of his presence. How this develops will be somewhat different for each of us. But eventually a profound sense or intuition of oneness starts to emerge. We begin to feel that we are one with Jesus, and that in and through Jesus we are one with God and with all of life.

The reason the path of spiritual devotion is so powerful is because it utilizes the emotional force of love. Maintaining a spiritual discipline is an incredibly hard endeavor for all people for two reasons: first, because the average person has no means of accountability for sticking to the process. We don't have coaches, bosses, or mentors observing, encouraging, and holding us accountable to a spiritual practice. Second, for most people the spiritual life remains vague and ill-defined. When we are learning how to play the piano, there are very clear signs of progress. However, in the spiritual life it is very easy to become discouraged because, as we grow, we become more aware of our limitations, more aware of our ego, more aware of our faults and struggles. In fact, this awareness represents progress and leads to a growth in humility. But in practice, we easily become disheartened and confused, and tend to let go of our spiritual practice. Love, however, is a powerful motivating force. As we fall in love with someone, we become attached not to a spiritual discipline, but to a relationship. And the relationship itself becomes the motivation for remaining in the practice and on the path.

Obviously, this spiritual path or process of devotion has no end. So it is no use thinking, "I can never get there," or "I may as well not even start." The true goal of the spiritual practitioner is to have his or her heart begin to open in love, and to begin to intuit, even in small ways, the presence of God, which gives rise to all of life and binds it together in one unending fabric.

The path of devotional worship of Jesus, as described above, is surprisingly not that common for most Christians. Most feel more comfortable worshipping God, as revealed to the world in Jesus. And, indeed, worshipping Jesus is not the only way for Christians to grow spiritually or to draw closer to God. Yet the practice of cultivating a relationship with Jesus as our living spiritual guide and hero possesses a power that is quite profound in that it draws upon the strength of human love to lead us ever deeper into the spiritual life. It is a path that requires experimentation and practice in order to discern its impact and it will not appeal to all. However, such experimentation is well worth the effort!

Having looked at faith, Jesus, and a variety of tools and methodologies that can facilitate the spiritual life and the journey into God, we can now consider how what we have learned speaks to the pressing issues that affect us in our everyday lives.

LIVING
THE VISION

Chapter 7

Morality & the Bible

[A teacher of the law asked Jesus...] "which is the greatest commandment in the Law?" Jesus answered, "'Love the Lord your God with all your heart, with all your soul, and with all your mind.' This is the greatest and the most important commandment. The second most important commandment is like it: 'Love your neighbor as you love yourself.' The whole Law of Moses and the teachings of the prophets depend on these two commandments."

Matthew 22:35–40

A professor of ethics once gave her class this moral dilemma as part of an examination. You are driving along on a wild stormy night. You pass by a bus stop and you see three people waiting for the bus: 1) an old lady who is about to die from a heart attack, 2) an old friend who once saved your life, 3) the perfect man or woman you have always been dreaming about. Which one would you choose to pick up, knowing there was room for only one passenger in your small, European sports car?

You could pick up the old lady, because she might be dying, and thus you should save her first; or you could take the old friend because she or he once saved your life and this might be your perfect chance to pay her back. However, you might never be able to find your perfect dream lover ever again.

The student who received the top grade, out of 200 classmates, came up with this answer: "I would give the car keys to my old friend and let her take the sick woman to the hospital. I would stay behind and wait for the bus with the man of my dreams."

During my childhood, I was fascinated by stories my father told about his experiences as a soldier during World War II. I could listen to them over and over again. My parents were born and raised in pre-World War II Germany. As a young man, fluently bilingual in German and English, my dad became quite interested in Canada. During the 1930s, he decided to visit Canada and while here applied for permission to stay. Although various other European visitors to Canada found whatever work they could and quietly disappeared into the fabric of Canadian society, my dad had a strong sense of personal ethics and never considered staying illegally. Canadian immigration officials informed him that he would be an ideal candidate for immigration, but unfortunately, due to the economic depression and the lack of jobs in Canada, they could not give him permission to stay. By that time, Hitler and the Nazi party were on the rise in Germany and my father was not happy about returning to that environment. He asked immigration officials if there were other options for him. They noted that England likely wouldn't take him for the same reasons as Canada, but that Spain might be open to doing so. However, Franco and his brand of fascism were on the rise in Spain and my father had no interest in going there either. In the end, he had no choice but to return to Germany. Upon returning, his moral and religious convictions led him into a precarious situation.

My dad was part of a church organization of which the Nazis became somewhat suspicious. One day, local Nazi officials called him to their offices for a meeting. They said they were concerned about possible anti-government activities by several members in my dad's religious community. They asked him to keep an eye on these people and to report back to them any suspicious activities. My father politely told them that to do so was against his principles and that he would have to decline. Apparently, at that point, the lead official interviewing him became very hot under the collar and screamed at him, "We can make things very difficult for you,

Mr. Hoppner. How would you like to spend the next few years in a German prison? You are a disgrace to Germany and not fit to be called a German citizen!" My father was shaking when he left the meeting, aware they could have followed through on their threats. However, their behavior also provoked him and he proceeded to write a letter to Nazi officials higher up the chain of command. In his polite but firm literary style, he noted that he was very insulted by the behavior of the local Nazi officers. In addition, he took great exception to their comment that he was not a good German citizen just because he lived by ethical principles that precluded him from spying on fellow members of his church. He never received a reply.

Some time later, like most age-appropriate German men of the time, he was drafted into military service. However, he always made it clear to his superiors that he had religious and political convictions and for the most part the non-Nazi officers respected him for this. To the day he died, my dad felt a deep sense of gratitude to God for being assigned to a supply posting, where he never had to shoot at or kill anyone.

Stories like these, as well as observing the way my father lived his life, made a deep impression upon my young psyche. My parents finally immigrated to Canada late in life, after the war was over. Although my family was never financially well off, my father always insisted that we give ten percent of our income to our church and to charity. As in his experience with the Nazis, in his everyday life, he truly lived his religious and moral convictions and impressed upon me the importance of doing likewise.

With this chapter, we begin to consider how the newly emerging paradigm of God and Christian spirituality affects our everyday lives and behavior. This leads us to the study of morality and ethics, an examination of what constitutes right and appropriate human action. As I observed in an earlier chapter, morality and mysticism constitute two sides of one coin. You cannot authentically have one without the other. Mysticism and the emerging spirituality provide the foundation for a new way of understanding God. God is not far away from us, up in the sky, but is present all around us and is in fact the very ground of who we are, our own deepest identity. But this new vision has profoundly moral implications, which we need to consider given the fact that we live in an age of such enormous ethical complexity.

The Bible as Moral Authority

Before we consider how the new vision of God and spirituality shapes our understanding and expression of ethics, we need to consider the place and role of sacred scripture in our decision making. Traditionally, when Christians have faced difficult moral situations, they have turned to the Bible for guidance and for answers. (Christians are not unique in this; people of other faiths typically turn to their own sacred scriptures for guidance under similar circumstances.) However, although the Bible certainly plays a role when it comes to Christian moral reflection and decision making, it is not the only thing to be considered. This is true for several reasons.

The authority of the Bible

Historically, most religious traditions have adopted a fairly high view of their sacred scriptures. That is to say, they have gone to great lengths to assert that their sacred scriptures were somehow either written by God or divinely inspired. The purpose of all such assertions has been to endow sacred scripture with absolute authority, the authority of infallibility.

So perhaps the very first thing to assert here is that the Bible was *not* written by God; it was written by human beings. People who continue to insist on the divine origins of the Bible can only do so by steadfastly refusing to face the evidence that modern scholarship has revealed about the Bible.

When we look to the Bible, or to any other sacred text as an absolute authority, we ascribe to it the characteristics of God. This is sometimes called bibliolatry: worshipping the Bible as God. But the Bible is *not* God and should not be *treated* as God. Rather, the Bible, and all other sacred scripture, is a lens through which we look at and think about God. The Bible shapes and colors how we think about God by causing us to look at God through the thoughts and images of our ancestors. Marcus Borg uses a poignant metaphor from the Buddhist tradition to characterize sacred scriptures. Buddhists often speak of the teaching of the Buddha as "a finger pointing to the moon." The temptation is always to focus on the finger, the teaching, instead of on the moon, that to which the finger points.[1] The Bible is not God, but encourages us to pay attention to God, to whom it points.

Furthermore, when we look to the Bible for absolute authority and truth, we deny the purpose and intent of faith in our lives. Faith exists in the absence of absolute proof. Faith is required because no absolute proof or authority is available to human beings.

In light of this observation, some people wonder, "Then what makes the Bible special and sacred?" Again, Marcus Borg makes the helpful point that our scriptures are not sacred because they have their origins in God, but because of the special status we give them in our lives and in our religious communities. When we call our scriptures sacred, it is not because God dictated them, thereby making them inerrant or absolute. We call our scriptures sacred because of the importance we attach to them, because of the place we ascribe to them within our religious tradition.[2]

Sacred scripture, including the Christian Bible, is a record of the experiences and reflections of our spiritual ancestors, as they sought to understand their relationship with God. In the Bible, we see the changing and developing thought of the ancient Hebrew people over the course of roughly 1000 years of history, culminating in the life of Jesus and the experience of the early Christian community. In fact, the Bible is not a single book, but a collection of books and writings. In other words, we might think of it more aptly as a library that includes many different kinds of literature, including stories and myths, rules and regulations, prayers of many different types, songs, love poetry, collections of proverbs and wisdom sayings, accounts of prophetic visions and mystical experiences, and, yes, some actual history, too. As with any library, not all the works are of equal artistic value or spiritual merit. But all these different works emerge out of and reflect the hunger of ancient Israel to know God, to understand God, and to live a life in harmony with God's will. That is what makes these scriptures not only important but also sacred to us today.

The Methodist heritage names four cornerstones for Christian life and decision making: the Bible, tradition, experience, and reason. It is a wise model, in which each of these four cornerstones relies on the others. None is intended to stand alone. At the same time, we cannot call ourselves Christian without including our sacred scripture, the Bible, within the equation. The Bible is one of our foundation stones, a source of tremendous wisdom that has shaped both our spiritual and our cultural identity. When we turn to the Bible to see what it has to say about moral and ethical issues, we do so out of respect and a desire to know what our Hebrew ancestors, our spiritual forebears, thought about such matters. We appreciate that they had a close relationship with God and possessed deep wisdom that might be helpful for us today.

The differences between biblical and contemporary times

There is another reason why the Bible, or any sacred scripture, cannot constitute the only or even the final word of authority when it comes to moral issues and decision making. Quite simply, although there is a commonality to human experience throughout history, many of the situations we face today have no precedent in biblical experience. The biblical writers knew nothing of high-tech medical life-support systems and therefore never had to consider the ethics of removing life-support from a loved one. The biblical writers lived millennia before the advent of nuclear weapons. They did not have to discern the ethical appropriateness of creating weapons of mass destruction as a strategy of deterrence.

In addition, many of the issues that biblical writers *did* need to deal with are simply no longer issues for us today. Reading through the ancient laws and regulations that governed Israelite society, which are found in the Book of Leviticus, we see how totally irrelevant much of that material is to our contemporary life. Among other things, Leviticus contains regulations for the purification of women after childbirth, laws concerning mildew in houses, rules for how to treat slaves, regulations concerning the execution of animals for burnt offerings, and so on. Of course, in some ways the underlying issues these laws were meant to address are timeless. Greed, jealousy, anger, and all the emotions of the human heart were the same for the ancient Hebrews as they are for us today. But in other ways we live in a world that is so totally different it is almost beyond comparison. So we turn to our ancestors for their wisdom on the larger spiritual issues of the human heart, but recognize that when it comes to concerns of culture, science, technology, and modern learning, we need to travel forward on the basis of our own understanding, not theirs.

The Greatest Commandment

The CEO of a large corporation died and came before Saint Peter. "What exactly have you done to earn eternal happiness?" asked Saint Peter. The CEO recalled that he had given 50 cents to a bum on the street just the other day. Saint Peter looked grimly over to his assistant, Gabriel, and asked, "Is that in the records?" Gabriel nodded, but Saint Peter told the executive it wasn't enough. "Wait, wait, there's more," pleaded the CEO. "Just a week ago I tripped over a homeless boy and gave him 50 cents too." Gabriel checked the records and confirmed the story. Saint Peter contemplated and then asked Gabriel, "What should we do?" Gabriel glanced at the CEO in disgust and said, "I say we give him back his buck and tell him to go to hell!"

For many people, the Ten Commandments (Deuteronomy 5:1–21, Exodus 20:1–17) best represent the timeless ethical wisdom developed by our Hebrew ancestors, a wisdom that crosses all the divides of culture, technology, and modernity in general. According to the ancient story, God gave the Ten Commandments to Moses for the edification and direction of the Hebrew people. This was the storyteller's way of ascribing to the Ten Commandments the moral authority they had come to bear for their society. Of course, the Hebrew Bible contains hundreds of other moral and legal rules governing all sorts of behavior, because this was the way ancient Hebrew society, including the one in which Jesus lived, approached morality and ethical behavior; it codified all behavior and established strict rules for as many circumstances as possible. But Jesus realized this was not the most helpful way to encourage moral or ethical living. He recognized that human experience is far too varied and complex to be governed by a list of rules – even a seemingly exhaustive one.

When he was asked, "What is the greatest commandment?" Jesus responded with the words quoted above: "Love the Lord your God with all your heart, with all your soul, and with all your mind." Then he continued: "The second most important commandment is like it: 'Love your neighbor as you love yourself'" (Matthew 22:34–39). In fact, neither of these is a rule or law, at least not like those found in the Ten Commandments or throughout Hebrew scripture. How can you legislate love, either for God or for neighbor? You can't. Jesus' point is that if love is present, then all those other rules and regulations, laws and commandments, become unnecessary. This is why he concludes by saying, "The whole Law of Moses and the teachings of the prophets depend on these two commandments" (Matthew 22:40).

St. Paul put it this way: "I may be able to speak the languages of men and even of angels, but if I have no love, my speech is no more than a noisy gong, or a clanging bell" (1 Corinthians 13:1). We can follow the law and obey the rules, but if we do not have love, we accomplish nothing of lasting value. In short, without love, a truly ethical life is impossible. If we really *do* love God and *do* love our neighbor, our actions and behavior will be molded by love, making all those rules and regulations unnecessary. Pay attention to these two commandments, and everything else will fall into place.

In other words, Jesus is suggesting that we not worry unduly about following the letter of the law. He and his disciples were notorious for breaking rules that to them made no sense. Rather, in place of the letter of the law, Jesus suggests the use of an overall attitude or perspective in life, a general way of viewing the world. And that perspective, which is reinforced in the Hebrew scriptures and in the entire Christian Bible, has to do with loving God and loving our neighbor.

When you love someone deeply, passionately, and continuously, you develop a profound sense of empathy for that person. You begin to view the world through their eyes. You seek to relate to them and to care for them taking their perspective and needs into account.

It is no different when we truly begin to fall in love with God. When we love God, we begin to hold God in our thoughts and prayers, in our minds and hearts, continuously. In the process, we begin to reflect on the world from God's perspective. And that perspective is different from our normal daily outlook.

When we begin to look at the world with the eyes of God, or to reflect on life with the mind of Christ, we cannot help but consider all of creation. We begin to view the collective struggle of humankind as a whole. In the process, our gaze becomes less personal and more impersonal. The word "impersonal" here does not imply a lack of love. Rather, it suggests the growth of an all-encompassing love.

As we grow in the spiritual life, through all the processes named in this book, we begin to recognize that our personal, individuated lives, though sacred and precious, are but very small pieces in the larger unfolding of history and universal life. We cherish our individual lives, but also come to identify with the broader life of humanity, and indeed of the universe itself. In the process, our individual lives diminish somewhat in importance and instead we learn to value more deeply that larger life of which we are a part. We come to see ourselves as but an individual thread in a complex and beautiful tapestry; as a single patch in a large and multifaceted quilt; as a single note in an exquisite symphony. Paradoxically, the thread, the patch, and the note, are also one with the tapestry, the quilt, and the symphony. Not only are they all interconnected and interdependent, but all of it is created out of the same underlying Spirit and power we call God. And so we come to see ourselves not only as a part of the larger fabric of life, but also as participating in the Source of that larger life. We are the creator and the created at one and the same time. Processes of prayer and contemplation, as well as processes of reflection and service, all lead to this awareness. This is the awareness that emerges out of a deep and profound love for God. This is the awareness that Jesus was seeking to cultivate in his listeners. And it is this awareness that provides the foundation for a truly moral and ethical response to life.

An Ethics for Complexity

Mary José Hobday, a Spanish, Native American says that her Native mother taught her many wonderful Native American concepts. But the concept of the Fourteen Generations remains one of the most broadening and challenging. The idea is deceptively simple, but wonderfully profound. It suggests that we need to pay reverence and respect to the seven generations that have gone before us and the seven generations that will come after us. According to this tradition, we need to keep seven generations, forward and back, in our minds and hearts in everything we do, and live accordingly.[3]

Good Will Hunting, a movie written by Matt Damon and Ben Affleck and produced in 1997, was nominated for nine academy awards. In the movie, the most brilliant mind at America's top university doesn't belong to a professor or a student, but to the kid who cleans the floors. Will Hunting, played by Matt Damon, is a headstrong, working class genius who is nonetheless failing the lessons of life. After one too many run-ins with the law, Will's last chance comes in the form of a psychology professor, played by Robin Williams, who ends up being the only man who can reach Will.

One of the most memorable parts of the movie, for me, is the scene in which Will is interviewed by officials from the National Security Agency (NSA), who want to hire him for his ability to solve mathematical equations, which form the root of all codes. After outlining all the possible benefits of working for the NSA, one of the interviewers says to Will, "Well, son, the question isn't why should you work for the NSA; the question is why *wouldn't* you work for the NSA." This is Will's response:

> Why shouldn't I work for the NSA? That's a tough one, but I'll take a shot. Say I'm working at the NSA and someone puts a code on my desk. Something no one else can break. Maybe I take a shot at it and maybe I break it. I'm real happy with myself cause I've done my job real well. But maybe that code was the location of some rebel army in the North of Africa or the Middle East. And once you guys have that location, you bomb

the village where the rebels are hiding. Fifteen hundred people I never met, never had no problem with, get killed. Now the politicians are saying, "Oh send in the Marines to secure the place," cause they don't give a damn. Won't be their kid over there getting shot, just like it wasn't them when their number got pulled because they were all doing a tour in the National Guard. It'll be some kid from Harlem over there taking shrapnel in the backside. He'll come back to find that the plant he used to work at got exported to the country he just got back from, and the guy who put the shrapnel in his backside got his old job because he'll work for fifteen cents a day and no bathroom breaks.

Meanwhile, my buddy realizes that the only reason we were over there in the first place was that we could install a government that would sell us oil at a good price. And of course the oil companies can use a little skirmish over there to scare up domestic oil prices – a cute little ancillary benefit for them – but it ain't helping my buddy at $2.50 a gallon. Then the oil companies take their own time, of course, to get the oil back. Maybe, they even took the liberty of hiring an alcoholic skipper who likes to drink martinis in places crawling with icebergs. It ain't too long till he hits one, spills the oil, and kills all the sea life in the North Atlantic.

So now my buddy's out of work. He can't afford to drive so he walks, which is a major drag because the shrapnel in his backside gives him chronic hemorrhoids. And meanwhile he's starving because every time he tries to get a bite to eat, the only cheapie meal they're giving is North Atlantic cod served up with Quaker State oil. So you want me to take your job breaking codes. I think I'll hold out for something better.[4]

We live in an incredibly complex world where it's so easy to go to our jobs and live our lives and never think about the consequences of our actions in terms of the well-being of humankind or the earth. With his brilliant mind, Will Hunting analyzes the larger implications of the activities of some "average guy" sitting in front of a computer screen cracking military codes. The movie suggest that we cannot afford the luxury of "simply doing our jobs," of living our own quietly isolated lives unaware of the world around us. All of the choices we make – from the career we pursue, to the kind of car we drive, to the food we eat, to the investments we hold – have implications for the larger picture. This is true, whether we choose to think about it or not.

When an internationally owned casino recently moved to the city where I live, many individuals thought only about the jobs it would make available, and the government relished the thought of a new source of taxable income. However, many other people pondered the larger picture, the implications of this development on many of the small, locally owned restaurants and clubs in the downtown that might lose business and income. They reflected, too, on the problem of gambling addiction, and the financial ruin, marriage breakdown, violence, alcoholism, and even suicide that it can lead to.

This is just one small example of the complexity of our lives and choices. Another issue currently facing Atlantic Canadians involves the domestic salmon fishery. Salmon bred and raised in fish farms have been escaping into the Saint Lawrence River and are interbreeding with wild salmon, weakening the wild salmon stock, which may potentially lead to its extinction. When we buy domestic salmon, we are, therefore, consciously or unconsciously participating in this process. Genetically altered foods represent a similar risk. At this point, we have no knowledge of the long-term impact of genetically altered food sources on human systems or on natural food sources.

Nothing is simple anymore. Economic systems have become complex. Science has become complex. Human relationships have become complex. Simple answers and black-and-white rules didn't work in Jesus' day and they work even less well today.

An ethics for complexity seeks to view life and the world from God's perspective. In any moral decision-making process, an ethics for complexity encourages us to consider not only our personal well-being, but the well-being of the whole, the larger fabric of life of which we are a part. Further, it causes us to consider the well-being of the whole, not just from the perspective of being a part of the whole, but also from the perspective of God as the very creator of it all. When we come to the point of loving God with our whole heart, and soul, and mind, we begin to take on God's perspective. In turn, we begin to love our neighbor as ourselves, because when we view our neighbor through the eyes of God, we see them as equally valued and loved by God. We see our neighbor as created by God and as permeated by God's Spirit, the same as ourselves. That "seeing" spontaneously leads to a deep and profound compassion, not just for our neighbor, but for all of creation. From this perspective, all our decision making will be informed by the question, "What is the best action to follow, for the greatest number of people affected by this decision?" I am included in that question, because I am one of the people whose needs have to be considered. But I am not the *only* person to be considered.

When we start to view the world in this way, we discover a profound truth. We discern that our own deepest happiness and well-being will be served if the happiness and well-being of the greatest number of people affected by the decision is also served.

When our love for God becomes so deep that we begin to see the world and all our decisions through God's eyes, we can no longer make decisions – be they about the vehicle we drive, or the products we purchase, or the jobs we undertake, or the ways we relate to our families – solely on the basis of immediate self-gratification. Rather, we will ask questions like the following: how does my decision to drive to work or to take the bus affect the environment; how do my purchasing habits affect the lives of people living in other parts of the world; does my job contribute to the peace and well-being of the planet, or to more suffering and destruction; how does my decision, either to stay in or to leave a difficult marriage, affect the larger well-being of all members of my family, my children included. And on and on it goes.

As we take on God's perspective, and as we begin to ask these timely but challenging questions, we discover that our own happiness and well-being cannot be sustained in isolation from the happiness and well-being of others. If what seems good for me is really bad for others, in the long term, it will ultimately be bad for me, too.

The command of Jesus to "love God with all one's heart and one's neighbor as one's self" leads us to view the world from the all-encompassing perspective of God. This perspective, which is encouraged and fostered by all advanced forms of spirituality and prayer, is our truest and most trustworthy guide in times of moral and ethical decision making.

Chapter 8

Service

Then the virtuous will say to him, "Lord, when did we see you hungry and feed you or thirsty and give you a drink? When did we notice that you were a foreigner and extend hospitality to you? Or naked and clothe you? When did we find you ill or in prison and come to visit you?" And the king will respond to them: "I swear to you, whatever you did for the most inconspicuous members of my family, you did for me as well."

Matthew 25:37–40[1]

There's a story about a rabbi who asked his students how they could best tell when night was over and morning had arrived. One responded, "When you can see an animal in the distance and can tell whether it is a sheep or a dog?" The rabbi said no. Another said, "When you see a tree in the distance and can tell whether it is a fig tree or a peach tree?" Again the rabbi replied no. So the students demanded, "Well, then, when is it?" The rabbi responded, "When you can look on the face of any boy or girl, man or woman, and see that she or he is your sister or brother. Because if you cannot do that, no matter what time it is, it is still night."

Marion Christie is the matriarch of Bedford United Church, the congregation I serve. She is a remarkable woman, and not just because she is 99 years old. Over the years, she has served on every committee and board of our church and has participated in all aspects of its life. She continues to attend church every Sunday and makes a particular point of coming out to support special events, such as concerts and plays put on by the youth, congregational meetings, and so on. Several years ago, with the assistance of another remarkable couple in our community, she wrote a history of our church and oversaw its publication. In addition, she continues to preserve the history of the community of Bedford, writing monographs and essays that have been produced in both book and digital formats. And, to top it all off, she still makes her own meals and on occasion cooks for other family members, too.

Marion is blessed with a quick memory and highly intelligent mind, a delightful sense of humor, an openness to life and new ideas, and a gracious spirit of hospitality that blesses all who know her. She sends out birthday and sympathy cards, drops off lemon meringue pies to families with loved ones who have just died or who are in the hospital, and generally supports and cares for so many people around her. I never cease to feel humbled in her presence.

Marion was born in 1906 and moved to the community of Bedford when she was eight years old. Her mother had died from tuberculosis, and her father, Andrew Robb, was determined that Marion and her sister would be brought up in the fresh air and natural environment of this small seaside town. Here, the family bought a house on a lovely piece of property overlooking the ocean. Marion has many fascinating and humorous stories to tell about her years growing up in that house, which had no indoor plumbing, no electricity, and no telephone. Marion says, "When my father had a bathroom installed upstairs, he had a large zinc-lined tank put in and we children had to pump to fill the tank, up and down, up and down. We got paid one cent for every 200 strokes, so we kept strict count, marking our score each time on a piece of cardboard on the wall."[2]

As a young woman, and generations before it was common for women to pursue a university education, she obtained first her B.A. and then her M.A. in history from Dalhousie University. In 1929, she moved from Halifax to Calgary, where she taught for two years at Mount Royal College before pursuing further studies in education. After another year of teaching in the west, she decided to come back home to the Maritimes. Here, she worked for a local newspaper, *The Chronicle-Herald*, as its social affairs editor, until, in 1935, she married George Christie, a school chum who had also been raised in Bedford. According to the custom of the time, once married, a woman was not allowed to remain on staff in a formal job. But Marion didn't let that stop her. Although she lost her job at *The Chronicle-Herald*, she obtained a contractual position with a local radio station, CHNS, where she hosted a morning talk show dealing with current events called, *Looking Over the Morning Herald, with Marion Robb Christie*. In addition to these activities, she, along with George, raised a large and active family of four children. And when her last child began school, Marion, at age 48, returned first to teaching, for close to ten years, and then to newspaper work, serving as the social affairs editor for another local newspaper, *The Daily News*.

Marion's husband, George, was a man equal in stature to his remarkable wife. Not only did he have an impeccable career, first with the County of Halifax and later with the Provincial Department of Municipal Affairs, but he also volunteered in a myriad of different ways. He served with the Bedford Ratepayers Association, was secretary to the trustees of the local school board, provided leadership in the Scouting and Air Cadets movements, and was a long-time chairperson of the local Brookside Cemetery Corporation. When he officially retired from the Department of Municipal Affairs, lest he become too bored, he immediately took on the responsibility of secretary for the Board of the Pine Hill Divinity School, the East Coast seminary for the United Church of Canada, where he served for ten years into his mid-70s. It is no wonder that George was honored so many times, receiving among many others, both the Provincial Volunteer of the Year Award, and the Governor General's Caring Canadian Award, both of which Marion also received. In addition, he served on every committee and board of Bedford United Church and was instrumental in the construction of an entirely new church facility in 1963. The large, new church was built on the Robb property, the one on which Marion grew up and which the family sold to the church after Marion's father died. For many years, George served as a greeter at the church entrance on Sunday mornings. He not only possessed a delightfully cheery twinkle in his eye that immediately attracted visitors, but also had a mind like a steel trap and never forgot a newcomer's name. Like Marion, George remained active in both the church and community, until he died in 2003 at the ripe old age of 96.

Marion and George are the finest examples I have ever met of people who have dedicated themselves to service on behalf of their community, their church, and their world. Both of them were imbued by their respective families and by the culture of the time with a strong ethic of service. Like other members of their generation, they were deeply loyal and committed to the institutions – civic and political, as well as religious – they considered so important to the healthy functioning of society. They passed on these same values to their children, who continue to this day to be active and significantly involved in civic, political, and religious life in Nova Scotia.

The emerging vision of God and religion named in this book has a very specific understanding of service as a spiritual path in its own right. In the expression of service, this new spirituality finds its most practical application in the world. Although many people who engage in service do not consider themselves to be particularly spiritual, this really does not matter. Marion does not reflect a great deal on her life of service as a spiritual discipline. It is simply something she does, because she considers it to be important. But the end result is the same. In this chapter, we will look at the understanding of service emerging from the new spirituality, why it is so important, the benefits it adds to our lives, and provide some cautions to observe in giving the gift of service.

Service as an Expression of Shared Life

To be sustained, and to ensure maximum impact, the impulse to serve other people and the world cannot stem merely from feelings of love or pity, or from other emotional sentiments. We all know that emotional states are subject to the winds of change and so cannot be relied upon to provide long-term, consistent motivation. Rather, the impulse to serve is strongest and most continuous when it originates from a profound insight, an intuitive awareness about the very nature of life itself.

In the story at the beginning of the chapter, the rabbi teaches his students that morning has arrived when we can look upon the face of any other human being and recognize in that person our brother or sister. True love and care arises and functions out of the recognition and acknowledgment of our shared humanity. When we, all of us, understand and feel the common bonds that connect us – that we are created of the same flesh and blood, and subject to the same forces of birth, growth, decay, and death; that we experience the same needs for sustenance, security, community, meaning, and love – we will begin to care for each other much more deeply and authentically. We will come to see that the things that bind us to each other, that unite us, are far more substantive than the things that separate and divide us.

However, when we read the story from the Gospel of Matthew quoted at the beginning of this chapter, we find an even deeper and subtler bond. Matthew presents a story about the end of human destiny, when all people are gathered together at a time of final judgment. In this story, Jesus is presented as God's cosmic judge and ruler, and names a profound mystical and spiritual truth. When he praises the virtuous people for having shown him such love and care in the world, they scratch their heads in puzzlement and ask, "Lord, when did we ever take care of you, feed you, treat you when you were sick, visit you in jail...?" And Jesus replies, "Whenever you did these things for someone else, you did them for me."

Matthew is simply noting a profound mystical insight held by the early church, but found in all the world's major religions. All life is an expression of the one ultimate life we call God. At the deepest level, deeper even than our shared flesh and blood, deeper even than our molecules and atoms, we are joined together by the very being and body of God's own self. The eternal, infinite divine Spirit lives in us all and gives birth and expression to us all. The Spirit is the true source of our varying identities. The Spirit is the one deepest identity we all share. In truth, when we care for someone else, we care for God; when we harm or injure someone else, we harm and injure God. Thus, the risen Christ can say, "When you did something for someone else, you did it for me. You did it for the one true life that we all share, the very life of God."

This is the profound insight that underlies the expression of all service in the world, for each other and for all of life. Over the centuries, it has given rise to the many and varied expressions of morality expressed in all the world's religious traditions. In the previous chapter, we noted that in the ancient Hebrew tradition, it gave birth to the Ten Commandments (Deuteronomy 5:1–21, Exodus 20:1–17). And in the life of Jesus it was expressed in the simple statement, "Love the Lord your God with all your heart, with all your soul, and with all your mind...[and] love your neighbor as yourself" (Matthew 22:34–40). We can now see why. My neighbor and I are literally one with, and expressions of, God. Ultimately, all of life constitutes one single fabric of being. Whenever we love any part of it, or serve any part of it, we love and serve all of it. This understanding, this intuition, which lies at the heart of the spiritual life, gives rise to a profoundly moral life. Morality, as we saw earlier, is simply the lived out expression of what becomes revealed in the spiritual depths of life.

But this understanding, this intuition, gives birth to something else besides an explicit morality. It generates a profound experience of compassion and caring within us for all existence. When we look at suffering, whether it's human suffering, or the suffering of non-human life, or of the planet itself – and recognize that we are connected to it by virtue of our shared life in God, then compassion emerges spontaneously as the human feeling or sentiment in response to this situation. We can no longer feel separate from others or from creation. We can no longer isolate other beings as objects with whom we have no connection or for whom we have no feeling. They are part of us, like a child will always be a part of his or her mother and father, and we will feel for them what a parent feels for his or her child. It is a love born of a profound sense of shared connection and shared life.

We see this morality and this deep and loving compassion fully revealed in the life of Jesus, renewing and refreshing his followers, like a cool ocean breeze on a hot Middle-Eastern day. Time and again, Jesus challenged people to consider life and morality more deeply, rather than simply accept everyday notions of right and wrong. And the compassion and caring he expressed for all people, from the rich to the poor, from those of high esteem to low, astounded everyone. In response to Jesus and to the needs of others, we also are inspired to manifest this kind of morality and compassion in our own lives. But there are other reasons to do so, reasons that paradoxically serve us more than those we seek to serve.

The Principle of Reciprocity

A Saudi Arabian prince once needed eye surgery. Not sure where to go, he was referred to a famous New York ophthalmologist. Prior to the surgery, the ophthalmologist wondered how much she should charge the prince. Her usual fee was $10,000. But in this case, she felt that maybe she could charge $20,000, $30,000, or even $40,000. Indeed, the prince could afford it. Finally, she decided to call the prince's New York lawyer for advice. The lawyer told her that a common practice in relationship to the prince was to place no amount on the bill. Instead, at the bottom of the invoice, it was customary to write, "The Honorable Prince Can Do No Wrong!" and let the prince pay whatever he liked.

The doctor was a little skeptical about this arrangement but finally decided to go along. Imagine her surprise, then, when a number of weeks after the surgery was completed, she received a copy of her invoice in the mail along with a card of thanks and a check for $100,000.

Delighted, the doctor promptly bought a new Cadillac, refurnished her condominium, and booked a trip around the world effectively spending all the money. A few weeks after returning from her world cruise, she received an invoice in the mail from the prince's New York lawyer. And the amount of the lawyer's bill? It wasn't filled in, but at the bottom were typed the words, "The Honorable Doctor Can Do No Wrong."

The interconnectedness and the oneness of all of life gives rise to a cosmic or universal law that I call the "principle of reciprocity." Whenever we give freely of ourselves in service to others or to the world, be it through our jobs or in our personal lives, we give in ways over and above what is formally expected of us. We give because we feel "called to do so," or because we know it is the right thing to do. Like the doctor in the above story, we give up the opportunity to ask for anything in return. But, also like the doctor, most of us *do* receive a return that often far exceeds our expectations, not necessarily in financial remuneration but in other ways. The principle of reciprocity is the root of the biblical saying, "As you sow, so shall you reap," or the more contemporary saying "What goes around comes around." Though it's not always immediately apparent, what we put out is what we shall receive in return. The universe is structured that way. So what are some of the benefits that accrue to us as a result of the gift of service that we give to others and to the world?

One of the most positive benefits to come our way when we give the gift of service is a sense of meaning. Life takes on meaning as we contribute to a purpose or cause larger than ourselves. No longer are we focused just on our own small lives, on our concerns and agendas. Instead, we work together with other people to effect change for the greater life of humanity and the world. In so doing, we feel we can leave a legacy of change and well-being for others.

In the process of giving the gift of service to others and to the world, we are also blessed in return with the gifts of new energy and hope. During the 1980s, immersed in the depths of the civil war in El Salvador, Maria Lopez Virgil, a social activist, was quoted in *The United Church Observer*.

> It is said that only those who walk can have the hope of one day arriving. Only those who participate. That is what is happening now in El Salvador with the prolongation of the war. The war doesn't end. But the exhaustion is felt more by those who have stayed on the sidelines, watching what has happened. They are the most tired. They are the ones losing hope, feeling desperate. But those that go walking, no, they feel they are getting closer. In the heart of the conflict, we don't feel tired. Outside of the country, there is more pessimism and more destruction caused by the war of El Salvador than there is here inside. And we are those who are in the war, in the heart of

the conflict. The farther one is from the conflict, the less one participates, the more tired one becomes. Curious, isn't it?[3]

Curious indeed. And the war did eventually come to an end by the efforts of people just like Maria.

Many people have become discouraged and overwhelmed by the pressing concerns facing the world today: concerns for the environment, about militarism, about poverty and social justice, and so on – and have essentially "given up." It's easy to fall prey to such feelings. However, it's important to remember that these feelings are profoundly self-centered and nihilistic, and do not take into account the incredible human potential to achieve change for the better. Worse, they leave people in a deeply lethargic position, which only serves to exacerbate the problems we face.

Contributing to social causes, or simply helping other people, motivates and energizes us. In the process of working to improve the world and the lives of other people, we find the gift of energy in ourselves. We free our energy for productive work. We also find hope. We may not be able to resolve huge problems overnight, but in the efforts we make, in the small changes for the better we see and help make happen, in our discovery that there are other people like ourselves working to make the world a better place, we find deep reservoirs of hope, optimism, and new life that in turn fill us with light where once there was darkness.

Another common benefit of giving ourselves in service is that we find and become part of an extended community of like-minded individuals. Most of us live our lives in fairly small circles of family, friends, and colleagues, who share a similar perspective on the world and who do not push us to grow or to learn. When we become part of a larger cause or organization seeking to make a difference in the world, we begin to learn and to grow from our association with other people. We also absorb energy and new hope, as mentioned above. Life simply becomes more interesting, more engaging, more meaningful, and more *fun*.

But there are still deeper benefits to giving the gift of service, which have to do with spiritual transformation. When we give of ourselves to other people and causes, we become motivated by values and principles that begin to alter our entire lives. First, in the process of working for justice, peace, or the environment, our lives tend to become simpler. After working at our jobs, spending time with our families, and giving of ourselves to various causes, we find there is no time left over for activities that waste time or possess little value in terms of meaning and joy. Second, we become less self-absorbed as we take on more concern for the larger world. And third, as we learn more about the needs and concerns of the planet and of other people, we develop an increasing capacity for empathy and compassion. The more we learn about the problems and concerns of others, the deeper we can feel with them in their struggles.

Fundamentally, regardless of which religious tradition we pursue, this is the spiritual transformation all paths point towards: increased inner and outer simplicity, decreasing self-concern and self-preoccupation, and a growing compassion for life and other people, a growing sense of connection to all of life and other people. Clearly, offering the gift of service is a time-honored and significant path of spiritual transformation in its own right.

Burnout and Rustout

A woman phoned her pastor and said, "I needed your advice on something yesterday, but when I phoned you weren't in." "I'm sorry, but yesterday was my day off," said the pastor. The parishioner snorted, "A day off? You know, the devil never takes a day off." The pastor replied, "That's true, but if I didn't have a day off, I'd be just like him."

For the most part, when people give of themselves in service, they receive gifts in return that add much value to their lives. However, we also need to be aware of the risk of "burnout" and "rustout." Burnout, in particular, happens when we take on too much. The world is full of need and trouble, and as compassion sensitizes our hearts, we try to address it all. The attempt can easily lead to progressive energy loss, fatigue, and emotional exhaustion.

It's important to be sensitive to this risk in our lives. In the long term, we will be of no use to others or to the world, if we do not care for ourselves as well. Sometimes, too, we may end up neglecting our family, or other immediate concerns that require our attention. We may find ourselves trying to heal others while inadvertently contributing to suffering in our own immediate circle of concern. It is important, therefore, to seek balance, to handle our responsibilities close to home before we seek to care beyond ourselves. And it is necessary to constantly renew ourselves, to care for our own health, for example. One of the most important habits of highly effective people, according to Stephen Covey, is that they "sharpen the saw"; they constantly renew themselves in order to be able to give more.

To be sure, on occasion, a particular piece of work will require an extraordinary commitment of time and energy on our part. It may be necessary at such times to negotiate with those closest to us, to be freed from certain other responsibilities for a limited period of time, so that we can take on the exceptional tasks we face. Sometimes, to do a new thing well, we have to let go of something else.

"Rustout" and the vacuum principle

Sometimes we find that we have been giving in a certain area or carrying a responsibility for such a long time that it no longer feels life-giving. However, we do not let it go because of a high sense of responsibility for and personal investment in the task. This is called rustout, a slow, progressive loss of enthusiasm and energy for the service in which we are engaged, combined with an inability to let it go.

In these situations, I like to refer to what I call the "vacuum principle." We all know that the universe abhors a vacuum. Where a vacuum occurs, something always seeks to fill that space. Likewise, where a need occurs or a job exists, if we step out, generally someone else will step in.

It's important to remember this, not just for the sake of our own health and vitality, but for the sake of those who might benefit from picking up where we have left off. In other words, if we don't step aside, there will be no room for someone else to take on that responsibility. Therefore, it is sometimes important for us to step aside from an area of responsibility so that we can find renewal and so that someone else can step into our previous position and contribute in new and creative ways, as well as learn and grow from the position according to their own needs.

Taking the Long View

Patiently, over the course of several hours, a small boy crisscrossed a beach looking for stranded starfish. Whenever he found one, he picked it up and threw it back into the water. Finally, a man who had been watching all this approached the boy and said, "Son, these starfish are a lost cause. There are simply too many of them. Do you really think what you're doing will make any difference?" The small boy held up the starfish in his hand: "It makes a difference to this one."

Inevitably, a life of service requires that we take a long-term view of our work. As much as we might otherwise wish, it is not possible to change the world overnight. Life is far too complex. Also, permanent change almost always happens as the result of many small, individual actions. I have a screensaver on my computer that says, "What matters most in life is not the speed with which you travel, but the direction towards which you are moving." This is so true. Undue worry about results of our work usually reflects a very self-centered approach to service that is more concerned with personal gratification than with significant long-term change.

This is not to say that results are unimportant. To be sure, we need to be concerned about the *kinds* of results we are looking for, and that the means we are using will lead to those results. But we also need to recognize that quite often we will never see the final results of our actions. Ideally, this should not stop us from making our contribution. Hopefully, we engage in service because we believe it is the right thing to do, not because we seek the gratification that comes from seeing results. Adopting this long-term perspective will enable us to slow down and to take care of our immediate responsibilities and ourselves at the same time as we engage in work for the larger world.

When offered wisely, service represents not only our legacy and an exceptional gift to the world, but it leads to a personal transformation that deepens our experience of the spiritual dimensions of life. No wonder service has been such an important component of all the world's major religious traditions.

Chapter 9

Love & Relationships

Then Jesus' mother and brothers arrived. They stood outside the house and sent in a message, asking for him. A crowd was sitting around Jesus, and they said to him, "Look, your mother and your brothers and sisters are outside, and they want you." Jesus answered, "Who is my mother? Who are my brothers?" He looked at the people sitting around him and said, "Look! Here are my mother and my brothers! Whoever does what God [asks] is my brother, my sister, my mother."

Mark 3:31–35

A couple had been married for 50 years and were sitting on the couch one night watching television. The man said, "Things have really changed. You used to sit so close to me." "Well, I can remedy that," the woman replied, moving next to him on the couch. "And you used to hold me tight," he said. "How's that?" she asked, as she gave him a hug. "And do you remember that you used to nudge my neck and nibble on my earlobes?" he responded. At this she jumped to her feet and left the room. Startled, he asked, "Where are you going?" "I'll be right back," she said. "I've got to get my teeth."

My mother and father were married at the close of World War II, on May 14, 1944, in Hamburg, Germany. According to custom, they first went to the City Hall for a civil ceremony, and then to the local church, where their pastor, family, and friends surrounded and blessed them in a religious service. My father was 36 and my mother 27. Following the wedding, they went on a short honeymoon to Lubeck, a beautiful, old-world German town where my mother's sister and her husband lived.

For my mother's 85th birthday, I enlarged an old, sepia-tint picture of their wedding. In the photograph, my father looks tall and proud in his army uniform and my mother radiant and happy in a simple but classy dress. They are standing arm in arm on a pathway that meanders around a lake in Lubeck. A happier and more romantic couple could not be imagined. When my father died on February 11, 1997, they had been married for 53 years. However, by all present-day criteria, it was a marriage that should never have survived.

Because the war was just ending when my parents got married, they had no money, little food, and accommodation was hard to come by amidst the bombed-out ruins. My father was fortunate to obtain a job with the British Control Commission in Germany, but was obsessed with the fear, held by many at the time, that Russia would soon invade the country. And so the day arrived in 1951 when my parents said goodbye to their families and friends and boarded a ship bound for Canada. By this time, they already had one child, my oldest brother Kye, and my mother was pregnant with Roger, my second brother. With only two old luggage trunks, they traveled to a brand new country, where they knew no one, and whose language my mother and brother could not speak.

When they arrived in Canada, my father discovered that work was scarce. A good job in a large city was not to be had. And so they ended up, first, in the small northern city of Sault Ste. Marie, and then in Wawa, a tiny mining town in northern Ontario, which, at the time, was only accessible by rail.

In Wawa, my father got a job with the local railway and the entire family attended a recently begun Pentecostal church, in which my father served as a lay minister. I was born during this time, unplanned to be sure, but loved nonetheless. In 1958, the pastor, who had come to strengthen the ministry in the fledgling church, left and yet another pastor arrived on the scene. But the church failed. Eventually, becoming discouraged with the church and with life in Wawa, my parents decided in 1959 to move back to Sault Ste. Marie, where another job with the railroad had become available. But their destiny in Wawa was not yet over!

In Sault Ste. Marie, they attended a large Pentecostal church where they had some friends. They bought a house on a lovely, quiet street close to a nearby river and looked forward to establishing a good life. However, after some time, the pastor in Wawa left and the Pentecostal leadership in Sault Ste. Marie asked my father to return to Wawa to provide interim ministry. When a job again opened up with the railway in Wawa, my parents agreed and back they went. Weeks later, tragedy struck.

It was a beautiful, sunny morning on Saturday, May 6, 1961. Kye asked my mother if he could go for a hike in the woods with some friends. Since he was quite mature and responsible for his age, mom agreed. And because she was babysitting the child of a friend and noticed Roger hanging about looking bored, she said to Kye, "Why don't you take Roger with you?" Kye grumbled, but agreed. Then, just before he left, she said to him, "Now don't you come home without your brother." And so the die was cast.

What my mother didn't know was that Kye and his friends were going to a small, mountain lake. Once there, they planned to cross on rafts to the other side, where they were building a log cabin.

Crossing the lake, Kye and a group of boys were on one raft, while Roger and a second group were on another raft. The raft on which Roger stood started sinking and the boys tried to jump to the other raft. Both groups of boys fell into the lake and most were able to swim ashore, including my brother Kye. However, when he got to the shore, he noticed that Roger was not there. "Where's Roger?" he asked desperately. No doubt remembering my mother's words – "Don't come home without your brother" – Kye quickly re-entered the lake to try to save Roger. In so doing, both he and Roger, along with another boy, drowned in the icy cold waters. In those moments, my parents' lives were changed forever!

After the death of my brothers, my mother was sick in her soul, and yet she realized that life needed to carry on. In the years that followed, my parents, filled with grief and with psychological and spiritual pain, struggled to come to terms with the enormity of what had happened. They also struggled financially, which made things even worse.

Eventually, of course, I grew up, my father retired, and my parents left Wawa for a better life.

Reflecting on their lives – particularly the struggle to make a new life in a new land and the loss of two sons – I sometimes wonder how they managed to stay married. What kept them together, when their lives were crashing apart all around them? It could only have been love!

Love is the most talked-about yet elusive quality of human life. Human beings are designed for relationship and we all yearn for love. Yet not until we have learned to share love with others, can we receive love in return. The new vision of God and emerging Christian spirituality help us understand why this is the case and how, indeed, we can learn to love.

Love as a Force of Attraction

There are many invisible forces in the universe, which act to sustain and hold life together. Fields of electromagnetic force allow us to experience the sun's heat and light, enjoy radio and television broadcasts, and use the cell phone communication networks that link us together. Gravitational forces keep us rooted to the earth and prevent us from flying off into space. They also hold the planets in their orbits and control the expansion of the universe. Strong and weak nuclear forces provide order and structure at the atomic and sub-atomic level, just as gravitational forces do at the macro level of the cosmos. If the universe didn't possess these unique fields of force literally everything would fly apart and deteriorate into chaos.

Love, too, can be envisioned as a force within the universe and within the body of God. Just as the absence of cosmic or subatomic forces would result in the disintegration of the universe, the same is true in human life when the force of love is absent. When love is missing, our lives fly apart and dissolve into destruction and chaos that can ultimately lead to death. But when the force of love is present, we are drawn into relationships that are life sustaining, healing, and renewing.

The Christian spirituality I have described in this book visualizes God as a multidimensional, weblike Spirit. Or, to use another image, we can imagine God as an infinite spiritual grid, rather like an electrical grid, with an elaborate network of intersecting transmission lines. Human beings represent points of life contained within and spread across God's weblike or gridlike body. Invisible spiritual transmission lines permeate the body of God and enable love to flow back and forth, from one human point to another on the spiritual grid of God's being, and indeed, toward life as a whole, including plants, animals, and even the earth itself.

This force of love consists of two components: feeling and intention. Feeling is emotional and reflects heart-based energy. Intention is characterized by thought and reflects mind-based energy. When the feeling energy of the heart is combined with our caring and loving thoughts, we generate the force of love. This force of love is then manifested in two ways. Most obviously, it is demonstrated *externally* in the way we *act* toward others and toward the world in general. Acts of kindness, justice, and caring for others and for the earth all result from this force of love. But this force of love, just like electricity, also exists as a form of *invisible, subtle energy* that is transmitted across the spiritual grid of God's being to other people and forms of life and can be profoundly healing and nurturing.

The question and challenge for all people is how to sustain this force of love under all conditions and circumstances, and throughout the passage of time. Someone once quipped, "Whereas love intoxicates, marriage sobers." As an emotional state, we generally experience love as ebbing and flowing, rising and falling, coming and going. But the spiritual process seeks to stabilize the feeling component of love by directing it towards God in an ongoing and consistent fashion. At the same time, it also seeks to stabilize and empower our intentions, thinking, and visioning of love for the world. Indeed, stabilizing our capacity for empathetic and loving *feeling* lends energetic support to the development of loving *intention*. When we combine loving feeling with compassionate intention, and stabilize both in our relationship with God, they act as a force within the body of God that draws people together in a variety of intimate, familial, platonic, collegial, and communal relationships.

Narcissus Revisited

Unfortunately, as was noted in Chapter 2, narcissism, self-centeredness, or simply self-preoccupation act as a hedge, wall, or barrier around the human psyche, preventing us from sending out or receiving the force of loving feeling and intention that resides in each of us, and that flows through the weblike body of God. If, like Narcissus in the Greek myth, we are deeply self-absorbed – caught up in self-love, or perhaps by grief, lack of self-esteem, anger, jealousy, or depression – we will have great difficulty receiving or giving love to others. The more we are wrapped up in our own inwardness and pain, the less we will be able to feel the love others hold for us.

Narcissus and self-preoccupation reveal themselves in the desire for self-fulfillment. As long as the self is preoccupied in a process of seeking its own gratification, its own rewards, its own happiness, its own love, that very act of self-absorbed seeking prevents it from actually knowing happiness or love. The spiritual life, on the other hand, is ultimately not about self-fulfillment, but about *self-transcendence*. This is why the fundamental impulse of religious and spiritual practice is to diminish and eventually uproot altogether the seeds of narcissism and self-preoccupation. Until we have become healed of the wound of narcissism, we can never fully experience the gift of love.

When narcissism, inwardness, and self-absorption are uprooted, we discover a paradoxical truth. On the one hand, we become whole and free in ourselves. We can stand alone, independent, knowing that we are held within the ultimate force of love in the universe, that which we call God. When the daily angst and activity of self-preoccupation is dissolved, we stand free, happy, and capable of feeling and sharing love. We observe the presence of love within ourselves and know that we participate in the love of God. Free of the activity of Narcissus, we no longer worry about being loved, because we know ourselves to *be* love.

At the same time that we now stand free and independent, we also become profoundly capable of relationship and feel ourselves called into relationship. Love does not exist for its own sake. Free of self-concern, we can now reach out unselfconsciously to others. Fully present to others, already full of love, peace, and joy within ourselves, we can demonstrate deep kindness and compassion without seeking anything in return. Indeed, we need not self-consciously do a thing. The force of love simply finds itself drawn into and expressed through our lives in and of its own accord.

People are attracted to such a condition, to such loving and free people. People who are already full of love and capable of conducting this love, who are deeply free of narcissism, always attract people and community to which they give themselves fully. Every great spiritual leader has attracted a wide community as a result of the presence of such a love and the capacity to convey this love to others. Indeed, in our own time, we only have to think about people such as Mother Teresa and Jean Vanier.

I am reminded of a delightful saying: "To be above with the saints we love, ah, that is glory. To live below with the saints we know, now that's a different story." Learning how to love the people we love is one of the most difficult things we can undertake, because it cannot be separated from the process of our own transformation and self-transcendence. It requires the cultivation and integration of wisdom into our living, throughout our entire lives. We shall now consider that undertaking in very practical terms.

Banishing Narcissus from Our Homes

Banishing Narcissus from our homes, establishing and stabilizing loving feeling and intention as a very real force in our lives, can involve many different processes. Self-help literature abounds with useful advice on how to communicate more effectively, nurture commitment, respect autonomy and mutuality, accept each other's limitations, and so on. My parents, however, did not focus their attention on those strategies. Instead, my parents prayed. The other ingredients of healthy relationships just mentioned flowed from their life of prayer.

My parents prayed within the dualist religious perspective that was part of their heritage. Despite the limitations of that perspective, they still experienced their prayer life as profound and freeing. First, they prayed to God out of passion for God and to know God. Their prayer to God was devotional and filled with longing. I do not know all the factors that contributed to that desire and hunger for God in the first place. It may have been something inherent in them. Or their own families may have nurtured it. It was certainly nurtured in the life of the worshipping congregations they attended over the years. And it may have grown as a result of the suffering in their lives and their sense of need for God. But regardless of how it originated, I *do* know that in the process of praying to God, of making prayer a daily habit and intention, their relationship to God and love for God deepened and grew. The presence of this love for God and their intentionality about worshipping God and praying to God strengthened their capacity to feel and to demonstrate this same love for the people in their lives. This capacity played an important role in the midst of the stressors and conflicts that emerged throughout their married life.

When my mother was angry with my father, she prayed to God. She asked God to release her anger and it would not surprise me if she also asked God to change my father. She also asked God to address the circumstances that led to the conflict in the first place, such as a lack of money, a sense of isolation from her family, or whatever it may have been. It's true that her circumstances did not change overnight, and I'm not sure how much my father changed as a direct result of her prayers. But I do know that pouring her heart out in prayer to God softened her feelings for my father, kept her heart open to him, and more often than not helped to reshape her perspective on what was going on in their relationship. For his part, whenever my father experienced disappointment with my mother, with his children or with life, he too poured out his heart in prayer to God. And he too found renewed perspective, a softening of his despair, and a sense of new hope. Both of my parents discovered a sense of inner peace and stillness in prayer, which took the edge off volatile emotions, facilitated a renewed clarity and objectivity in their thinking, and enabled their sense of love and care for each other to resurface. Their love for and relationship to God, which they nurtured daily, was able to dissolve the hard edges of narcissism and self-absorption, and freed their love to flow back and forth between them.

Within the emerging understanding of God and Christianity I have been describing in this book, we approach prayer more deeply and systemically from a *non-dualist* perspective, but it still leads to similar results.

From the perspective of the new paradigm, we no longer only pray to God as a Great Spirit, who is separate and removed from us, and who reaches down into our lives to effect change. We also relate to God as the Great Spirit reality in whom we live, breathe, and have our being. God is all around us and within us; we live in God. We may still pray to God as an "other," as a being over and against us, as separate from us, but we also learn to rest in God, as the very deepest part of our own being. One of the primary ways we do this is through the "prayer of quiet," which I describe in Chapter 5.

Feeling love for God

One of the things that distinguishes the Christian "prayer of quiet" from the forms of prayer found in some of the other religious traditions of the world is that the attention we direct towards God as the great mystery and ground of our being is linked with loving feeling. Christian prayer and meditation typically has a devotional component associated with it. As we pray or meditate, we endeavor not only to direct silent attention to God, but we also open our hearts to feel love for this great and wonderful reality. As this daily prayer and meditation is sustained over weeks, months, and years, the loving feeling that we bring to resting in God starts to grow and takes on a life of its own. It becomes rooted within us, and in the process we develop a very real and continuous love for and sense of the presence of God in our lives.

It is *this* love that has such a powerful impact on our relationships. It is next to impossible to feel a continuous sense of love for God and a sense of God's presence in our life, and not have that love flow into our relationships.

Awareness and the capacity for loving intention

It is important to repeat that this form of Christian prayer and meditation is not the talk prayer I describe in Chapter 5. In the prayer of quiet, we are not talking to God using thoughts or words. Rather, we are simply directing loving feeling and attention towards God, in silent awareness, or by repeating over and over again, like a mantra, a name for God that has particular meaning for us. This process is designed to disengage the mind, but something else occurs as well. We begin to identify and recognize awareness as a constant unchanging dimension of consciousness in all our thoughts and emotional states. Indeed, we begin to recognize that this underlying awareness is an intrinsic and unchanging component of our being, whereas our thoughts and emotional states are transient and constantly changing. When we identify with the underlying condition of awareness and develop the capacity to stand back within that condition of awareness, we are engaging what is often referred to as the "witness consciousness," or assuming the position of the "observer." Resting in pure awareness, we develop a capacity to observe or witness our own mental and emotional states apart from any sense of identification with them.

In Chapter 3, I referred to Stephen Covey's concept of "response ability" and to the gap that lies between a stimulus we receive and our response. Our "response ability" consists of our capacity to seize that gap and thereby to obtain the freedom to choose how we will respond to the stimulus. This is a challenge for most people because it requires a very high level of personal awareness. But it is this awareness that we develop in the "prayer of quiet." In the "prayer of quiet," we learn to observe and monitor our mental and emotional states; to release and disengage those that are negative and unhealthy for our lives, diminishing their control over our behavior; and to shift our attention to God. In other words, we develop the freedom to choose which thoughts and emotional states we will cultivate in our lives, including our loving feelings and intentions for God and for others.

The prayer of quiet in practice

As this capacity for love and awareness grows, we begin to feel its impact in our everyday circumstances and relationships. In times of relational conflict or stress, rather than immediately reacting to the circumstance out of anger, frustration, or some other painful emotion, our attention automatically shifts to the observer or witnessing mode that we practice daily in the "prayer of quiet."

Let's take a very simple example of this to see how the process works. Let's say you have just come home after a long and busy day at work and encounter your partner, who also has just arrived home after a hectic and stress-filled day. He or she immediately snaps at you because you forgot to put the garbage out that morning. Immediately you face the temptation to lash back in anger, perhaps reminding your partner that if he or she had made the kids' school lunches the night before instead of leaving them for you to do at the last minute, you wouldn't have forgotten. This could be the beginning of an evening of escalating emotional reactivity and hostility. But instead, before you react in this manner, your witness self kicks in, you observe what is going on, and you choose to simply ignore your partner's comment, or to respond more quietly and empathetically.

It is important to realize at this point that your emotional response to your partner's verbal attack doesn't disappear. The "prayer of quiet" does not lead to an emotionless life. In this example, you will probably still feel angry and defensive, but because your witness self immediately kicks in and observes both the attack and your emotional response to it, you can step back and choose how you will respond.

It is also important to realize that just because you are aware of what is going on within yourself and can step back before responding doesn't mean you won't choose to respond in anger as a form of retaliatory attack. This is why it is important to realize that the Christian prayer life is not just about developing awareness. It is also about cultivating a feeling of love for God and about directing attention to the presence of God everywhere, including within the person who may have just hurt us.

In this circumstance, then, awareness, which has emerged in your daily meditation practice, enables you to step back, to claim the gap between the stimulus and the response, and to choose a response that honors and respects the presence of God in your partner.

The subtle dimensions of meditational prayer in human relationships

The example above shows how we can avoid returning hostility for hostility in our relationships. And, as we take this first step, we enable the other person to respond more peacefully and benignly as well. This is a very practical result of such prayer.

But now, let's take the example a step further. Let's say that before going to sleep that night, you spend some time in your usual evening meditation. During those 20 minutes or so, you first pray to God for your partner using traditional talk prayer. You pray for God's strength and wisdom to guide your partner through the difficult time he or she is facing at work. You pray for God's blessing on your relationship with your partner and ask God to keep your love for each other soft and strong. After this short time of "talk prayer," you then visualize a current of white light and love energy flowing from your heart to your partner, surrounding her or him in a cocoon of energy.

Remember the "genius of the AND." There is nothing inappropriate or ineffective about talk prayer. We are both part of God, yet separate and distinct nodes within the web or the grid of God's being. Talking to God can indeed evoke an intensification of God's energy for other people. When we pray to God to bless someone, we act as co-creators with God to make that happen. The universe *does* respond to our initiative. But then, as in our example, you can go a step further. You can literally send forth loving energy from your being, through the weblike body of God, across those spiritual transmission lines, to your partner. You can surround your partner with the loving energy of your feeling and intention. In so doing, at subtle subatomic levels of energy and being, you are impacting your partner's capacity for love, wisdom, and spiritual stability.

In Chapter 5, we considered how such prayer could affect physical healing in others from a distance. It's important to remember here that the healing we seek to nurture in others may not just be physical, but also spiritual, emotional, and relational healing too. In this example, your freedom to respond with love and peacefulness to your partner's attack immediately neutralized the negative and destructive power of that exchange in the relationship. But your further pursuit of prayer on behalf of your partner may have helped him or her, in a very subtle way, to be more loving and resourceful in the future. When my mother prayed for my father in times of conflict and stress, those prayers may indeed have affected his capacity for love and wisdom in relationship to her and our entire family.

And, of course, when you pray for your partner at night and visualize sending out loving energy to him or her, you are also reinforcing and re-arranging neural patterns and networks in your own brain that will assist in governing your future responses to your partner.

None of this diminishes the need, in contemporary relationships, to learn about communication skills, conflict resolution, negotiating roles and boundaries, healthy sexuality, and so on – all of which are necessary ingredients of healthy and loving lives. But it is the spiritual disciplines referred to above that make these other aspects of loving relationships effective. If we haven't learned to cultivate and grow the feeling energy of love in relationship to God, and the awareness that comes with it, we will lack the power to drive the intention for these other dimensions of healthy relationships. Let's take a brief look at some of those other aspects now.

The Many Facets of Love

Commitment

When we are committed to a relationship, we invest the time and energy needed to sustain not just ourselves, but the relationship as a whole. We see clearly that our own well-being in the relationship depends on the well-being of the other person or party. And so we work to encourage and enhance their well-being too. But when deep commitment to a relationship is *not* present, Narcissus raises his head. Self-concern pushes forward its own agenda at the expense of the other person, perhaps even to the point of harming the other person. This leads to anger and to emotional distancing, which erodes commitment to the relationship. As this commitment disintegrates, so does our intention to treat the other person with kindness, civility, and compassion. As the hedge of Narcissus builds around us, it makes the sending or receiving of love more and more difficult.

The same is true in political and international relationships. In general, international relationships are based on self-interest rather than on any real commitment to the welfare or well-being of the other country. Establishing relationships on the basis of economic self-interest does not represent real commitment to a relationship. Certainly, the poorer nations of the world continually criticize Western countries for engaging in this kind of relationship. We pretend we are doing them a great service, when in fact we simply seek the economic gain such relationships may bring. When there is no real commitment to the well-being of the people of another country, there can be no lasting relationship or peace.

The same is true in our relationships with other forms of life and with the water and the air, and with the earth itself. When we feel no real sense of relationship with the earth, or commitment to the well-being of the earth, it becomes easy to use the earth solely for our own self-interest and benefit. Indeed, this is how we have treated the earth for so long. For the most part, we have lost the biblical notion of caring for the earth as God's stewards, of caring for something precious that God has created. Again, this reflects the perspective and activity of Narcissus, a preoccupation only with what concerns us to the exclusion of the needs of others and of life as a whole.

If we felt committed to a relationship with the animals, the fish, the plants, the air, the water, and the earth itself, we would seek the well-being of these creatures and things in addition to our own well-being; we would seek to enhance our mutual relationship.

Communication

Effective communication is another facet of the force of love. Truly relational communication includes both the capacity to listen and the capacity to speak in a spirit of openness.

One of the seven habits of the successful life, as noted by Stephen Covey, is the capacity to "seek first to understand and then to be understood." This places the priority in communication on listening first, and speaking second. And the fundamental requirement of good listening is a quiet mind, which is an important goal and outcome of the "prayer of quiet," as mentioned above. In order to truly listen to another person, we must be still within ourselves; we must be able to silence the inner voice that constantly chatters even while we are trying to listen to others. When we suspend the activity of the inner and outer voices, an inner quietness emerges that helps us to hear the other person clearly. In the process, we also suspend judgment and criticism, which enables us not just to hear the other person, but also to be sympathetic to what they are saying. True listening does not just entail hearing the words spoken by the other person, but also perceiving and appreciating the feeling and the context out of which the words are spoken.

Listening isn't something we do only in our relationships with other people. We can also practice it in our relationships with animals, plants, and the entire earth. Suspending the inner voice, learning to be inwardly still, enables us to hear the sounds of the earth and also to see the earth clearly, to recognize and to understand its true condition and our true relationship with it. This profound inner silence and clarity leads to wisdom and compassion.

Just as listening is important, so too is speaking. In order to live in life-sustaining ways, we need to be able to talk. More precisely, we need to be able to talk about two central components of human relationships: feelings and values. Again, both of these become progressively clearer to us as we engage meditative or contemplative prayer.

Feelings or emotional states drive so much of our behavior. Anger, jealousy, fear, and insecurity, to name just a few, emerge in all relationships and can lead to highly destructive behavior unless they are vetted in conversation and understood. Likewise, expressing our sense of caring, desire, or love for others is important in order for them to appreciate the real foundation of the relationship. Previous generations often had great difficulty communicating feelings. Such communication was typically considered a female trait and of little relevance for men. Fortunately, today we understand that communicating our feelings is important for both sexes.

In addition to expressing feelings, communicating our values is critical to the demonstration of love. If we can't communicate and reach some level of mutual understanding of the things that are important to us, we will always be in conflict. As I write these words, Iraqi suicide bombers are blowing themselves up in attacks against Americans, and sometimes against their own people. Conflict continues to rage around the planet, even in this supposedly enlightened age. The fundamental ingredient missing from so many of these situations is shared communication about deeply held values and perspectives.

In the West, dispute resolution processes that involve shared communication are becoming more and more popular as an alternative to litigation. The same kinds of processes need to become just as deeply rooted in the arena of international relations as in the arena of intimate and familial relationships. Differences in values tend to be the greatest source of conflict between people and nations. Learning to appreciate other people's values and why they hold them will be essential if we are ever to reduce the level of conflict in the world.

Autonomy and mutuality

Autonomy and mutuality are two more, interrelated aspects of healthy relationships. Kahlil Gibran once wrote these famous words pertaining to marriage.

> Love one another, but make not a bond of love:
> Let it be a moving sea between the shores of your souls.
> Fill each other's cup but drink not from one cup.
> Give one another of your bread but eat not from the same loaf.

Sing and dance together and be joyous,
   but let each one of you be alone,
Even as the strings of a lute are alone though they quiver with
the same music.

Give your hearts, but not into each other's keeping.
For only the hand of Life can contain your hearts.
And stand together yet not too near together:
For the pillars of the temple stand apart,
And the oak tree and the cypress grow
   not in each other's shadow.

Gibran's poetry expresses a profound understanding of life and human re-lationships. From birth onwards, healthy children exhibit an ever-greater need for independence and autonomy. Parents know that to raise a healthy child they must encourage and facilitate the child's growing independence in ways that are appropriate to the child's age and abilities. To keep chil-dren forever dependent is to stunt and hinder their ability to grow to their fullest potential as persons.

At the same time, however, children must also learn that their lives and growth depend in all sorts of ways upon their parents, teachers, friends, and a whole host of other people. They must come to understand that life consists of an intricate web of mutually supportive relationships and that although we seek independence and self-determination, ultimately our lives and our growth can never be separated from the people and the society in which we live. In other words, we are all *interdependent*. And so we move from being totally dependent as infants, through a stage of seek-ing greater and greater independence as adolescents, to the recognition as adults of the ultimate interdependence of all life. This reflects the "genius of the AND" that we referred to earlier. Healthy adults recognize that we must be independent, even as we are interdependent.

In practical terms, this means that partners will allow each other to pursue independent goals and needs that might be quite separate from the relationship. Indeed, each partner can provide the support, encouragement, and assistance necessary for the other to pursue their own agendas. While one takes a course in the evening, the other looks after the children at home. At the same time, both partners may also have many interests and responsibilities in common and may take time to pursue these together. In this entire situation, then, there is both mutuality and autonomy. There is a free flow of the force of love back and forth between the partners, which contributes to an enormous sense of freedom and creativity. And there is a mutual intention, and allowance made, for each partner to unfold and grow into everything that life calls them to be.

Accepting imperfection

The expectations we bring to a relationship can be the greatest obstacle to the free flow of the force of love in that relationship. If we expect that our partner will be perfect in all ways and that the relationship will fulfill all our needs for happiness, then we will experience great dissatisfaction when these expectations are not met. When we become dissatisfied with the relationship and with our partner, we become self-absorbed and inward in our reflections. This self-absorption, this inwardness, is a form of narcissism, which prevents us from sending love to our partner and from receiving love in return.

People are not perfect. And no relationship can fulfill all of our needs for happiness. If a person has not found a sense of peace and happiness within him or herself, he or she is not likely to find it in relationship with someone else. And of course, none of this implies that we must put up with abuse or allow ourselves to be consistently taken advantage of. If injustices and abuses occur on a regular basis in a relationship, it neither can nor should survive. It's just that I have seen so many relationships between otherwise decent and caring people founder on the rocks of discontent. Instead of focusing on the strengths and gifts that each person brings to the relationship, partners become fixated on each other's faults and ascribe responsibility for all the unhappiness within themselves to the other. All of this, as we have seen, results from inwardness and self-centeredness. This inwardness and self-absorption is what the "prayer of quiet" seeks to uproot and eradicate.

When we are able to recognize that our loved ones are not perfect, but that they are expressions of God nonetheless, then the overall context of the relationship changes. We start to see our partner's goodness and this in turn draws forth from us a response of deep love and appreciation.

Kindness and compassion

The fundamental requirement of relationships, however, the one that most contributes to the free flow of the force of love between people, is kindness and compassion. In fact, kindness and compassion are synonymous with love itself. Compassion consists of the ability to feel what the other person is feeling and to respond appropriately according to what they need at the time. Kindness and compassion can gently cut through another person's hedge of narcissism and self-preoccupation. Kindness and compassion enable us to touch other people in ways that are healing. Often, this enables them to respond in a similar fashion, thereby freeing the love within them to flow out towards others.

Like begets like. When we act towards others with anger, cruelty, derision, or hurt, we elicit the same response in return. This is why Jesus never responded to violence with violence. Dr. Martin Luther King Jr. captured the essence of Jesus' attitude perfectly when he said, "Returning violence for violence only multiplies violence, adding deeper darkness to a night already devoid of stars." Jesus said, "As we sow so shall we reap." Plant a crop of kindness and compassion, and that is likely what we shall reap in return. The very best way to help other people find and express the force of love in their lives is to share our own loving kindness and compassion first. But in order to do so, we need to develop the freedom to respond in such a way. As noted earlier, this capacity is developed in meditative and contemplative prayer, as we cultivate loving feeling for God and develop awareness that leads to stabilized loving intention.

Conclusion

Despite the difficult and indeed life-changing circumstances of my parents' lives, they possessed something that was stronger than any force working to pull them apart. They both possessed a profound passion for God. They both yearned to experience and to know God. They prayed to God constantly. They loved God more than anything else. In the midst of the darkest nights, their attention always turned to God. In the moments immediately following the death of my two brothers, when my mother felt she could easily have slipped into insanity, it was the turning of her heart to God, the shifting of her attention to God that saved her.

This focus on God ensured that the walls and hedges of Narcissus did not take root in my parents' lives. It ensured that, no matter how difficult life became, they did not become buried in themselves, within their own grief, anger, depression, or solitude. Yes, they experienced hard moments when the feelings of love ebbed. They experienced periods of sustained anger and disappointment too. But by constantly cultivating their relationship with God, my mother and father retained the capacity to love and care for each other, even in very difficult circumstances. This love ensured that the fundamental ingredients of commitment, listening and communication, shared power, the acceptance of imperfection, and most of all, of kindness and caring for each other always remained. Their love lasted over 50 years, through good times and bad, because they never ceased to remain connected to the source of all love.

In our own lives, the force of loving feeling and intention needs to flow like electric current back and forth between us. Love was not intended to reside like water in a static pool, contained unto itself. When love flows freely across the weblike Spirit of God's being, it creates health, happiness, joy, and well-being. Where it gets blocked, problems, tensions, and struggles emerge that can be terribly destructive to life. That's why learning to use the tools and the understandings that contribute to the free flow of love is critically important. Chief among these is developing love for God and the capacity for awareness, self-understanding, and the freedom to respond to life in accordance with our values. Jesus said the first and most important commandment in life is to love God with all your heart, with all your soul, and with all your mind. If that piece is in place, the second commandment – to love our neighbors as ourselves – will follow naturally, and life will take on the joy and the radiance that God intended it to have.

Chapter 10

Suffering & Healing

Then Job answered the Lord. "I know, Lord, that you are all powerful... You ask how I dare question your wisdom when I am so very ignorant. I talked about things I did not understand, about marvels too great for me to know... In the past I knew only what others had told me, but now I have seen you with my own eyes. So I am ashamed of all I have said and repent in dust and ashes." ...The Lord blessed the last part of Job's life even more than he had blessed the first... And [Job] died at a very great age.

Job 42:1–6, 12, 17

Never again will they hunger or thirst; neither sun nor any scorching heat will burn them, because the Lamb, who is in the center of the throne, will be their shepherd, and he will guide them to springs of life-giving water. And God will wipe away every tear from their eyes.

Revelation 7:16–17

A husband and wife had to interrupt their vacation in order to see a dentist. The woman said to the dentist, "I want a tooth pulled, and I don't want a needle because I'm in a big hurry. So just pull the tooth as quickly as possible and we'll be on our way." Now the dentist was quite impressed and said, "You're certainly a very courageous woman. Which tooth is it?" The woman turned to her husband and said, "Show him your tooth, dear."

Suffering more than any other aspect of life puts the spiritual journey and religious faith to the test. The emotional and psychological pain that my parents felt upon the death of their two sons was terrible. But the spiritual pain they felt was even worse. They believed in a God who was in control. They believed in a God who was fair. Even more, they believed in a God who loved them. Yet there seemed to be nothing fair or loving about a God who allowed two little boys to drown. However, like Job, their experience of God over the years ensured that, in the end, even though they could not understand their plight, they nonetheless continued to trust in God. They took solace, too, from the biblical passage from Revelation, quoted above, that some day, in some way, God would make everything right. God would wipe every tear from their eyes, if not here on earth, then in heaven.

My own experience of that tragedy was quite different. As a five-year-old, left behind and lacking in experience of both life and God, the belief that I might see my brothers in heaven held little consolation. Indeed, it only added more confusion and darkness. And, as for the Bible, it seemed to come up very short of answers.

But answers there are. Suffering and faith can go hand in hand and it is to that possibility that we now turn.

God and Limitations

Rick and Debbie were a young professional couple who began their married life with great joy and expectation for the future. They took several years to become established in their work, to travel and simply to enjoy each other before deciding to settle down and begin a family. After a short while, Debbie gave birth to a healthy, nine-pound baby girl whom they named Nicole. As Nicole grew into a happy and healthy little toddler, Rick and Debbie decided to have another child to complete their young family. A short while later, they were blessed with the birth of a beautiful little boy, whom they named William. Life was full and happy. But then things changed.

When William was about one year old, he started having seizures. At first they were short and infrequent. But soon they increased both in frequency and intensity. With the onset of each seizure, Rick and Debbie would rush William to the hospital emergency clinic, where they spent many seemingly endless and anxious hours waiting for the seizures to subside so they could take him home again. Doctors conducted a battery of tests to obtain a diagnosis, but couldn't seem to pinpoint the specific cause. They knew it was some form of epilepsy, but which type and which treatment was required eluded them. Finally, after months of testing, they diagnosed a rare form of epilepsy for which there was no known cure. There was, however, a new form of treatment being attempted that entailed a very strict dietary regime extremely high in fats. Rick and Debbie were trained in the preparation of this diet and it began to have some effect on William. Still, William's development was delayed and from this time on he would never live the normal life Debbie and Rick had hoped he would have. As for Rick and Debbie, they would never be the same again either. They put their career plans on hold. Family responsibilities became very demanding and social relationships shifted. Everything changed in the blink of an eye.

As horrible as the death of a child is, it is not the only tragedy that can shake parents' lives and faith to the core. One evening, Rick and Debbie and I sat down to try to make sense of this change to their lives. They were struggling desperately to come to terms with William's illness within the context of their faith in a loving and caring God. The first emotion they expressed was total frustration at the unfairness of it all. Not only was this disease unfair to them, it was brutally unfair to their little boy. What had he or they done to deserve this?

Upon receiving an award, the late Jack Benny once said, "I really don't deserve this award. But I have arthritis and I don't deserve that either." Life is not fair. The sooner we accept that fact, the sooner we will find some measure of peace. Life is filled with limitations and frustrations and randomness and sometimes chaos. Some people get awards. Some get arthritis. And some get both. Some people are born in a shantytown in Guatemala, and others are born into the affluent south end of Halifax. Some people are blessed with loving families and opportunities for growth and education, and others are born into poverty, alcoholism, family violence, and a total lack of support or encouragement. One child is born healthy and normal, another is born with disease. There is no rhyme or reason as to where we are born that we can discern. Random luck, fate, or chance, seem to convey both blessing and misfortune. And even God can not change that fact.

But why couldn't God change this fact? Isn't God the omnipotent creator of the universe? If sickness and disease, accidents, and life in general happen as random events, does that mean that God is not in control of the world and its unfolding? Rick and Debbie and I talked about that too.

The Bible confesses that God is first and foremost the creator and sustainer of life. The very first words of the Bible state, "In the beginning, when God created the universe, the earth was formless and desolate" (Genesis 1:1–2a). Prior to creation, life had no form, indeed no existence whatsoever. God existed only as infinite, Spirit-Energy unqualified by any parameters of space or time, or anything else for that matter. Then, at some point within infinity, God decided or spontaneously moved to create life.

In order to establish life, structure and order were required. "The raging ocean that covered everything was engulfed in total darkness and the power of God was moving over the water. Then God commanded, 'Let there be light' – and light appeared... Then [God] separated the light from the darkness, and [God] named the light 'Day' and the darkness 'Night'" (Genesis 1:2–5). To give birth to creation, God had to establish parameters and the existence of opposites. Day and night, up and down, male and female, responsibility and freedom, love and hate, order and disorder, yin and yang; all were required.

Unfortunately, parameters entail limitations and limitations involve suffering. To be born and to grow in time, we must also eventually decay and die in time. To experience light and happiness, we need also to live with darkness and sorrow. And, as the Genesis story so poignantly reveals, from the very beginning of time, to experience love we also have to live with the possibility of hate. Adam and Eve loved Cain and Abel, but Abel learned to love and Cain learned to hate. God had no choice in the matter. To create life, all the possibilities for both good and bad, light and dark, were required. They emerge together as part and parcel of one whole, as two sides of one coin.

Next, I had a question for Rick and Debbie, one sometimes posed to me. Despite William's disease and your suffering, would you rather not have given birth to him? This is a concrete expression of the larger philosophical question, "Is life worth having given the enormous suffering that not only people, but animals and all life forms experience in the process of living?" Many people have asked this question. Obviously God thought life was worth creating despite the inherent possibilities for suffering and pain, otherwise God would not have created it in the first place. When confronted with the question, Rick and Debbie came to the same conclusion – having William had undoubtedly been worth it, regardless.

Together, we were able to reframe their perception of baby William. Yes, he did not turn out to be the perfectly healthy little boy they had originally hoped for. But he was a beautiful little boy nonetheless. He exhibited great courage and tenacity in the face of his illness. He had a wonderful personality and could make them laugh and experience deep joy. And despite his struggles, and the efforts required on their part with him, Rick and Debbie had come to love him with a depth of care and concern that brought out the very best in them. Yes, they felt blessed to have this little bundle of life, despite the suffering involved.

As a minister, I work all the time with people who have experienced the death of loved ones due to sickness, accidents, crime, and so on. I often ask parents of a child who has died, "Would you rather not have given birth to your child, and thereby been spared the pain and grief of his or her loss?" Without exception, the answer has always been a resounding "no." My parents would have answered the same way. Despite the pain of losing Kye and Roger, it was better to have brought them into the world, to have known and loved them, than never to have had them at all. Despite the pain, the suffering, and yes even the horror that often goes hand in hand with life, most people still recognize life to be a very precious gift. On occasion, people will commit suicide, succumbing to despair and the feeling that life is no longer worth living. But humanity as a whole does not feel this. The radiant, yellow-white sun rising over the ocean, giving birth to another glorious morning, makes the darkness of the night not just bearable, but infinitely worthwhile.

God gives us this wonderful gift of life. At the same time, God is unable to dictate what the circumstances of our lives will be. In that sense, God is not in control. God is fair and loving. Life is not. But life is wonderfull and worthwhile nonetheless.

This is not to suggest that there may not be some deeper mystery to life and to the unfolding of human circumstances that we do not understand. In all my conversations with my parents over the years, I could never shake their belief, and neither did I want to, that somehow there was a deeper pattern, a deeper meaning at work in the unfolding of their lives and in the death of Kye and Roger, which they simply could not understand, but which was fully comprehensible to God. Indeed, this may be true. But even without this deeper pattern or meaning, we still understand life to be a miraculous and wonderful gift, beautiful and precious, and yes, certainly worthwhile.

The Causes of Suffering

To make sense of suffering, it is helpful to distinguish between the different causes of suffering. Doing so brings understanding and can shape our attitudes and actions in regard to suffering.

First, there is suffering that occurs as a natural consequence of life itself. Where we are born, and into what family, will determine the economic and educational resources that are available to us and, to some extent, the degree or kind of suffering we will face. The genetic inheritance we receive can lead to great suffering in the form of all kinds of illnesses, diseases, and medical conditions, both chronic and degenerative. Likewise, natural disasters, such as weather-related events, or earthquakes or volcanoes, and epidemics of disease such as AIDS, are all natural sources of suffering. Then again, we all live with the natural consequences of daily struggle and aging. All of these sources of suffering arise as a natural consequence of life itself.

Of course, much suffering in life has its origins in our lack of knowledge. A lack of knowledge about the impact of technology on the environment, for example, has caused climate change and climate disasters, and has resulted in extensive suffering, with more to come in the future. A lack of technical understanding and know-how can lead to failures in technology, resulting in accidents and crashes. Then, too, there is the suffering that originates from a simple lack of wisdom and maturity. People who drive fast and recklessly are likely to cause accidents, as are people who drink and drive.

In addition, there is suffering that originates as a result of human poverty and the lack of equitable distribution of resources. And there is the suffering that originates from the human capacity for hatred and evil. Crime and war draw on the most base and evil instincts in human beings. As I write these words, the world is remembering the 60th anniversary of the liberation of Auschwitz, which saw the most brutal and systematic torture and execution of human beings on a mass scale ever perpetrated. One would think we would have learned our lesson. But contemporary examples such as Rwanda and the Sudan reveal this tendency to be ever present.

Suffering originates from all sorts of things and in all sorts of places, some of which are randomly generated by life itself, and some of which are, intentionally or accidentally, caused by human behavior and activity. And so it is impossible to eliminate suffering from life completely. We can learn to live in harmony with nature and with each other, but nature will still visit natural disasters upon us because such is part of the natural logic of creation. We can learn to live in peace and love with our fellow human beings, but can never escape the emotional agony and grief that arises from the death of a beloved child, spouse, or friend. And, inevitably, aging will challenge us with the loneliness and with the gradual decline of our capabilities. We simply cannot avoid the reality of our mortality. This is fundamentally part of what it means to be human.

Life as a Creative Struggle

There was never a philosopher, who could bear a toothache patiently!

William Shakespeare

The inevitability of suffering has led many people, and even some religious groups, to take a very fatalistic view towards it. However, this was not the stance of Jesus, the Buddha, or of most other spiritual geniuses throughout history. Rather, they seem to have approached life as a creative struggle, one in which we grow and learn and become ever more loving and compassionate.

Christine and Paul were another young professional couple who got married and spent some time traveling and becoming established in their careers before deciding to start a family. When they did, they gave birth to a lovely, healthy little girl whom they named Alyssa. When Alyssa was about three, she started having health problems. Christine and Paul took her for tests and shortly thereafter she was diagnosed with leukemia. Christine quit her job to look after Alyssa full time. The family moved to a larger city in the region, where more specialized health care was available for their daughter. Thus began an 11-year roller coaster journey. In spite of everything, Alyssa grew up to become an amazing young girl. Despite (or perhaps because of) constant treatment and going in and out of remission several times, she developed a courage, tenacity, and fearlessness that was quite remarkable. To be sure, she was still a normal little girl who could drive her parents nuts, and who could be saucy, naughty, and delightfully funny. But in other ways she was mature and profound far beyond her years. Her parents gave their lives to her and when she died at the age of 14 they were devastated.

God could not give us a life without suffering. God could not give us a world free of pain, randomness, or a world of total fairness. But God *could* give us the possibility of transforming suffering and pain into something life-giving and meaningful, something filled with the possibility for new hope. God has structured this potential into human beings and into life itself. About a year after Alyssa died, Christine and Paul, in conjunction with the children's hospital where Alyssa spent so much time, established a special memorial trust fund in her name, to provide assistance for the families of other children going through similar treatment programs. Out of the midst of life's deepest horror, they sought to create new meaning and hope worthy of the very special child they had lost.

God intends us to be co-creators of life with God. We are called to work with God, to take the stuff of life so filled with darkness, pain, and mortality, and to transform it into something filled with light, joy, and eternity. This is the destiny God has given us. When we work to fulfill this destiny, we find hope, energy, joy, and meaning. Mothers of children killed by drunk drivers formed an organization to raise public awareness and to work for change. Thousands upon thousands of people affected by apartheid in South Africa did not just accept their fate but, despite great persecution, creatively challenged the system until it eventually collapsed. Against great odds, millions of people and hundreds of organizations today are challenging the common despair that the earth is beyond repair and are working hard not just to turn back the tide of environmental destruction, but to renew and repair the earth. All around the planet, people are engaged in one creative struggle or another to alleviate suffering not just for human beings, but for all of life and indeed for the earth itself. The problems we face are immense and complex. But the human spirit reaches out to transform problems into possibilities for new life and new hope. This is our birthright. This is our destiny. This is the mandate given to us by God, the very source of life.

In all of this, there is a correlation between faith and the creative struggle to bring healing into life. People who are deeply open to God seem to be more empowered to alleviate suffering and more governed by love and a sense of compassion in their efforts. This may be especially so for people who see God as the connecting force and reality that holds all of life together in a single unity. What we do to one part of life, we do to all of life, including ourselves. This vision, more than any other, leads us to work for healing change in the midst of struggle and suffering.

A Holistic View of Healing

We turn now from the question of suffering to the possibility of healing. In Old English, we find that the word for health also possessed the meaning of wholeness. To be healthy meant to be whole, sound, or well.[1] What today is becoming increasingly clear, in medical and non-medical circles alike, is that health is about much more than human bodies free of negative symptoms. Health relates to the totality of what we are as human beings, both as individuals and as communities living in relation to the entire cosmos.

I like the words of Joel Goldsmith, which no doubt express what many doctors have felt from time to time: "The problem with merely patching up bodies is that you don't know who you are putting back on the streets." For example, is a person healthy if his body is functioning well, but he then goes out and shoots someone? Of course not! This person is sick. Human beings are incredibly complex bio-chemical, electrical, skeletal constructs, with mental, emotional, social, and psycho-spiritual dimensions. Consequently, when we speak about health – really meaning wholeness – we have to refer to all these dimensions of our lives.

We see this clearly in the very holistic ministry of Jesus. Jesus healed broken bodies, disturbed emotions and psyches, and tormented spirits. He also sought to transform and heal both Judaism and the society of his day as a whole.

In the wonderful story of the paralytic who is brought to Jesus on a stretcher, Jesus says, "Courage, my child, your sins are forgiven." But the scribes, who overhear him, think he is blaspheming, so Jesus says, "Why do you think such things? Is it easier to say, 'Your sins are forgiven,' or to say, 'Get up, pick up your mat, and walk'? But to prove to you that the Son of Man does have the authority to forgive sins, I say to you, 'Get up, pick up your mat, and go home'" (Mark 2:1–12). And immediately the man is healed. Throughout his ministry, Jesus made little distinction between healing bodies, caring for psyches, and saving sins or healing broken spirits. It was all part of a larger process of necessary healing in people's lives.

As a minister, I frequently work with people who have lost a spouse through death and who then have become very introverted, shutting out life and love. Typically, they experience depression and, as a result, tend not to eat or sleep very well. As a result of lack of proper food, exercise, and sleep, their immune systems weaken and they become sick with pneumonia or other illnesses. These people need more than an antibiotic! First, they need to courageously address their grief, and then they need to start living again. (And they may need help to do both these things.) In other words, the physical symptoms of the pneumonia point to a much larger malaise in their emotional and spiritual lives.

These examples, from the life and ministry of Jesus and from my own contemporary ministry, make clear that healing is a multi-faceted process. Today, even the very materialistic medical science establishment, prodded on by pioneers such as Bernie Siegel, Carl Simonton, and Elisabeth Kübler-Ross, has come to acknowledge that deep-seated and uninspected emotions can manifest in physical symptoms.

Everything is connected in this matter of health. We ignore any one dimension of our being to the risk and detriment of all the others. This is true not just within our own bodies, but on a global scale as well. It has become widely recognized that cancers have increased dramatically because of environmental pollution, and, in the case of skin cancer, because of the destruction of the ozone layer. Heart disease, too, is so common because of frenetic lifestyles that include too little exercise, and diets that contain far too much alcohol, tobacco, sugar, and refined foods. As for the frenetic lifestyle itself, *it* stems from a lack of peace in our collective social consciousness, and from a lack of spiritual values that would lead us to live in deeper harmony with ourselves, with each other, with nature, and with God.

I like the joke about the doctor who called up his patient to complain about a bounced check. He said, "I say, Jack, your check came back." To which Jack replied irritably, "You're right. And so did my bursitis." For too long, we've relied on doctors and other experts to fix all our ills rather than take responsibility for our own lives. It is time – and it has been happening – to take back control and responsibility for the health and wholeness of our own lives. But this requires maturity – especially spiritual maturity.

The common understanding of the word "holy" has had to do with a traditional kind of piety, with saying prayers and with reading scriptures.

But when we look at the etymological origins of the word "holy," we discover that it, too, is connected with the word "wholeness."[2] If something was holy it was to be kept whole or intact, should not be violated or broken apart. Thus, to keep life holy means to look at the larger picture, to consider not just my own needs and circumstance in life, but the needs and circumstance of the totality of life in which I live. To be a holy person or a spiritual person in today's world requires that we consider not just the well-being of our own lives, but that of the entire human race, and indeed that of the planet as a whole. The new vision of God we have been considering in this book calls us to do just that; it reveals to us that all of life emerges from and is interconnected within this vast spiritual reality. When we consider the truth of God, we can no longer avoid our responsibility for all of life.

Healing Principles and Techniques

At this point, it may be helpful to look at some of the principles and techniques that can guide our approach to healing.

Positive and negative feedback

Carl Simonton, a pioneer of the use of visualization and guided imagery in the treatment of cancer, believes that health is the natural state of humanity. He notes that when we are healthy, we feel happy and positive. He refers to these feelings as a positive-feedback system. Through them, life is telling us that we are in harmony and doing well. Likewise, illness is a negative-feedback system telling us that something is wrong and that we need to change what we are doing and how we are living. One of the first principles of healing, then, is to learn to listen to the negative feedback, the painful symptoms that we experience, not only in our individual body, emotions, thoughts, and spirits, but also in our collective social life together and in regards to the planet as a whole. We need to listen to what this negative feedback is telling us about our life.[3]

Many years ago, I started experiencing back pain. That led me to the discipline of yoga. Today, if I do not exercise and work out regularly my back starts to ache. I have learned to hear that ache as a voice saying, "Start exercising." Negative feedback in the form of physical, emotional, or spiritual pain is simply the way our lives speak to us and tell us that something needs changing. And our first task is to be willing to listen to this feedback, to attempt to understand what it is saying to us.

Never jump to conclusions

Very often, when people first start receiving negative feedback indicating that something is wrong, they jump to conclusions. "This lump must be cancer. Cancer means I'm toast!" Of course, the lump may have nothing to do with cancer. And even if it is cancer, there is no reason to assume that it is malignant. Human beings have a tremendous capacity to exercise imagination for both good and ill. Very often, when we first experience symptoms our imagination starts working overtime developing as many worst-case scenarios as possible. None of which may be true. The very first thing we need to do when suffering of any sort occurs is to obtain an accurate diagnosis of what is wrong. In law there exists that fundamental tenet of presuming innocence till proven guilty. In issues of health, you should presume health until you know for sure what is wrong.

Look everywhere

When looking for the source of our suffering, when developing a diagnosis, we should look at *all* facets of our lives, searching for an imbalance, a lack of harmony, a lack of wholeness. This involves a process of learning. Since all facets of our existence are interconnected, symptoms appearing in one dimension may affect another. It is important to look for these connections. For instance, a heart attack is often a symptom of clogged arteries. But are clogged arteries really the problem? What caused the clogged arteries? Do we need to change our diet? And if so, are there lifestyle factors – perhaps working too many overtime hours – that lead us to eat too much fast food? And why are we working so hard? Is it because we love our work, or because we are avoiding a relationship, or because we feel a sense of emptiness in our life? These are the kinds of questions we need to ask ourselves.

The point is, when symptoms occur – be they physical, emotional, or spiritual – we need to examine our whole lives, not just the area affected by the symptoms, for aspects of imbalance or lack of health. And then we need to address *all* of those areas. If we are willing to listen to our symptoms, if we are willing to use them as an opportunity to inspect our lives as a whole, then we can turn symptoms, pain, or handicaps into wonderful opportunities to grow and to mature, and to develop life skills we might never have dreamed of.

Search out resources for healing

In carpentry, having the right tool for the job makes all the difference in the world. The same is true in the process of healing. Having the right resources can make all the difference. So often, though, wonderful resources for healing surround us on all sides, but we do not take advantage of them.

In the past, religious people often held a superstitious belief that God would intervene directly in their lives. In extreme cases, they may have even declined "outside" help, believing it to be unnecessary, believing that "God will provide" – miraculously. But when we understand that *all* of life is an expression of God, then doctors, researchers, advocacy groups, the Internet, and books can all be seen as agencies of God's grace and healing power. God is life affirming and life positive. Anything that contributes to healing and wholeness in life is valuable and sacred.

Today there are so many different approaches to and techniques for physical, emotional, and spiritual healing. And for each of these techniques, there exists a practitioner or group who can help us achieve the goals we have set for ourselves. Like the people who sought out Jesus for help, all we need to do is ask.

At the same time, people often believe, erroneously, that it is the doctor or therapist who does the healing. This is not the case. Any doctor, psychotherapist, or spiritual director worth his or her salt will tell you that they do not do the healing. Rather, they administer medicines or teach techniques that enable our body, our innate intelligence, and the divine source of life to facilitate the healing. Ultimately, the power and source of healing lies within us. Our own body and spirit know what we need for healing and are capable of providing it. We just need to learn to trust our own inner wisdom and instincts.

If we are willing to learn from our symptoms and to courageously look at all facets of our life and health, we will come to learn a great deal about ourselves. In the end, *we* will be the best judge of what we need. We need to be intelligent and practical about using all available resource people, but ultimately, we are the ones who make the decisions and who must seek to understand what it is that we require for healing. There is no great, all-powerful healer outside of us. Our healer dwells within. Ultimately, it is the life force that originates in the ground of our being, the mysterious source of life we call God.

Do not compare yourself to others

People who are sick often console themselves by observing that there are other people much worse off. In fact, though, someone will always be worse off than us and someone will always be better off. If we're around people who are worse off, we may be able to take some consolation in that fact. But if we are around people who are better off, we can drive ourselves into deep despair. The best course of action is to recognize that God is not responsible for our circumstances and loves all people equally. God wants us to find the healing we need in our suffering; to grow through our circumstances into a whole, happy, and loving life, wherever we are.

I often use the analogy of playing golf. Golf isn't the least bit fair when we start comparing ourselves to other players. Some players have more natural ability than others. Some get good winds and others get lousy winds. The point in golf is not, or should not be, to compare my score with yours, but to constantly seek to improve my own game and my own score. The point in *life* is to take responsibility for my life where it is here and now, and to seek to grow and learn from that point. None of us start life in the same place. Life doesn't offer an equal playing field. So we need to play our own game the best we can. We need to deal with our own suffering and come to terms with it regardless of the situation of other people.

This means that we need to find our own meaning in our suffering. Many people feel that God has given them their particular blend of suffering to teach them some lesson in life. As we have already seen, God is not responsible for our circumstances, neither our joy nor our suffering in life. But God has given us the capacity to make sense of our lives, to find the lessons we need to learn, to look for the meaning that life holds for us. Finding meaning in suffering is important. Creating meaning from our suffering is important. It is not necessary to project the source of that meaning onto God. God wants us to learn and to grow and to become agents of God's presence in the world. That is enough. Anything that helps us to grow in that way will be in line with God's will for our lives.

The healing power of love

Bernie Siegel tells a story about a colleague of his, a psychiatrist, who had been working for three years with a severely burned woman, trying to teach her that she was lovable in spite of her scars. After hearing Siegel lecture on the topic of love in healing, the psychiatrist gave the woman a big hug the next time she came in for her counseling session. The psychiatrist said the woman improved more with that hug than with three years of therapy. George Goodheart, a professor of dentistry at the University of Pittsburgh, has said, "It is no exaggeration that many people get better simply because they like their doctor." The gospel demonstrates time and again how God's power for healing became manifest in and through the love of Jesus, and through people's trust in *God's* love and power flowing through Jesus.

Healing techniques and abilities cannot be separated from love, because a fundamental quality of the source of life is love, and it is this Source that ultimately does the healing. In being loved and in sharing love, we become conduits for God's healing power.

So often in the midst of our suffering, we become completely caught up in our own circumstances. This subjective absorption in our pain in turn creates even more suffering. One of the very best ways to transcend our own suffering is to become an agent of love and healing for others. The people who provide the most effective support to those who are suffering are those who have been through a similar situation. And, in the process of helping others, we too become healed. We become less fixated upon ourselves, more self-forgetful, and in this way find relief from our own suffering. We also find a sense of meaning and purpose as we serve others. In sharing love with others, we not only contribute to *their* healing, but *we* become healed in return.

Cure or Healing

Arnold Palmer once attended a convention of blind golfers. He asked the golfers how they knew where to hit the ball. One golfer explained that the caddy goes out ahead and rings a little bell as he stands near the hole. The golfers then hit the ball toward the sound of the bell. Arnold asked how well this process worked. The golfer responded by challenging Arnold to a round of golf, and just to make it interesting, suggested a $10,000 bet that he could beat Arnold. Well, this just blew Arnold's mind. He pressed the blind golfer, but the man insisted he was willing to bet that amount on his ability. So the deal was struck. Arnold said, "Okay, what time do we tee off?" The blind man replied, "10:30 tonight."

The last thing I want to discuss is the anguished cry I have heard from many people who have prayed to God, who have tried to follow the principles of healing mentioned above, but who still suffer. What does it mean when the tumor, or the emotional anxiety, or the spiritual emptiness doesn't go away?

It is important at this junction to clarify the difference between being cured and being healed. Like the blind golfer above, we may never be able to eliminate our own "blindness," the challenges we face from our lives, but we can learn to live with a sense of happiness and well-being despite those challenges. We may not be *cured*, but we may be *healed* of self-pity, despair, and unhappiness.

It is helpful, too, to distinguish between pain and suffering. Pain is the immediate physical or emotional sensation we experience as a result of some physical or psychological injury that occurs in our lives. Suffering consists of all the additional subjective pain we add to the original pain as a result of our internal resistance to and struggle with the injury. When we cannot come to terms with what has happened; when we blame others for our condition; when we despair over the changes that are now required; when we refuse to accept that a new, more difficult phase in our lives has begun; all the mental and emotional reactivity we bring to the new situation adds an additional level of pain, which we call suffering.

However, if we have used the principles referred to above, we may not always be cured of the original injury or disability, but we *can* be healed of our suffering.

Over the years, I have worked with numerous terminally ill patients. Many of those who died grew and healed in a variety of ways, even though their bodies were not cured. Elisabeth Kübler-Ross worked with many children who were terminally ill with leukemia. She noted that the longer these children suffered physically, the more the spiritual dimension of their lives opened up. She experienced them as very wise, old souls who had much more knowledge of life than their years would suggest. She also discovered that they were very willing to share their wisdom. Although they were not well from a purely medical point of view, to her, they had found healing.

Healing takes place in many different ways, in many different dimensions, but it is always a form of learning. If we are open to learning about our lives and our limitations, about what we need to heal and about sharing love, about learning to turn to the great source of life and about entrusting the unfolding of our lives in God, if we are open to learning about all those things, healing will occur. Maybe not perfectly or completely, or in all the areas we would like, but it will occur.

Chapter 11

Sin & Evil

God placed human beings in the Garden of Eden to cultivate and guard it. God said to them, "You may eat the fruit of any tree in the garden, except the tree that gives knowledge of good and evil. You must not eat the fruit of that tree; if you do, you will die that same day."... Now the snake asked the woman, "Did God really tell you not to eat fruit from any tree in the garden?... God said that because God knows that when you eat it you will be like God and know what is good and what is bad." The woman saw how beautiful the tree was and how good its fruit would be to eat... So she took some and ate it and gave some to her husband and he ate it too. As soon as they had eaten it, they were given understanding and realized that they were naked... That evening they heard God walking in the garden, and they hid themselves from God in the trees.

Genesis 2 & 3, selected verses, paraphrased

Mr. Abraham, a devout Jew, was having a pair of trousers made by a tailor. One day, driven to distraction by the tailor's endless delays, he cried out in exasperation: "Tailor, in the name of heaven, it has already taken you six weeks working on my pants." The tailor replied, "So." "So you ask? Six weeks for a pair of pants? Ribono shel Olam. It took God only six days to create the universe!" "Nu, so what," shrugged the tailor, "and look at it."

As a young and newly ordained minister, I undertook studies in counseling at a professional training institute in Sudbury, a small city in northern Ontario. Part of the program involved counseling clients who registered with the center. This counseling was not provided on-site. Rather, each member of the program needed to find a local church or parish that would provide free space in which they could work. I was very fortunate to meet Jerry, a young Roman Catholic priest, who generously provided me with a room in a quiet part of the church building.

One of my clients was Tony, an Italian who owned his own construction firm. He had come to the center to request counseling and was referred to me. At our first session, I asked him why he had come. He divulged that his second wife had left him and he was trying to figure out how to get back together with her. Thus began a series of six hour-long sessions.

I discovered that Tony was the son of Italian immigrants to northern Ontario, who had made good in the construction industry. At the age of 20, Tony launched out on his own career, starting a small signage business. After a couple of years, he married, but the relationship did not last and his wife left him after eight months. She complained that he was too overbearing and controlling, and said that she didn't really love him. The business was failing, too. So when Tony's parents asked him to come back and work in the family construction company he agreed. As his father grew older, Tony assumed the reins of responsibility and took control of the business. In his late 20s, he married again. He met his second wife in a bar. She was divorced and had two young children. Four years after they were married, she left complaining that he was too hard on her kids and that he spent all his time at work. Some time later, Tony came to the institute.

As Tony and I explored his life, I discovered that his younger brother had committed suicide when Tony was young. Tony revealed that they had had a very overbearing father and that he had not originally wanted to stay in his father's business. I learned that he and his two sisters didn't get along with each other and seldom spent time together. When we talked about his second wife and the children, he would become weepy and emotional and declare how much he missed them. But then I started probing a little deeper.

I asked him about the children. He said they were good kids but that his wife didn't know how to discipline them. I asked him about his relationship with his wife. He said she complained he worked too much. "But," he went on, "she doesn't understand the demands of the business." I asked him how the complaining affected him. He said it would really irritate him, particularly if it happened when he came home after a long day at work and if the kids were out of control. I asked him if he ever yelled at his wife. He said, "Sometimes." I asked him if he had ever hit her. He said "No." But then he reconsidered and confessed he had pushed her around a few times. I asked him how he did that. He said it was never anything serious, more in jest really. He would bump her with his belly. Tony was a big man with a big stomach. I could visualize him towering over his wife yelling at her and hitting her with his large protruding belly. I asked him how he thought those incidents made his wife feel about him. He admitted it probably didn't endear him to her. When our time came to an end, and we booked next week's session, I had no idea it would be our last.

As part of our sessions, Tony and I sometimes talked about dreams. For any therapist or counselor, dreams can be a very valuable tool to explore emotional content of which a person may not be fully conscious. In standard psychological theory, dreams are understood to reflect various parts of our own psyches. Furthermore, the events taking place in our dreams reflect the processing by our unconscious minds of situations and concerns we are dealing with in everyday life. Tony and I had spoken about this and had discussed a couple of his dreams in earlier sessions. When Tony came to session six, he had a dream to share with me.

He proceeded to tell me how, just the night before, he had dreamed that he was in a quiet, secluded room. The door to the room was made out of steel and possessed a deadbolt. The walls were covered with padding. Along one wall hung a rack with all sorts of torture instruments, including knives, whips, and chains. A single, stark electric bulb lit the room. Someone was hanging from the ceiling by a noose, with blood dripping out of their mouth. He wasn't sure if it was a man or a woman or whether they were dead or alive. He was standing in front of them with a whip in one hand and a knife in the other.

You can imagine how hearing this dream made me, a young student counselor, feel. I was alone in a secluded room, with a man who had already demonstrated some fairly controlled but still violent tendencies in his relationships with two previous wives. I was spooked. But it wasn't just the dream that spooked me. As Tony told me the dream, I had the distinct impression that I was listening to a different person. Every now and again, he would sneak a look at me, and then turn his gaze away. In those furtive glances, I got the distinct impression that he was analyzing me, gauging my responses. In addition, his eyes looked cold, empty, and distant.

One of the first lessons new counselors learn is to pay attention to their own feelings when working with clients. Transference and counter-transference are technical terms that suggest that the relationship between a counselor and a client is not strictly an objective one, dealing only with the client's issues. Rather, in the counseling environment, a relationship is established between the client and the counselor that has its own dynamics. This relationship, in itself, can be a source of great insight and assistance in dealing with the client's larger issues. It can tell the therapist a great deal about the client's relationships in his or her everyday life.

In this situation with Tony, while paying attention to my own emotions, I realized I was scared. I felt, overwhelmingly, that I was encountering a part of Tony's being that was truly evil. I use that word sparingly and cautiously. But there is no other way to describe it. It wasn't just the dream itself. It was the way Tony told the dream, the way he looked at me in such a cold and calculating way. It was the look in his eyes that appeared dead and devoid of emotion. I was scared and I trusted those feelings. I steered the session away from the dream, kept it fairly light, and decided I did not want to see Tony again. As it turned out, I had no need to do so. Later that week, Tony called the institute and cancelled his next appointment. He never returned.

When I discussed the case with my supervisor and peer group, I shared my thoughts about this client. I sensed that, in session five, I had probed more deeply and seen more of Tony's dark side than he wanted exposed. I suspected that the dream he shared with me in session six was intended, whether consciously or unconsciously, to scare me and to cause me to back off. It worked. Perhaps with more training, and in a safer-feeling environment, I would have probed deeper. But obviously Tony did not want me to go there. He did not want to face the depths of darkness and evil in his own soul. To this day, I have not forgotten the cold, empty, calculating look in his eyes. Tony convinced me that evil really can and does exist.

Since time immemorial, the presence of evil and sin in human life has provided the most perplexing and disturbing conundrum for people of faith. How, for example, does one reconcile the reality of the horrors of Auschwitz or Rwanda, with the existence of the loving God proposed by Christianity and other world religions? Throughout history, philosophers and theologians have attempted to deal with this paradox, generally with unsatisfactory results. However, the understanding of God and spirituality emerging today sheds new light on this thorny dilemma.

The Garden of Eden

The writers of the Book of Genesis were deeply perplexed about the presence of sin and evil in the world. Being storytellers, they used a story about a mythical first couple named Adam and Eve, to suggest that sin and evil have their origins in human disobedience and pride. As the story unfolds, we see that God gave Adam and Eve (who symbolize all of humanity) the possibility of living forever in Eden – a garden of bliss, a place of happiness and reliance upon God. However, Adam and Eve refused to accept the condition that God placed upon the offer, which would have limited their ability to acquire knowledge and wisdom. Instead, they wished to be omniscient, all-knowing, like God. And this led to their downfall. After disobeying God's command not to eat from the tree of knowledge, they were expelled from the garden.

The story itself is wonderful and full of insight into the nature of human character and the reality of human desire. But it leaves many more questions unanswered than answered. In fact, if we analyze the story more closely, we might be inclined to blame God for the whole mess. Why did Adam and Eve have this insatiable quest for knowledge in the first place?

Why couldn't they simply be happy with their lot, as God had given it to them? And why did God stick that "Tree of Knowledge" in the garden to tempt them with its lovely fruit? And how did the snake get into the picture? Couldn't God have removed the snake in advance of creating this wonderful place? For centuries, people have felt guilty as a result of reading this story. Historically, the church has often manipulated this sense of guilt to control people's lives. Today, it is high time to look more deeply at the origins of sin and evil. The new vision of God enables us to do just that.

God and Evil

Before we truly can understand how sin and evil originated in the world, we need to reconsider the nature of the reality we call God. Clearly, the notion of a kind, benevolent parent sitting somewhere up in a cosmological heaven is far too simple.

Throughout this book, we have observed that God is better described as an infinitely extending Spirit energy, out of which all life comes into existence. Although, in the case of human beings, God has created a personalized form of life, God cannot be thought of solely in personal terms. God is far too vast, far too incomprehensible for that. Rather, God is the power and the context out of which existence and personal life come into being.

Each and every part of creation is a part of God, is composed of the very Spirit energy and power of God. Just like sandcastles are made out of the sand on the beach; just like snow people are made out of the snow in the field; each and every aspect of life is created out of the most basic, foundational substance of life, which is the Spirit energy of God. This is why *all* of creation is sacred.

But as life takes shape and form in God, it also assumes limitations. And, particularly in the case of human beings, we also develop a sense of separation from God. We lose the sense of oneness and connection with God that is part of the larger divine consciousness. This, then, is where we stand.

Emerging from divinity, from infinity,
we enter a realm of limitations, parameters, and randomness.
Conception, gestation, birth and growth
are followed by decay and death.
Chaos organizes into structure
then collapses into chaos once again.
Divine remembrance leads to Divine Self-forgetfulness.
All this is required as life takes shape
    and form in finite space and time,
a stepped down version of the infinite,
      unqualified energy and bliss of God.

As we noted in the previous chapter, given this circumstance, suffering is unavoidable. Likewise, sin and evil become inevitable. Subject to all the constraining parameters of life, to the vagaries and randomness of life; and circumscribed by our limited self-awareness, cut off from God's own self-awareness as infinite bliss, power, and love; we become capable of horrendous evil. Life is an expression of God. And evil is a possibility in life when it forgets its origins and true nature in God. Saddam Hussein is an expression of God's life gone terribly wrong, but he is still an expression of God.

The Origins of Sin and Evil in Human Life

Flip Wilson, a comedian from the 1960s, was well known for his famous quip, "The devil made me do it." As a corrective to the belief that some nasty little demon out there makes us do things we really don't want to do, Mahatma Gandhi once said, "The only devils in the world are those running around in our own hearts." Traditionally, religious people have explained the presence of sin and evil in the world as the result of some dark, external force in the universe called "the devil," who plays upon human hearts and minds, inciting us to behavior that ranges from simple pettiness to horrific evil. More thoughtful modernists have turned to the human psyche for explanations regarding the origins of sin and evil. Most people today subscribe to the belief that the "shadow," a term coined by the famous psychologist Carl Jung, no longer lives "out there" but resides within the human heart and psyche. Wars and horrors in the wider world are nothing other than the collective expression of all the darkness of our individual human hearts. However, the truth may lie somewhere in between.

Biological origins of sin and evil

As a possibility within life made out of God's own being, evil becomes a potential built into the very biology of human beings. In 1995, the Canadian public was drawn in horrified fascination to one of the country's most notorious criminal trials. Paul Bernardo and Karla Homolka were two outwardly normal and socially successful adults who, in their secret lives, raped, tortured, and eventually murdered two young women. At the time, Michael Harris, a writer for the *Halifax Daily News*, wrote an article entitled "The Eerie Normalcy of Psychopaths." He said:

> As the nation circles the Paul Bernardo trial like a moth drawn to a lurid but irresistible flame, the real horror sits amongst us, remorseless, calculating, and largely invisible. Working on the not-unreasonable theory that anyone who could so terrorize his helpless victims before carving them up like sides of beef is not like the rest of us, it is a good bet that Paul Bernardo – if he's guilty of the crimes he's accused of – is in all likelihood a psychopath.
>
> The bad news is that by conservative estimates, there are two million "high functioning" psychopaths in North America, some of them plotting their next crime, but many of them running corporations or clawing their way to the top of government bureaucracies. They are strangely equipped to succeed, because they give absolutely no thought to the people they destroy along the road to power.[1]

Harris goes on to quote one of the world's leading experts on these remarkable and frightening people, Dr. Richard Hare of the University of British Columbia, who offers this working definition of psychopaths:

> Psychopaths are social predators who charm, manipulate, and ruthlessly plough their way through life, leaving a broad trail of broken hearts, shattered expectations, and empty wallets. Completely lacking in conscience and feeling for others, they selfishly take what they want and do as they please, violating social norms and expectations without the slightest sense of guilt or regret. The most obvious myth about psychopaths is that they are like mad dogs, drooling for their next victim. In fact, they are not insane, do not always commit crimes, and if they do, the planning involved often borders on the brilliant.[2]

Harris notes that for a long time psychopaths were viewed as monsters. However, it might be more useful to view them as genetically defective machines. Researchers of psychopathology have discovered that the psychopath's brain appears to be unable to deal with the processes of emotion. Unable to feel for others or for his own self, a psychopath's self-image is determined by his possessions and external signs of success rather than by loving relationships and compassion for others. Harris concludes, "It pays to remember, you don't have to watch the Bernardo trial to experience the chilling presence of a psychopath; he may be your boss, or the person next door." Or the person you are counseling, as may have been the case with Tony, whom I described earlier.

If psychopathology *does* result from the inability of the psychopathic brain to process emotion, then evil is partly a result of a defective biological organism. It becomes a random potentiality of our structural existence. Science is discovering today that much more of our personality and emotional makeup than previously believed is determined by our biological, genetic, and chemical makeup. A person without emotion could obviously become a very evil person. A person with very volatile emotion could also become an evil person at times. A person with limited intellectual capacity may easily be swayed and manipulated to participate in evil.

This fact does not justify or condone evil, or suggest that society should put up with it. In fact, society needs to be very vigilant regarding evil behavior and needs to control and contain it when possible. But until medical science can accurately predict such behavior on the basis of genetic clues in an infant's makeup, until medical science can eradicate those biological features, psychopathology will continue to be a reality in the world, as will so many other forms of sin and evil that have a physiological basis.

Sociological origins of sin and evil

In addition to its biological origins, sin and evil may emerge as a result of complex social forces. A good example of this was the 1994 massacre in Rwanda. A bulletin from the development organization *Inter Pares* offered this analysis of that situation:

> Images from Rwanda still haunt us long after the TV cameras have left. For several months in 1994 the world's attention was directed to an African tragedy that, at first glance, was rooted in tribal conflict and despotic corruption. But even when genocide is the appropriate term to describe the crimes perpetrated, and all evidence points to a systematic and well-planned strategy, it would be dangerous to over-simplify the Hutu-Tutsi rivalry. And it would be especially misleading to talk about a spontaneous and unpredictable explosion of ethnic hatred as the chief cause of the catastrophe.
>
> To understand the 1994 crisis, we must recall Rwanda's history and transcend the clichés that have defined the country. While ethnicity plays a role in the conflict, it is colonialism that institutionalized ethnic distinctions in Rwanda. Despite the stereotypes, actual differences between the Hutus and Tutsis are ill defined, and certainly are not racial. They share the same language and traditional religion, and can often be members of the same clan. Historically, there has been a significant degree of inter-marriage, and stories abound about

how Hutus and Tutsis lived peacefully as neighbors up to and during the massacres.

It was the Belgian colonizers who implemented formal distinctions and separate identity cards for the two groups, and pursued a policy of "ethnic" favoritism. By independence in 1961, the politicization of "difference" for political gain had grown deeper and deeper, resulting in periodic massacres of Tutsis. The creation in 1979 of the Tutsi-based Rwandan Patriotic Front (FPR), and its war against the Hutu government, ultimately led to the crisis in 1994.

Another factor contributing to this spiral of events has been the well-documented complicity of the international community in the militarization of Rwanda, especially through loans and arms sales by France, Zaire, and South Africa.

The Rwanda crisis also has economic roots. In the late 1980s the country was ravaged by an economic crisis. The price of coffee, which represents 80% of the country's exports, fell dramatically, and internationally imposed economic austerity measures resulted in even more misery and hardship.[3]

Sin and evil, and the conflict from which they often emerge, stem not just from a personal and flawed biology. They have social, economic, political, and relational causes within the family and society as a whole. Poor and unloving parenting; the presence of greed, injustice, and poverty in society; and corrupt political agendas; all tend to contribute to conditions that generate violent, aggressive, sinful, and evil behavior.

Non-incarnate evil forces

Human biological and sociological imperfections can lead to tremendous evil in the world. But what about that "devil" to which Flip Wilson referred? All the great spiritual traditions recognize the possibility that evil, disembodied, psychic forces may exist and may affect human beings and societies.

Whether there exists a single, evil entity we can call the devil or whether there exist many disembodied forces for evil that can mysteriously affect human beings cannot be verified. But a great deal of evidence seems to point in this direction. Renowned psychologist Dr. M. Scott Peck, who dealt with psychological maladaptation throughout his long career, acknowledges that there are psychological conditions that can only be attributed to evil, independent, psychic forces affecting human beings.[4] We have all seen examples of exorcisms in movies and on TV. Although most of these are glamorized and popularized, there exists a wide body of literature and experience that points to some measure of reality in these accounts.

All of this demonstrates that evil is a complex phenomenon that can arise from a variety of different sources. Paradoxically, however, all these sources derive their life from God. Jesus is an expression of God's desire for life that has turned out wonderfully well. Adolph Hitler is an expression of God's desire for life that has turned out terribly wrong. But both are expressions of God's being in life. And this has profound implications for how human beings deal with evil and sin.

The Collective Nature of Sin and Evil

A nun died, but upon reaching heaven discovered her accommodation wasn't ready. Saint Peter said, "Go back to earth and call me in two weeks." The following week, the nun called: "Saint Peter, this is Sister Penelope. I'm in California. Everything is fine, except that I had a drink the other day." Saint Peter replied, "That's no big deal. But your room isn't ready. Call me next week." The call comes the following week. "Saint Peter, this is Sister Penelope. I wish you'd hurry. Last night I went dancing." St. Peter says, "Dancing isn't so terrible. Call me again on Tuesday. Tuesday, another call is made. "Pete, this is Penny. Cancel my accommodation. I'm not coming!"

Before considering our response to sin and evil, a further word must be said about the collective nature of sin and evil referred to above. Religious people often think of sin in highly personal terms, as the daily faults and shortcomings that so preoccupy us. Negative thoughts about other people, an uncalled-for scream at a child who is misbehaving, not declaring income on a tax return, using recreational drugs such as alcohol or marijuana, or perhaps engaging in a secret sexual liaison: these are the kinds of things we often define as sin. And they *can* be serious, and *do* reflect problems, weaknesses, and spiritual immaturity in our lives. But, in the context of the big picture, these personal faults and shortcomings pale in comparison to the larger atrocities committed by human beings: for example, the medieval crusades during which thousands of so-called Christians butchered people in the name of Christ; the extermination of Jews and other unwanted social classes in Nazi death camps, such as Auschwitz; the system of apartheid in South Africa during the latter half of the 20th century; the systematic torture and execution of indigenous people in Latin America during the 1980s; the progressive destruction and elimination of species as the human race spreads over the planet; the pollution and the destruction of the ozone layer; the continuing international scandal of global poverty and the extreme disparity of resources between the rich and the poor. These are the much more serious sins committed by human beings today and they far outweigh the small, daily transgressions that so often concern us.

This larger sin and evil occurs when individual human beings create systems – be they military, economic, religious, or otherwise – which then take on a life of their own and both shape and determine our individual destinies. In apartheid South Africa, there were many wonderful and caring white people who tried to live kindly and compassionately with their black and colored neighbors, but whose very participation in the ongoing life of that apartheid society contributed to the huge injustice taking place. When it comes to evil systems, there comes a time when, if we are not actively struggling against them, we are actually supporting and perpetuating them, whether we intend to do so or not. Simply by being part of North American society today, we contribute to the increasing harm being done to the planet. Driving a car, living in a large home, eating foods that have to be transported by aircraft from other parts of the world, placing chemical fertilizers on our lawns – all these contribute to the increasing levels of harm being done to the planet.

Dr. Martin Luther King Jr. once said, "All life is interrelated. All people are caught in an inescapable network of mutuality, tied in a single garment of destiny." It is impossible to separate personal sin from collective sin. Likewise, it is impossible to separate personal salvation from collective salvation. There are indeed connections between my individual functioning in life, between my thoughts and behaviors, and the functioning of the larger society of which I am a part. Society is made up of all sorts of people just like myself, with various faults and shortcomings. In order for the larger society to change, *I* must change. But for me to change, the larger society must change too. Again we go back to the "genius of the AND." This is not an either/or situation, but a both/and situation. I need to work on my own limitations and shortcomings, as well as work with others on those of society as a whole. Change needs to take place in both arenas at the same time because sin and evil are not just individual issues but collective ones too. This leads us directly to the question of how we address sin and evil in our lives and in the world.

The Great Undertaking

Overcoming evil in our lives and in the world does not just entail an esoteric process of spiritual transformation, although there are spiritual practices that need to be part of the process. Overcoming sin and evil requires very practical self-awareness and down-to-earth behavior modification.

Just as Stephen Covey has noted the importance of positive habits in the lives of highly effective people, we also must recognize the impact of negative habits in our lives. Most of what passes for individual evil and much of what passes for collective sin in our world is the result of habitual functioning or behavior that has become so ingrained in our psyches that we are neither aware of it nor capable of doing anything about it. When this is the case, we become addicted to certain ways of thinking and behaving in the world. This means we are no longer free. Swearing routinely when something goes wrong may start out as a one-time event, but over time becomes an ingrained habit. Buying a chemical fertilizer for my lawn may start out as a one-time event to get rid of those pesky weeds, but may end up being an annual ritual. Drinking after work may begin as a one-time social event with my peers at the office and end up becoming a routine way of relaxing. Hitting my spouse in a fit of rage may over time escalate into an ongoing pattern of spousal abuse. Driving the car to work may be an expensive way to travel but one that becomes so convenient we never think about other options. Human beings are indeed creatures of habit and routine. Our lives become shaped and molded by these patterns, to the point that they identify us and limit our freedom. The transformation that we all seek is at heart a transformation of these habitual, addicted ways of thinking and functioning. Therefore, I want to look, first, at some methodologies for effecting change and transformation in our personal lives, and second, for effecting change and transformation in society at large.

Dealing with Personal Sin and Evil

Before we point a finger at other people or at society at large, we need first to accept that evil lives in each of us. Certainly, it is always easier to demonize enemies and to blame things on someone or something outside us. But Russian writer Aleksandr Solzhenitsyn laments, "If only it were so simple. If only there were evil people somewhere insidiously committing evil deeds, and it were necessary only to separate them from the rest of us and destroy them. But the line dividing good and evil cuts through the heart of every human being. And who is willing to destroy a piece of his own heart?"[5]

Jungian analyst Robert Johnson states that "to honor and accept one's own shadow is a profound spiritual discipline." M. Scott Peck, in his book *People of the Lie*, characterizes evil as the ability to lie to one's self, to deceive one's self, regarding one's true nature and character. I believe that in the case of Tony, whom I wrote about at the beginning of the chapter, this was the fundamental source of the evil in his life. Certainly, I have come to discover this in my own life, too. Learning to recognize the darkness and evil in my own psyche encourages me to be much gentler and more cautious when confronting other people and their sins. But it is also a prerequisite to embracing the transformation that each of us requires.

When we have acknowledged darkness and flaws in our own lives and character, we need then to ask ourselves and to clarify what the important values, principles, and spiritual priorities are in our lives. Writing them down in a notebook or a journal helps the process. Being able to name them is the surest way to become clear about them. If I don't know what I believe, or what is spiritually or ethically important to me, I will never be able to resist temptation or addicting habits when they arise.

Clarifying our moral and spiritual principles and values helps us to cultivate conscience. Conscience is a very subtle spiritual faculty, which makes it easy to override with desire. Desire causes us to rationalize, which is nothing other than to create "rational lies." We need to cultivate conscience regularly, to ask ourselves, "Is this something Jesus – or whoever my spiritual hero is – would do, if he or she were in my shoes?" Or, how does God view this behavior or these thoughts? These questions will keep conscience alive and sensitive.

Avoiding exposure to temptation, people, or activities that can feed a habit or addiction is another useful strategy. If eating too many sweets is a problem, don't buy them and bring them home. If watching too much television is a problem, get rid of the TV for a year or two. If you are trying to stop smoking, for goodness sake, don't hang around with people who smoke.

Closely observing our thoughts and emotional patterns is another very important part of the process of spiritual and character transformation. Negative, desire-filled, and hurtful thoughts can be addictive. Learn to observe negative thoughts, or those filled with desire, as they arise and create some distance from them. Just watching such thoughts helps us to gain some control over them. Engaging in forms of meditation, as named earlier, will help us to do this. Replacing negative thoughts with positive affirmations, or with a spiritual mantra, is a powerful way to overcome their addictive power. We can also read a book or engage in some activity that will take our mind off destructive thoughts when we are immersed in them. The same can be done with emotions. Toxic thoughts and emotions can wreak havoc in our lives. By actively observing them, we can start to gain some control over them.

Praying is one of the most powerful ways to replace negative thoughts and to turn around negative behavior. When we pray about something, the process of prayer itself brings awareness to what is going on and undermines both the thinking and the acting, maybe not overnight, but over time and with persistence. We need to pray much more than we do. Alcoholics Anonymous discovered that the only way some addictions can be overcome is by turning to a Power greater than us. Learning to take the addiction or problem and to put it into the hands of God, however we understand God, takes away some of its power and its self-defeating energy. It also opens us to the possibility of God's transforming grace working mysteriously in our life. In the end, the more we open our lives to God, the more we start to understand and feel God to be the very ground of our lives, the more evil and sinful thoughts will simply fall away on their own.

Dealing with Collective Sin and Evil

But how do we address those larger social evils and sins in which we all are engaged almost against our will?

Perhaps the first thing we need to do is be willing to question the status quo and assumptions about the way things are. A "hermeneutic of suspicion" is a contemporary phrase that has been used to name this attitude. We need to be willing to analyze our world through suspicious eyes, not in order to become paranoid, but because we know that, generally, things are the way they are because the largest and/or most powerful groups of people acquire the most benefit from keeping things that way. In other words, I think we can safely assume that the CEO of the Royal Bank of Canada is not going to ask whether getting a million dollar salary, or the bank making billions in profit, is ethical.

People or groups in power will seldom question their power or privilege or their way of thinking about how things should be. Global trade agreements represent a good example of this. Those who argue most fervently and persuasively in favor of such agreements are, of course, the large and wealthy corporations that have the most to gain. We need to ask ourselves, what are they not telling us in these discussions? What are the drawbacks of such agreements, for a society's sovereignty, for everyday people, or for the environment, to name just a few potential areas of injustice? So many of the discussions around these agreements take place behind closed doors and in secret. And the implications are extensive. We need to be constantly vigilant and suspicious of the motivations of people and institutions that hold great power and wealth. We can safely assume that such groups always have a vested interest in maintaining or increasing such power and wealth. We should not become paranoid, but we should be very, very suspicious.

Such suspicion can encourage us to learn about the big issues affecting our world and society. Life and problems in our contemporary world are seldom simple and straightforward. Rather, the issues we face are usually very complex and we seldom see the consequences of decisions easily or quickly. Making rash statements or rashly opposing issues without knowing our subject matter destroys our credibility and makes people less inclined to listen to us.

Once we have taken steps to really learn about an issue that may have sinful or evil consequences for our society, we need to get over our reticence to speak out, and to challenge darkness and evil when we see it. Not in a finger-pointing way, but in a wise and understanding manner that recognizes that we, *too*, are part of the problem. The following quotation, by the German theologian Martin Niemoeller, writing during World War II, speaks powerfully to this need.

> In Germany, the Nazis first came for the Communists, and I didn't speak up because I wasn't a Communist. Then, they came for the Jews, and I didn't speak up because I wasn't a Jew. Then, they came for the trade unionists, and I didn't speak up because I wasn't a trade unionist. Then they came for the Catholics, but I didn't speak up because I was a Protestant. Then they came for me and by that time there was no one left to speak for me.

However, speaking out is very difficult to do by ourselves. It takes enormous courage and it also requires perspective that comes from having more people involved. Many people like to speculate or dream about what it would be like to be prime minister or president, to have the power and the control to change things in society. But change does not happen that way. To change society we can't just change structures; we also have to change people. And even the President of the United States or the Prime Minister of Canada cannot do that.

One of the best ways to change society, to transform the darkness in our society, is to form communities in which people grow together and through which people work to effect change. We are all in this together. In communities such as churches, justice groups, political action groups, and so on, we acquire much more strength and wisdom for the fight against evil in our society than we ever could by ourselves.

Finally, it is important to say the following about the transformation of the darkness, the sin and evil both in our personal lives and in our collective lives. When our lives are empty of meaning or relevance, we tend to become attracted to all sorts of behaviors and distractions that are unhealthy for us. Of course there are pleasurable activities in life that we all enjoy from time to time. But life is not truly about the pursuit of pleasure. Life is about meaning and about making a creative and positive contribution. Gambling, drinking, engaging in too much sex, and pursuing pleasure and stimulation of all sorts, is often the way people escape the sense of boredom, loneliness, and emptiness they feel inside. So the real challenge for the addicted life is to find meaning, a reason for living, a way to make a worthy contribution, and to give ourselves over to that. In the end, life is about self-transcendence; it is about transcending the limitations of our small egos by giving ourselves over to something larger than ourselves. That "something larger" can be a social cause or a spiritual pursuit. Either way, it is in this pursuit that the universe and God pushes us to grow and to develop.

In the final analysis, it is true that life is not fair and is shot through and through with suffering, sinfulness, and evil. Yet life is a profound and wonderful gift nonetheless. Since God is the originator of all life,

God experiences its unfairness no less than we do. God experiences the suffering, the evil, and the sinfulness in our lives, because our lives are literally an incarnation in matter, space, and time of God's own life.

But God has a great passion for life. God yearns for life to become fully transparent to God's own infinite Spirit. And God desires that human beings, even with all our structural limitations, become aware of our inherent divinity and learn to conduct the infinite Spirit energy of God through our lives. God hungers to bring into the domain of manifest limitation, into the domain of finite mortal life, the compassion and love and bliss that reside within God's own heart at infinity. What a grand undertaking indeed!

THE VISION
INTO
INFINITY

Chapter 12

From Death to New Life

When I was a child, my speech, feelings, and thinking were all those of a child; now that I am a man, I have no more use for childish ways. What we see now is like a dim image in a mirror; then we shall see face to face. What I know now is only partial; then it will be complete – as complete as God's knowledge of me.

1 Corinthians 13:11–12

A story is told about Krisha Gotami, a young mother, who once approached the Buddha. Her first child had just died and she was beside herself in grief and despair. She pleaded with the Buddha to provide her with a medicine to restore her child to life. With enormous compassion, the Buddha explained to the woman that he could make such a medicine, but in order to do so, he needed her to fetch him a mustard seed from a home that had never experienced death. The woman traveled back to her city, desperately knocking on one door after another in search of a mustard seed from a home that had never known death. As her search proceeded from one city to another without avail, she began to understand. She saw that life is constantly changing and that death is an integral part of life. She realized that nothing is permanent, and that death can occur at anytime, at any stage or point along life's journey. It is said that the woman returned to become a disciple of the Buddha and near the end of her life attained enlightenment.[1]

I will never forget my first experience with a stillborn child. I received a phone call from a local funeral director who told me about a young couple, Linda and Bob, whose first child died in a premature birth. They were absolutely grief stricken. They had no church connection but were looking for spiritual assistance and guidance to conduct a funeral service for their baby. Would I come to lend a hand? I met them at the funeral home where they showed me their little baby girl. They had named her Natasha. She was beautiful. A tiny, perfectly formed baby girl who fit into the palm of my hand. Over the next two days, Bob, a carpenter, made a small pine box for Baby Natasha. Then they wrapped her little body in silk and placed her in the box. Together we met in a country graveyard to say our farewells to her. But before we did so, I invited Linda and Bob to speak. They talked about the incredible happiness they had felt when Linda first learned she was pregnant and which they continued to experience through the early months of pregnancy. They spoke of all the hopes and dreams they had held in their hearts for this child. We then said thank you to God and to life for having given Natasha to them. And we said thank you to Natasha, for having shared her life with them, even if only for a short while. Then we said goodbye to Natasha and wished her well in whatever form her journey of life would carry on. And we said goodbye to all the hopes and dreams for Natasha's life that Linda and Bob had carried in their hearts for the past eight months. We said a prayer, and then we placed the little pine box with her body into the ground.

I met with Linda and Bob a couple of times after that, to help them move through their grief, but then we lost touch for a number of years. One day, however, I met Linda coming out of a local program center for children, where I was picking up my own daughter after her dance class. I didn't even recognize Linda at first, but she knew me and greeted me warmly. Bouncing along beside her were two lovely young daughters, chattering away, full of life, and completely oblivious to this stranger with whom their mom had stopped a moment to chat. Linda thanked me again for my help those many years earlier and introduced me to the two girls, whom she and Bob had adopted, and with whom life was now so full and happy. And then we said goodbye, both of us so much richer for having shared those moments of loss together, years ago.

There is nothing harder to deal with in life than losing a child. I know this from the experience of my own parents and from that of the many parents with whom I have worked over the years. The death of a child challenges our understanding of nature and of how life is supposed to unfold. Parents are supposed to die before their children, not the other way around. The death of a child can also challenge our understanding of God as a loving parent and as the benign and wise creator of the universe. And yet it happens to countless parents each and every day.

Death, whether it involves a child or anyone or anything else we love, is one of the greatest challenges to our human experience and to our desire to understand that experience. The death of a loved one, or even our own impending death, evokes within us the very deepest and most painful of human emotions. And it pushes us, like no other event, to seek meaning and reconciliation with life in all its apparent randomness, paradox, and inconsistency. No wonder the "problem" of death is a central focus of every religion the world over. But here, too, many of the traditional responses, emerging out of ancient worldviews no longer speak to modern people. Once again, the new vision of God and the emerging Christian spirituality can shed fresh light on this age-old dilemma.

Coming to Terms with Death

When my two brothers drowned, my parents turned for solace to their belief in an afterlife. In the early days after the drowning, my mother and father both experienced significant dreams about Kye and Roger. In the dreams, the boys spoke to them and told them that they were now working for God in heavenly realms and that my parents need not worry about them. They were fine. To his dying day, my father looked forward to meeting his sons once again in those heavenly realms, which God has in store for us all after we die. For my parents, not to believe in an afterlife was tantamount to not believing in God. And to think that they might never see their two sons again would have been painful beyond endurance.

Christians have always believed that after we die, after coming face to face with God, we will find peace with respect to the experience of loss that death represents. Christians have also believed that in the afterlife, coming face to face with God, we will learn the answers to our questions about life's suffering and injustice. This yearning is expressed with great poignancy in those wonderful words from St. Paul's famous chapter on love and quoted at the beginning of the chapter. These words brought enormous comfort to my father and remained in his heart forever. These are the words I had imprinted upon his tombstone. Like Paul, he understood that we couldn't hope to comprehend the reasons for life's suffering. But he, too, hoped that after we die we will be granted God's own perspective and understanding, which will make sense of everything.

Absorbed in this worldview throughout my upbringing, I fully embraced my parents' belief in the reality of the afterlife. This is why, as a young seminarian, I was shocked to discover that some of my Christian peers pursuing a vocation in ministry, did not hold the same convictions about the afterlife that I held. Although I was open to a contemporary theological education, this was one belief for which I could see no alternative. To be a Christian, you had to believe in an afterlife.

Indeed, the central teaching of the Christian faith, the resurrection of Jesus, was built on this belief. Some of my fellow students, however, saw the Resurrection in purely metaphorical terms. For them, the Resurrection did not refer to the literal coming back to life of Jesus after his death on the cross, but rather to the possibilities for new life that are constantly emerging out of death. So in regard to Bob and Linda's experience, described above, they would have said that resurrection referred to the new hope and joy that Bob and Linda found with two adopted daughters in the years following Natasha's death. My "non-believing" colleagues would not have been convinced that any future reality or life lay in store for Natasha herself. This was not a viewpoint I could accept or even consider at the time.

For me, if there was no continuation of personal existence in some form after we die, then death represented a massive failure and affront to life and to God.

Throughout my years in ministry my perspective on death has changed a great deal. Although I am still predisposed to believe in an afterlife, I have come to realize that the spiritual journey is not about finding absolute certainty or proof of such an existence. Rather, the spiritual journey leads to a deep acceptance of mystery, a capacity to live with ultimate questions without finding answers, and a profound peacefulness and serenity in the midst of life's paradoxes, conundrums, evil, and suffering. This, too, is where the new vision of God and the emerging Christian spirituality lead. But before we can get to a more detailed discussion of that point, it is important to consider at greater length this question of the afterlife.

The Biblical Understanding of the Afterlife

Someone will ask, "How can the dead raised to life? What kind of body will they have?" You fool! When you sow a seed in the ground, it does not sprout to life unless it dies. And what you sow is a bare seed, perhaps a grain of wheat or some other grain, not the full-bodied plant that will grow up. God provides that seed with the body God wishes; God gives each seed its own proper body...This is how it will be when the dead are raised to life. When the body is buried, it is mortal; when raised, it will be immortal.

1 Corinthians 15:35–38, 42

We know today that biblical understandings of the hereafter developed and changed over a long period of time. The Bible represents the evolving thought of the small Hebrew nation as it dealt with a variety of questions, including that of the afterlife. In addition, we know that their thought was influenced by ideas from many other groups and countries surrounding ancient Israel. The Bible reveals, then, the very complex development of a wide assortment of beliefs and ideas over the course of a couple thousand years. I will describe this development in broad outline, knowing that in doing so I cannot do the subject full justice.

According to the earliest Hebrew notions, when God created human beings, God breathed into us the "breath of life." This ancient idea of the "breath of life" is not the same as the modern notion of a soul that leaves or separates from the body after death, and which carries with it the human personality and identity. Rather, the "breath of life" was understood to be an animating principle or force that enables human beings to live. In ancient Hebrew thought, when a person died, that force of life simply went back to God. It did not retain the identity or individuality of the person. So one of the earliest biblical notions of death was that it consisted of the withdrawal of this life force back into God, thereby bringing an end to that individual's existence.

Existing side by side with this belief was a commonly held notion that the dead person, with the force of life now gone, could continue to exist as some kind of ghostlike being in a shadowy underworld called Sheol. Lacking the animating life force and the physical body, this was considered a half-baked existence that also eventually came to an end.

In ancient Hebrew thought, then, the afterlife didn't count for much if anything at all. The important thing was this life here and now. The way to continue beyond death was by having children, preferably lots of them.

Eventually, however, the ancient Hebrews developed a greater interest in the afterlife. This stemmed, perhaps, from a growing recognition that, even for the best of people, this life is often difficult and unfair. Surely, God must have devised a way to balance the scales. A life beyond this life would solve the problem. If you didn't get your just deserts in this life, you would get them in the next. This belief led to the notion of a judgment day, a heaven, and a hell.

But a judgment day, including a heaven and a hell, could only exist in the context of some sort of ongoing life. Thus developed the idea of resurrection, which, by the time of Jesus, assumed many different forms. Some people, such as the Pharisees, believed in an immortal soul that would leave the body at death and then be reinserted into the resurrected body here on earth during some grand future era begun by God – something like reincarnation, except that you got your old body back, albeit recharged and tuned up by the life force of God. Other people, such as the Essenes, believed in the idea of a soul or an eternal self that would carry on in a new resurrected body, not here on earth, but in the upper heavenly planes beyond the earth, above the vault of the heavens, where God was believed to reside. And then there were people, such as the Sadducees, who believed that when we died we returned to the earth and that was the end of our existence.

Jesus' teaching on the afterlife

It was in this intellectual climate and ideological milieu that Jesus lived and taught. Clearly some of the stories and parables ascribed to him make reference to an afterlife where the human personality lives on, either in an embodied or a spiritualized form, either in a heaven or a hell. Luke's parable of the rich man and Lazarus is a good example (Luke 16:19–31). Biblical scholars note that we cannot determine with absolute certainty which of these stories actually originate with the historical Jesus and which are products of the early church and are ascribed to Jesus. What is clear is that nowhere does Jesus engage in a systematic discussion of what he believed about the afterlife. Indeed, the gospels do not provide us with that kind of record of his life and teachings. What we have of the actual teachings of Jesus come to us, primarily, as short and pithy sayings and stories, strung together by the writers of the gospels to fit with their own theology and need to create an attractive narrative of Jesus' life. In all likelihood, Jesus simply entertained the various notions of the afterlife that were circulating in his day and used them as examples and illustrations in his teaching.

Rather than focusing on the afterlife, it appears that Jesus was more interested in considering the realm of God in this life, here and now. In that vein, his teaching reflects an attitude similar to that of the Buddha and of other great spiritual masters, who considered discussion of the afterlife an unhelpful distraction from the "present tense" business of living.

The resurrection of Jesus

With garden resurrections every year,
Life after death is not so queer.

Agnes Ryan, *Poems*

This leads us to the resurrection of Jesus. What did that experience consist of? We don't know for sure. The gospels contain a number of different stories that describe it, but they were all written many years after the death of Jesus. Mainline biblical scholars are absolutely certain that the accounts of Jesus' resurrection, as we find them in the gospels, are primarily storytellers' versions of what happened. But that something *did* happen in the early days after the death of Jesus seems apparent.

The story in Luke's Book of Acts, about how the Holy Spirit came to the disciples while they were praying in the upper room may provide a clue, since many charismatic Christians claim to have similar experiences still today and tend to associate them with the risen Christ. They interpret them as a gift of the Holy Spirit sent by Jesus himself. But regardless of what the early disciples actually experienced, their interpretation or reading of that experience was that Jesus was still alive. And this experience of the ongoing presence of Jesus, or of the power of God's Spirit, which Jesus promised to send them, transformed them from frightened cowards into dynamic, courageous proponents of the love of God revealed in Jesus. Somehow, they came to believe in a very real and powerful way what Jesus had proclaimed in his ministry: that "God is not God of the dead, but of the living." Somehow, they became convinced that the life of Jesus had continued on in God's vast power and love, and that this power was also available in our lives.

No doubt there are those who would wish for more details and for journalistic proof of what happened at the garden tomb 2000 years ago. But the Bible is not that kind of historical record. Rather than giving us a video camera account of biblical events, it provides a secondhand witness of how those events impacted the lives of the people who experienced them.

The only ultimate proof for any of these things needs to come from within us. The records of others can be encouraging, or even confirm our own experience and thought, but they cannot be a substitute for our own experience. The early disciples had their upper-room experience. St. Paul had a mystical experience of the risen Christ on the road to Damascus. I, and other people mentioned in this book, have also had mystical and charismatic experiences that have been profoundly confirming and reassuring. But my spiritual experience cannot provide proof for your faith or for your life. Each of us needs to find the verification for our faith within ourselves and in our own experience of life and God.

Heaven, hell, and the hereafter

A priest was preparing a man for his long day's journey into night. Whispering firmly into his ear, the priest said, "Denounce the devil! Let him know how little you think of his evil!" The dying man said nothing. The priest repeated his order. Still the dying man said nothing. The priest asked, "Why do you refuse to denounce the devil and his evil?" The dying man said, "Until I know where I'm heading, I don't think I ought to aggravate anybody."

A consideration of the biblical understanding of the afterlife would not be complete without addressing, at least briefly, the question of heaven and hell. When we talk about heaven and hell, we are really talking about cosmology, the study of how the universe, and not just the physical universe, is structured by God.

In the earliest traditions of the Bible, we discover a very simple three-tiered view of cosmology. The ancients believed that the sky was a dome separating the earth below from God's heavenly realm above the dome. God lived in heaven above the dome, and we human beings lived below here on earth. The ancient Israelites also came to believe that below the earth there existed a shadowy realm called Sheol, where the departed spirits of human beings lived for a time, without the breath of God, before dissolving into nothingness. Eventually, as noted above, this view of Sheol developed into an understanding of hell, a place of eternal torment and damnation.

At the same time that we find in the Bible this simple three-tiered cosmology, we also find articulated in Psalm 139 and in various other places that God is infinite Spirit, present everywhere, animating and giving life to all creation. For many contemporary Christians, this has led to some confusion. On the one hand, we believe in God as infinite Spirit, present everywhere and in all things, but on the other hand we still believe in a heaven and a hell; heaven being where God lives, and hell being where the devil and his legions live.

However, when we think of hell and the devil as possessing eternal significance and self-sustaining power, we place them on a par with God. This is dualist thinking and is out of step with the deepest biblical witness. God, by definition and by faith, is the single, ultimate power and reality of existence, who brings all of life and creation into being. Nothing can exist unless it is given life by God and is sustained in life by God. That includes this world, and all other worlds and beings too, particularly, whatever hell or whatever devil or dark force might exist. Hell, whatever it may be or wherever it may be, receives its life and being from God and is sustained by God. The devil, whatever it may be or wherever it may be, also receives its life from God and is sustained by God. To say anything other is to acknowledge that the devil and the forces of darkness in the universe are equally powerful to God and possess God's self-existent nature. This, by the way, was a doctrine called Manichaeism, which circulated in the early church, but was quickly discarded as bad theology.

Contemporary cosmology is based firmly in the biblical notion of the ultimacy and the singularity of God's Spirit. There is only one God, who is the creator and sustainer of all of life and of the entire universe, including the good and the bad, the dark and the light. One God is responsible for it all. We discussed earlier that the presence of suffering and evil in the world does not mean that there is a horrible dark force that exists on par with God. Rather, it simply suggests that a defined and limited creation will necessarily contain within it seeds of suffering and evil. The two go hand in hand.

This leads us back to our discussion of the afterlife. Whatever may happen to us in the afterlife, or wherever we may go, it still all happens in God, is given life by God, and is governed by the possibilities of God's grace and love. Indeed, there may be very dark realms as well as angelic realms that exist in the afterlife. But according to the psalmist, wherever we go God is still present and available to us. Hell, whatever it may be, possesses no ultimate power and no eternal hold on us. Even there, God's presence and grace are available.

In some Christian denominations, it is believed that when Jesus died, and before he returned to heaven to be with God, he went down to hell to break open its gates and to redeem the souls locked there in torment.

Although this is a story, it reflects a deep truth articulated so beautifully by St. Paul, when he said in his greatest theological work, the Letter to the Romans,

> Who, then, can separate us from the love of Christ? Can trouble do it, or hardship or persecution or hunger or poverty or danger or death?... No, in all these things we have complete victory through him who loved us. For I am certain that nothing can separate us from his love: neither death nor life, neither angels nor other heavenly rulers or powers, neither the present nor the future, neither the world above nor the world below – there is nothing in all creation that will ever be able to separate us from the love of God which is ours through Christ Jesus our Lord.
>
> Romans 8:35–38

Paul didn't always get it right, but here he reveals his most profound awareness and intuition of the nature of ultimate reality expressed in and through Jesus. There is one God, one love, one power that sustains everything, and we can never be separated or lost from it, neither in this world or the next. We are now ready to proceed with a description of the emerging view of the afterlife based in contemporary cosmology, spirituality, and interfaith study.

A Contemporary View of the Afterlife

Nothing is ever really lost, or can be lost,
No birth, identity, form – no object of the world.
Nor life, nor force, nor any visible thing;
Appearance must not foil,
    nor shifted sphere confuse thy brain.
Ample are time and space – ample the fields of Nature.

> The body, sluggish, aged, and cold – the embers left
>   from earlier fires,
> The light in the eye grown dim, shall duly flame again;
> The sun now low in the west rises for mornings
>   and for noons continual;
> To frozen clods ever the spring's invisible law returns,
> With grass and flowers and summer fruits and corn.
>
> Walt Whitman, *Leaves of Grass*

In this era of instant global communication and the world-wide exchange of information, of interplay between cultures and different religious traditions, of widespread dissemination of near-death experiences and the analysis of such experiences by the modern discipline of parapsychology, and of scientific investigations of cosmology and quantum physics, an entirely new vision of the afterlife has begun to emerge, which stretches our thinking and imagination.

Shortly, I shall present a fairly personal, composite picture of this emerging vision, which draws heavily on contemporary Buddhist teaching; North American shamanism; near-death literature – including the experience of renowned psychologist Carl Jung; present day cosmology and quantum physics; personal stories shared with me by many people, including my father; my own dream life; the teaching of Da Free John; and last but not least traditional Christianity itself. I mention all these sources to indicate the incredible wealth of experience and thinking that is available and that relates to our understanding of the afterlife.

As we begin to weave together the different strands of tradition and teaching related to the afterlife, what becomes apparent is the multi-dimensional nature of the reality in which we live. And it is not just esoteric spirituality or religion that speaks to this aspect of the universe. So do contemporary physics and cosmology. Brian Greene, one of the world's leading physicists, referred to by some as "the new Stephen Hawking only better," tells, in his highly acclaimed book *The Fabric of the Cosmos*, of the vision he had as a teenager that drew him into a life of science. He says,

I remember thinking that if our species dwelled in cavernous outcroppings buried deep underground and so had yet to discover the earth's surface, brilliant sunlight, an ocean breeze, and the stars that lie beyond, or if evolution had proceeded along a different pathway and we had yet to acquire any but the sense of touch, so everything we knew came only from our tactile impressions of our immediate environment, or if human mental faculties stopped developing during early childhood so our emotional and analytical skills never progressed beyond those of a five-year old – in short, if our experiences painted but a paltry portrait of reality – our appraisal of life would be thoroughly compromised. When we finally found our way to earth's surface, or when we finally gained the ability to see, hear, smell, and taste, or when our minds were finally freed to develop as they ordinarily do, our collective view of life and the cosmos would, of necessity, change radically.[2]

From this vision as a teenager, Greene went on to become one of the world's leading string theorists. String theory reveals that the universe consists of 11 dimensions, not just the three spatial dimensions and one time dimension with which we are all familiar. Explaining why we are not aware of these extra dimensions Greene says,

It is not necessarily that the extra dimensions are extremely small. They could be big. We don't see them because of the way we see. We see by using the electromagnetic force, which is unable to access any dimensions beyond the three we know about. Like an ant walking along a lily pad, completely unaware of the deep waters lying just beneath the surface, we could be floating within a grand, expansive, higher-dimensional space, but the electromagnetic force – eternally trapped within our dimensions – would be unable to reveal this.[3]

All of the psychic, mystical, and spiritual experience of humankind, from the beginning of time, reinforces this view that reality, including our own selves, is multidimensional in nature. What we experience as our physical lives in this world may simply be one expression of a much greater number of expressions of reality, of different dimensional ways of experiencing life. Indeed, as we experience these physical lives, we may be participating in other non-physical dimensions at the same time. Out-of-body states, near-death experiences, telepathy, premonitions, dreams, healing energies and the like, suggest powerfully that there are non-material dimensions to the body, to consciousness, and likely to existence itself.

When conducting funerals, I often use the words from the Gospel of John and ascribed to Jesus during the last supper with his disciples. Jesus says, "Do not be worried and upset. Believe in God and believe also in me. There are many rooms in [God's] house, and I am going to prepare a place for you. I would not tell you this if it were not so" (John 14:1–2). These words reflect a perspective that sees the universe and the hereafter as multidimensional in nature. God's house, the universe, contains many different rooms, or many different dimensions. Some of these dimensions are material in nature; others are more psychic or spiritual in nature.

Traditional religion has conveyed the impression that the universe is divided into only two dimensions: the material and the spiritual. The emerging vision of contemporary spirituality suggests that materiality and spirituality are simply different points on an eternal and infinite continuum of the power and being of God. There may be many different expressions of a material universe, many different expressions of a spiritual universe. The universe may be like an onion, with an infinite number of different layers, skins, or dimensions, each consisting of a different degree or intensity of spirit, light, energy, and matter; and all governed differently by time or no time, but each contained within God and sustained by the power and life of God.

Today's emerging spirituality and paradigm of God suggests that when we die, we don't actually go anywhere in space or time, but simply transition into a different form or dimension of being, like shifting from living in one skin of the onion to another that may be more or less psychic

240

or spiritual in nature. In that dimension, we may indeed still have a body, but of a different nature than the one we have here.

Keeping all this in mind, we are now ready to consider a composite vision of what the afterlife *might* look like from the perspective of today's many and varied disciplines and spiritual traditions.

Jack was approaching death. At a certain critical point, his internal organs and systems started to shut down. His heart stopped pumping and he stopped breathing. According to his prior wishes, his doctors did not try to revive him.

Jack experienced the process of dying as a gradual dissolution. First, awareness withdrew from his body, beginning with his extremities: his feet, legs, arms, and hands. Finally he lost awareness of his chest, back, and head.

Inwardly, as brain activity carried on for a few more moments, Jack thought about his loved ones and felt many different emotions: sadness, fear and strangely also curiosity. But then the memories and thoughts subsided, the emotional states came to an end, and Jack fell into a deep darkness and peace similar to falling asleep. And in that sleep, time came to an end.

Then, as though waking from sleep, Jack became "conscious" again. He wondered, "Where am I, what's going on?" He had no physical body, but he felt very much alive. As he looked around he felt as though he was floating, suspended like a cloud. He seemed to be nothing more than a speck of awareness in a vast bright space, similar to a never-ending blue sky on a sunny day. For a moment, Jack experienced total serenity, beyond anything he had ever known. And for the first time ever, he felt totally free. It was a moment of absolute quietness, with no inner thoughts whatsoever. Suddenly, into the peace arose a feeling of fear, a feeling of losing himself, and at that moment Jack's thinking became frantic: "What's going on? Am I dead or alive?"

As Jack's mind raced, he found himself speeding through a long black tunnel towards an incredible white light, a long way off. Traveling towards the light, he relived his entire life, as though watching a 3-D movie. From the moment of his birth to the moment of his death, he relived every single word, thought, action, and emotion, as realistically as when he was on earth. But something else was added. He also experienced every word and action through the people and life forms surrounding him in life. He felt the impact of all his negative actions, both large and small, on the people and life forms that had surrounded him at those moments, and on the planet itself. Likewise, he experienced the impact of all his *good* actions, both large and small. He felt both joy and remorse. He saw connections and understood why he had lived as he had.

Throughout the process, Jack saw loved ones reaching out to him from the sides of the tunnel, offering their love and best wishes and extending forgiveness. Jack felt all the unfinished business of his life coming to a close. As he drew closer to the light, Jack saw Jesus beckoning to him, inviting him to keep coming forward. Moving faster and closer, Jack finally swooned into the light. Again time stopped and Jack felt immersed in the most incredible love and understanding he had ever known, beyond anything he could ever have imagined.

Suspended as a point of awareness in this incredible light, Jack had another remarkable experience. A vast panorama of existence opened before his eyes, stretching across eons of time and space. Jack recognized himself as other people on earth, in times past and in future times. However, he recognized himself, not just as people, but also as a vast variety of different life forms on different planets, in different dimensions and realities. He understood how all the different lives were connected.

Jack understood that every single life he had ever lived was pushing him to grow into an ever-greater expression of the infinite life and love and bliss of God, in manifest form. And Jack saw, too, the lessons he still had to learn. He felt them deeply to the core of his being. Then, still embraced in God's love and light, Jack "fainted" once again.

Not long afterwards, a new baby was born on earth, a new angel came into being on some heavenly plane, a life form emerged in some very dark and sorrowful domain, unaware that it had lived before or that it would live into eternity, preparing to grow up, to experience life, and to learn and grow in life as it needed to do. One of them was Jack; perhaps all of them were Jack.

Let's take a somewhat closer look at Jack's journey, beginning with the dying process itself. At the point when Jack's heart stops and he loses all awareness – physical, mental, and emotional, he transitions into what could be called the afterlife phases.

Although the Bible reflects a variety of different perspectives on the afterlife, a clear belief to emerge from later Christian writers is that we continue to experience a personal sense of self beyond the confines of the body, after death. Of course, this notion is present in the Bible, as well. The story of Jesus meeting Elijah and Moses on the mountain during the transfiguration clearly suggests that, at the very least, the author of that story believed in some sort of "personal" existence in the afterlife, otherwise he wouldn't have named Elijah and Moses. And Jesus, however he appears to his disciples, does so in a form that they recognize as being him.

But this begs the question how, if we don't have a physical body, we can continue to exist as a personal life form after we die? Buddhist teaching, which is much more sophisticated and developed in this area than Christian thinking, states that we awaken after death as an individuated point of energy and awareness, which could be called the soul. As this individuated point of awareness, we have the option of merging with the ultimate God reality of unconditioned, undefined, and infinite clarity, power, and bliss. In this state, we lose all sense of individuated life and, rather, assume as our larger identity the totality of God's being. Indeed, this fundamental God condition is our own true identity and reality, both in this life and in the next. As the soul, an individuated point of awareness, Jack initially and briefly experiences this divine condition, as though floating in an infinite blue sky. It is a condition not unlike that of people experienced in meditation, who learn to rest in the deep stillness and silence of God.

However, both Christian and Buddhist theology suggest that, if we are not prepared in this life to remain centered in God, to enjoy and love God on a continuous basis, to merge into oneness with God, then we will not be able to do so in the next life. Jack believed in God, but he wasn't sufficiently prepared in this life to recognize or to remain centered in God, and therefore could not, as an individuated point of awareness, merge into the bliss and unconditional nature of the infinite God state.

As an individuated point of awareness, he still possessed mind. In short order, his mind commenced a tumultuous process of fear and desire and this immediately led to another stage of his destiny. Prayer and meditation are the key disciplines that enable people to learn to relax, to remain rested and centered in God. Since we take into the next life the same habits and qualities of mind and heart with which we leave this life, if we haven't learned to love God and to remain rested and centered in God here and now, we won't be able to do it in the afterlife. If Jack had been able, his soul could have merged with the bright blue sky, forever resting in the sheer bliss, wonder and oneness of God. That's what Christians would call the "realm of heaven." But Jack wasn't capable of this and so his destiny led him towards more experience. Thus his journey down the tunnel began.

In the near-death-experience literature, this phase of the journey begins with the flight down the dark tunnel and leads toward an incredible light. In the tunnel, the traveler is greeted on all sides by loved ones who have transitioned before. The presence of these loved ones is welcoming and reassuring and points to the ultimately loving nature of the great power that designed the process. These images of loved ones may be just that, reassuring images. Then again, in some mysterious way, they may represent the actual presence of loved ones. Either way, more important in the tunnel than the presence of the loved ones is the whole-life review.

Remember that the belief in an afterlife judgment day emerged in ancient biblical times and in human conceptual development as a requirement to make sense of the moral inequities of this present life. Human beings have a profound moral sensibility and a deep desire for justice, even if we do not always reflect that reality in our everyday lives. This fundamental sensibility prevents most religious people from believing that the God who created the universe could be immoral or amoral. If in creating life, God had no choice but to include both possibilities for light and darkness and good and evil, we believe that God must have built into existence provision for the balancing of the scales between good and evil. Every person must, at some point in his or her life journey, face the moral and spiritual deficits of his or her being. It is the struggle with this dilemma that is reflected so powerfully in the Book of Job. And so, eventually, there developed the belief in a judgment day.

In the new vision of God, however, and again being mindful of "the genius of the AND," we are both separate from and part of God at the same time. In the new understanding, God is not conceived solely as a loving or judging parent or authority, someone over and against us, but as our own deepest nature. Indeed, the whole purpose of life is to enable the fullness of God's infinite being to be reflected in and through conditional and incarnate forms. This view, combined with the near-death experience of the whole-life review, suggests a much more significant and meaningful form of judgment. Rather than being judged by an external being, we are granted the perspective of our own deepest nature. For a brief moment in time, we are able to live out of our dual nature, both as the infinite, unconditioned reality of God, and as a limited, conditioned expression of God. We experience ourselves not as either/or, but as both/and. We experience infinite love and acceptance at the same time that we experience deep and profound sorrow, remorse, and understanding. We see ourselves both *through* and *as* the eyes of God – God not separate from us, but God as part and parcel of our own being.

In the tunnel, this is what Jack experienced. He saw his entire life through the perspective of his own divine nature. He saw how every thought, action, and emotion was connected. He saw, too, the impact each had on the lives of people and the life of the earth around him. He made peace with loved ones who had been part of his life. His life came to a wonderful completion. And because Jesus had been so important in his life, he met Jesus and found Jesus welcoming him into the light of God. If Jack had been Buddhist or Hindu or Muslim, a central figure in one of those religions would have been present to greet and welcome him into the light. Then, as this part of the review concluded, he swooned into a sense of the totality of God's light and being.

A multidimensional perspective of the universe suggests that individuated life beyond this dimension does not lead to a single heaven or hell, but rather consists of a much longer journey of growth and development, one in which there may be many different lives in store for us. This does not necessarily refer to reincarnation, as it is traditionally understood. We may have many lives, but they may not all be as human beings or occur on the earth. Our lives might continue in angelic realms, or in any number of other dimensions that God might have in store for us beyond death. And these lives may not all follow sequentially in time, as we understand it. Again, we are reminded of Jesus' words, "In my father's house are many mansions." But there is a complicating factor in this perspective.

That factor is that when we are born into this life, we have no memory of previous lives. Thus, the question arises, "Of what value is an ongoing journey if we have no memory of previous phases of the journey?" The long-term memory must surface during the between-lives-state and belong to the soul. It is the soul condition that has access to our eternal and infinite memory. We cannot have that memory in this material, bodily based existence, because it would be too difficult to carry with us. Just think how hard it would be to carry on through our limited human lives with the memory of a billion years behind us. Many days I can't remember to take my keys with me when I leave the house, let alone deal with this kind of memory. The brain simply does not hold the capacity for such memory. It wouldn't make sense or be possible. Therefore, we don't have the memory here. But in our soul condition, between incarnate lives, we may be able to access the infinite memory of God.

Accounts of the near-death experience never end in the actual light. Before the near-death traveler gets to the light, they are turned back to this life. And so this part of Jack's journey is strictly hypothetical. But it seems to make sense within a larger vision of what God might be attempting to do with our lives. When Jack plunges into the infinite light and power of God's being, he accesses the entire memory of his individuated journey in God, one that spans infinite lives, in multiple dimensions. He understands how all these lives are connected and how, through them all, God is seeking to be expressed. And then he collapses into a deep, peaceful, and dreamless sleep once again. This then leads to the next stage in his individuated, personal journey of life.

What happens to the soul after its "life review" in God?

Traditional Christianity has been confounded by the question of what determines where we go after we die. The great scandal that plagues fundamentalist Christianity is that, depending on whether or not you accept Jesus as your "Lord and savior" before you die, you will either go to heaven or to hell. In these churches, unless the words "Lord and savior" are expressed in precisely this way, the person is bound for hell. More thoughtful people have pondered the injustice of such a worldview. Why would a loving God base someone's eternal destiny on his or her conduct in this one short life? People are born into this world with totally different backgrounds and opportunities to grow in faith and love. Many people are good and loving, but never accept Jesus as their "Lord and savior," either because that religious language makes no sense to them, or because they simply feel no need to do so. Many other people are born and raised in non-Christian traditions for whom becoming Christian makes no sense. Still other people are raised without loving families and faith communities of any sort to nurture them along a spiritual or religious journey in life. It makes no sense to believe that God would condemn all these people to eternal hell and damnation.

This is why the emerging view of the afterlife concludes that if there is an ongoing, afterlife existence for human beings, it must be one that takes into account the wide discrepancy in opportunity for spiritual growth and learning in this lifetime, and must provide opportunities for growth that are more specifically geared towards our individual human differences and journeys. Furthermore, it must do so in a way that accepts and respects the pluralist nature of human religious expression, of which we are so aware today.

In Buddhist belief, where we go when die, into what realm of existence we transition, is determined by the quality of our hearts and minds at the time of death. If our hearts and minds are characterized by thoughts and tendencies that are loving and peaceful, we will be drawn toward a loving and peaceful dimension of existence within God. If our thoughts and tendencies are darker, more self-centered, filled with evil and greed and so on, then we will be drawn towards darker realms of existence and being within God, realms more characterized by pain and suffering. If you are a beautiful and loving human being from within any religious tradition, you may be drawn into an angelic dimension and live as a form of angel. If you are an evil and dark human being, you may be drawn to some demonic, hell-like form of existence and live as some sort of dark entity.

However, it is most important to note that all these dimensions exist within the body, the power, and the being of God. This means that, from within any one of these dimensions of existence, God's love and grace can be accessed. A demon in the deepest depths of hell can open its heart to God, call upon God for grace, strength, and forgiveness, and be transformed within God. That demon may need to live through its own lifespan in that place or dimension until it is ready to transition into a new life form in God, but the possibility is always there. This is to say that God's redemptive grace and love, God's redemptive presence and spirit, is always available anywhere and anytime, because all of life is surrounded and permeated by God, held in being and sustained by God. And so wherever Jack ended up after his life review in the tunnel, the review of all his lives throughout eternity, and his final swoon in God, whether it was back on earth, in an angelic realm, or in some demonic and dark world, his soul would never be lost to God. God would always be available to him whenever and wherever he opened his heart and being to God.

We cannot leave this vision of the afterlife without sharing one final comment and caution. If some form of individuated soul existence does continue for each of us after this bodily existence has ended, and if that soul *does* migrate into some other embodied form in some dimension of existence, we may continue to remain subject to the suffering of change and time. Individuation, as noted earlier, presumes change and suffering. Any form of existence that is governed by any parameters of space, time, and embodiment, is governed by change that entails suffering. The only form of existence that entails no suffering is God's own infinite, unbounded spirit Being of infinite bliss. But this form of existence also involves no individuation or personal being. Perhaps the last step towards this form of life is to exist as an angel in the very highest realm of being, where our minds become so accustomed to being suffused by the energy, spirit, and love of God that the next step is simply to let go of any final sense of individuality and to merge into the oneness of infinite being and bliss for all eternity.

For some people, God would seem much kinder if that possibility were immediately available to all of us upon dying. It is to that possibility that we now turn.

Another Possibility for the Afterlife

There is neither a here nor a beyond, only the great unity.
Rainer Maria Rilke, *Sonnets to Orpheus*

As I have indicated throughout this book, the afterlife is a reality pointed to by a vast range of human experience, but experience that is for the most part anecdotal and subjective rather than scientifically verifiable. Psychic experiences such as clairvoyance, precognition, and telepathy; mystical experiences, shamanism, near-death experiences, the resurrection of Jesus, and even dream states, all point to non-material dimensions of existence that may govern or interact with human life in this material world. But regardless of the reality of such additional dimensions of existence, there is another possibility for Jack's afterlife journey – not characterized by an infinite process of transformation.

It could be that, at the end of the tunnel, following his whole-life review, when Jack's soul swoons into the incredible light and love of God for the last time, there is no review of previous lives and neither is there reincarnation or migration of his soul into any other lives. It could simply be that this is the end of the road. After we die to this bodily based life, we experience a review of our life through God's eyes and from God's perspective, and then simply fall back into the great, undifferentiated bliss, unity, and love of God's being.

In this understanding of the afterlife, every life belongs to God. When our bodily based, individuated life comes to an end, we simply wake up to the awareness that this individuated life always belonged to God and now folds back into God. For a brief moment in time, we are conscious both as the individual we were and of the totality of God that is, and then our identity expands permanently to identify with God's infinite being. Period. End of story. For many people this is a much more appealing ending to our earthly lives.

However, once again, the dilemma for traditional Christianity with this scenario is the need for some motivation to live justly and compassionately in this life. If there are no consequence in the next life for our behavior in this life, if we simply dissolve back into the great ocean like a river running to the sea, why should any of us engage in a loving and just life? Why not simply live selfishly and narcissistically for ourselves?

The answer is so simple and straightforward that we often miss it. Love and compassion, caring for others, and engaging in service are their own reward. Conrad Black, with all his wealth, may seem to live a happier and more fulfilled life than the east-coast fisher eking out a modest living while caring for his or her family and community, giving to his or her church and the wider world, and so on. But the secret of life, the one people find so hard to comprehend, is that true joy in life comes from our connection with community and with the world, and lies in the process of shared love and purpose, not in material acquisition.

Making Peace with Life and Death

O Lord, you have always been our home.
Before you created the hills, or brought the world into being,
you were eternally God, and will be God forever.
You tell [human beings] to return to what [we] were;
you change [us] back to dust.
A thousand years to you are like one day;
they are like yesterday, already gone,
like a short hour in the night.
You carry us away like a flood; we last no longer than a dream.
We are like weeds that sprout in the morning,
that grow and burst into bloom, then dry up and die in the
evening.

Psalm 90:1–6

When my brothers died, perhaps because I was raised in a very devout and religious home, I needed to search for an understanding of God that would make sense of that event for me. This search consumed much of my young adult life. During that search, however, I took for granted my parents' belief in an afterlife and the conviction that an afterlife would provide resolution for all the contradictions and questions posed by existence. That belief has, for me, survived the test of time. In fact, it has strengthened due to the stories and accounts shared with me by other people, as a result of my own experience, and because contemporary science itself is today considering the possibility of a multidimensional reality. But, paradoxically, just as I have come to believe even more strongly in the afterlife, that very reality no longer seems so important to me. This is because of the new vision of God and Christian spirituality that is emerging today.

In this book, we have discovered that God does not live up in the sky or far away from human beings. Indeed, we have discovered that God is as close to us as the air we breathe. Not only is God close to us, God is part of us. At the same time that we appear to be quite separate and distinct from God, in truth we are part of and one with God. We are expressions of

God in the same way that waves are expressions of the ocean. Every wave is different, having its own size, color, sound, and other qualities. At the same time it is not separate from the ocean. When the wave dies, it simply enters back into its eternal, larger aspect. The wave doesn't grieve that it is losing existence when it dies. It simply takes back its larger identity.

The emerging Christian spirituality tells us that the religious journey is not about ensuring that we go to heaven when we die because, indeed, we already live in God now, and we always will. Rather, the new spirituality tells us that the religious or spiritual quest is about discovering and becoming aware of God as the ever-present ground of our being, the eternal spirit in whom we live, right here and now and always. It tells us that we can learn to live beyond the self-contained nightmare of separateness and narcissism, and enter into the glorious vision of unity and oneness in God and with each other. Spiritual discipline and wisdom enable us not just to think about, but also to become aware of and to identify with God; not as some great being up in the sky who is separate from us, but rather as that power, spirit, and identity who is most truly what we are and who we are.

When we start to absorb this wisdom into our hearts and minds, when we learn to meditate upon and realize the truth that God is our own deepest identity and condition, we begin to relax. Then our mortality no longer scares us, because we recognize that that which is mortal and that which changes is simply the temporary identity we assume for expression in this dimension of existence. When this identity ends, we revert to our prior identity that is the self-radiant, blissful, self-sustaining, and eternal life of God.

We discover, too, that this spiritual awareness of our oneness with God may not necessarily lead to absolute answers to all the mysteries of life and the hereafter. But it *does* allow us to relax with the questions, to let go of the need for answers to all our questions. It allows us to stop questioning death, as though death were a problem. For God, death is not a problem or a question. For God, death is simply part of an ongoing, universal process of change and transformation. In truth, the human mind will never be able to comprehend the totality of existence, or have answers to all the questions of life. But we can learn to relax into the great mystery of life, to surrender into the great source we call God, with trust and with faith, and there be at peace.

It is this kind of peace that Moses exhibited at the boundary of the Promised Land. At the end of a long and eventful life, during which he led the Israelite people out of slavery in Egypt, through the desert wilderness for 40 years, and finally to the border of the Promised Land, God tells Moses that he is to go no further. The end of his leadership, the end of his time has come. The leadership of Israel needed to pass on to a new and younger generation. In the story, Moses climbs the mountain at the border and surveys the whole land the people are soon to enter. And then, with his vision and energy still intact, he dies. Having glimpsed the Promised Land, he is able to let go of his responsibilities and finally be at peace.

Psalm 90, quoted above, is attributed to Moses. Among other things, it helps us to understand the deep sense of peace with which he died. In the psalm, Moses reveals a profound wisdom. Like Krisha Gotami in the story at the beginning of this chapter, he has come to learn that life is short and fragile. He understands that life is governed by change, impermanence, and death. In the midst of this change and impermanence, however, he celebrates God who is eternal. His heart and mind are rooted and grounded not in the ever-changing aspects of life, but in God this eternal non-changing ground of all being. With his heart and mind rooted in God, he finds peace and acceptance.

It is not easy to surrender our constant fascination with the immediate, constantly changing, surface aspects of life. Indeed, the entire content, culture, and structure of our lives is preoccupied with and built upon these aspects. In the midst of their daily struggle to make a living while dealing with the harsh political and economic realities of first-century Palestine, not to mention the demands placed on them to placate the gods through the religious observances of the day, Jesus called his people to a deeper life and vision. In Matthew's gospel we find these wonderful words.

> This is why I tell you not to be worried about the food and
> drink you need in order to stay alive, or about clothes for your
> body. After all, isn't life worth more than food? And isn't the

body worth more than clothes? Look at the birds: they do not sow seeds, gather a harvest and put it in barns; yet [God] in heaven takes care of them! Aren't you worth much more than birds? Can any of you live a bit longer by worrying about it?... [God] knows that you need all these things. Instead, be concerned above everything else with the Kingdom of God and with what [God] requires of you, and God will provide you with all these other things.

Matthew 6:25–27, 33

Jesus doesn't just tell people to stop worrying about life, as though that in itself was a panacea for all that ails us. Rather, he invites people to give themselves over to the kingdom of God, a reality he knew not as an afterlife state, but as a condition of being here and now. He knew that people would still go hungry, be without work, and find themselves in difficulty with the political and religious authorities of the day. Jesus knew the realities of life only too well. But he also knew that, despite these realities, our immersion in the deeper dimension of life we call God gives to us perspective and peace.

This immersion in God does not remove from us the responsibility of working to change this life, of struggling against political oppression and injustice, and of working to bring healing to human lives and to the planet as a whole. Again we are dealing with the "genius of the AND." We are called to both. We are called to a way of responsible and creative interaction with life while at the same time surrendering our attention and care into God, the deeper ground of our being. This is precisely how Jesus lived. He engaged life and the human struggle fully. During the day, he dealt with daytime responsibilities: teaching, healing, and challenging political structures. But by night he prayed, immersing himself in the divine dimensions of life from which we ultimately come and to which we ultimately return.

In the process of living his daily life, Jesus encountered many difficulties and challenges that led to his inevitable confrontation with the authorities and that resulted in his being brutally murdered. Jesus knew from the beginning that this was a possible outcome of his life. What was true for everyone else in his society was also true for him. John the Baptist was also brutally murdered for confronting the religious and political authorities of his day. But Jesus' life had also been given over, remarkably given over, to God. And that giving over became apparent, not just in his living and dying, but in his ongoing presence with and impact on the disciples following his death.

Jesus' life involved great sacrifice. But it is not just the sacrifice we normally think about. He was indeed willing to sacrifice his physical earthly life for the sake of the larger mission of living out his vision of God's peace and justice here on earth. Many people who have come after him, such as Mahatma Gandhi, Oscar Romero, and Dr. Martin Luther King Jr., have done likewise. But Jesus engaged another profound sacrifice too. This was the sacrifice of his heart and mind in God. This was the sacrifice of his human ego, self-preoccupation, and narcissism, in the giving of his attention and love to God. It was that sacrifice that enabled the other sacrifice to take place. "Love the Lord your God with all your heart, and soul, and mind. Then love your neighbor as yourself." The order of these two commandments is so important. In learning to love God, in learning to give our attention fully over to God, we develop the capacity to truly love each other. We also develop the capacity to live life simply, freely, and without worry for this life or for the next. A heart made pure by devotion to God and a mind made singular through attention given over to God is a life freed of the millions of competing demands made by a daily surface existence.

The true significance of Jesus' resurrection was not, as Paul believed, that death was now conquered. Death isn't something to be conquered. Death is a natural part of life. Rather, Jesus' death and resurrection teaches us the supreme principle of life. If we will surrender our anxiety and need to cling to life and instead resort to a supreme trust and relaxation into God, then we can trust both life and God.

In any case, we have little choice. We can suffer through life, feeling separate and lost from our true home – the one we have in and name as God; we can feel the weight of our mortality and limitations; or we can daily exercise the law of sacrifice, of release of our self-centered and preoccupied attention into the great mystery of God, and in that sacrifice find peace.

Conclusion

Christianity did not begin as an organized body of doctrines, beliefs, or even spiritual practices. And it did not begin with a pre-existent Bible. Christianity, at the very moment of its inception, began with a human life, a remarkable life, the life of Jesus. Attempts to totally mythologize the life of Jesus, either making him a supernatural incarnation via the virgin birth, or merely a symbol for a cosmic, universal truth do us a disservice. Although the record of the New Testament obscures somewhat the historical life of Jesus, that life shines through nonetheless. Jesus was real. He was born, lived, loved, taught, and made a remarkable impression on those who knew him.

However, he lived in a volatile time and place in history that was brutal in its exercise of power. Anyone who opposed the power structures of the day, either religious or political, was quickly and violently dealt with. Jesus was no exception. And his was by no means the first or the last crucifixion on a Roman cross, of which there were thousands. But his life and his story, unlike the thousands of others of his day and age, stood out, made a significant difference, and continues to do so to this day. Obviously, this is partly due to the fact that a later religious and political power, the emperor Constantine, absorbed his story and made it part of the general culture. But even before that event, the life of Jesus had made a significant impact on his followers, who ensured that his story was passed on. Beyond any doubt, part of that impact was connected to the ongoing experience of and relationship with Jesus that his followers had after his death.

As the life and story of Jesus became absorbed into the general culture of later generations and as the Christian church began to develop and evolve, beliefs became codified into doctrines, and doctrines became the litmus test of belonging to the emerging Christian religion and culture.

Today, it no longer matters whether people belong to a Christian church or whether they identify themselves as part of the Christian culture. In a global society, people are free to hold whatever religious beliefs they like, and even our Western culture is no longer explicitly Christian, although it still possesses many of the trappings and even some of the values of Christianity.

In some respects, this has been a great loss because it has led to the breakdown of a cohesive set of religious and cultural values around which our society can coalesce. On the other hand, it has been very freeing. And for truly religious people, including those committed to spiritual practice, it has enabled us to see through and to look past the enormous overlay of thinking and belief about Jesus, to try to discover the person at the center of it all.

This is what many Christians and non-Christians alike are seeking to do today. Indeed, many in the organized Christian church are involved in this endeavor and that is one of the things this book seeks to encourage.

The Christianity that has developed over the 2000 years since the time of Jesus has been an enormous gift to our cultural and religious heritage. But, in many ways, it is a gift that now hampers our ongoing religious and spiritual development. A literalist reading of the Bible, for example, no longer serves our contemporary, knowledge-based culture. The doctrine of the atonement that states that Jesus had to die on a cross as a sacrifice for our sins perpetuates unhealthy understandings of God and the glorification of violence, as exhibited in Mel Gibson's film *The Passion of the Christ*. The belief that Jesus is the only way to God creates walls and divisions among people in a day and age when we desperately need to learn to live and work together.

The way forward is not to hang on to this gift from the past, but to let it go – at least those parts that no longer serve us. The way forward lies in reaching out to our sisters and brothers around the world, and to the other religious traditions of the planet; it lies in learning together about the truths that we all share about the religious and spiritual journey, and then in applying those universal truths to our particular path. We do not need to abandon our specific path, but we can learn to understand and use it in different ways to facilitate spiritual growth and awakening.

Drawing on the experience of other world religions and other ancient and contemporary spiritual movements too, this book has shown Jesus to be a remarkable spiritual genius, in the same lineage as Krishna, the Buddha, Mohammed, and others. His capacity to know and to experience God was extraordinary. That experience made God both intimately personal and transpersonal to him. For Jesus, God was not removed from human life, but a reality so intimate that he could relate to God as a loving parent. Reference to mystics and contemplatives since the time of Jesus, both within Christianity and within other religious traditions, helps to clarify the nature of Jesus' experience of God. Jesus was not the first or the last to experience God in this way, but his experience remains rare and precious. Furthermore, the fact that Jesus is not the only human being to have had this depth of experience of God need not be a source of anxiety or concern, but is actually a confirmation of the truth of what he revealed.

Marcus Borg makes the following point in his book *Meeting Jesus Again for the First Time*. He says, "Rather than being the exclusive revelation of God, he [Jesus] is one of many mediators of the sacred. Yet even as this view subtracts from the uniqueness of Jesus and the Christian tradition, it also in my judgment adds to the credibility of both."[1] I would suggest that the uniqueness of Jesus does not lie in the nature and profundity of his experience of God, but in his particular historical and cultural demonstration of that experience. What Jesus demonstrates for us is that God has chosen and can choose to be revealed in any time, place, and culture in God's effort to reach out to humanity and to renew human spiritual life.

Of course, many Christians struggle with the idea that the Christian path is not the only way to God. If other paths are also valid and have a contribution to make, why then should someone choose to be part of the Christian community? There are many good reasons for belonging to the Christian community as well as to any other religious community. I would like to name a few.

Five Values of Christian Faith and Community

The importance of a path

A wise sage once said to an aspiring spiritual seeker, "God will not judge you by your spiritual accomplishments in life, but by whether or not you were true to your path." Although giving some time to experimentation and to trying different practices and approaches at the beginning of the spiritual life is important, at some point we need to choose a direction and a path. Experimentation, exploring, and dabbling enable us to see what is available in the spiritual marketplace. But in order to grow deeply in the spiritual life, we must give ourselves over fully to a path and to a practice.

All across North America, retreat centers are opening up. Many exist within monasteries and other religious institutions. Others, however, approximate luxury spas. With beautiful rooms overlooking the ocean, whirlpools, hot tubs, and gourmet food, these places offer a smorgasbord of spiritual practices, including yoga, different forms of meditation, chanting and drumming, sweat lodges, and shamanistic experiences. Sam Keen has made the astute observation that "all of us affluent people like to do our discipline in armchairs, diet on gourmet food, and do our wrestling with the shadow in full light."[2] The "spiritual spa" can be useful at the beginning of the spiritual journey. But, again, to grow and mature into a truly wise and spiritual person, commitment to and consistency along a particular path is necessary.

As we commit to a particular religious path, the teacher, the practices, or the organization as a whole begin to take up more space in our life. They begin to ask more and more of us in terms of talent, time, and commitment. As we commit to regular weekly worship; to participating in disciplines of prayer and study; to giving of our time, service, and money to a spiritual community; and to serving the world in humanitarian ways, we are confronted with our own self-concern and preoccupation. We begin to encounter a resistance to the spiritual life, to serving others and God. It is in confronting this resistance in ourselves that we begin to see the various "shadows," as Sam Keen calls them, that prevent us from growing spiritually.

Contributing and serving on a particular religious path provide the very challenges that enable us to grow. Yes, we can go on retreats and explore a whole variety of different and exciting possibilities in the spiritual marketplace. But none of these things ask for any real commitment from us. Until we make commitments and face them with maturity, no real growth is possible. Getting up on Sunday morning and going to church, perhaps also teaching Sunday school, can be a profound indicator of how serious we are about the spiritual life. We may find that we would much rather sleep in on Sunday morning after staying out late with friends on Saturday night. Likewise, finding a time to spend in prayer each day can be enormously difficult for a spiritual aspirant. But if we cannot find ten minutes a day to pray, how can we ever hope to know God? Engaging in some kind of service to others – serving in a food bank, or even making financial commitments to particular causes – can unleash in us a tremendous amount of resistance. But if we cannot engage in such simple acts, how can we grow in the depth of love revealed in Jesus? These are the kinds of practical, everyday challenges we face when we make a commitment to a particular religious path and organization, and which cause us to grow.

The spiritual life is about joy and freedom; it is about release from guilt and the sense of obligation and requirements. At the same time, no real growth is possible without discipline, without commitment, without a deep and profound love that lifts us out of ourselves. We simply do not acquire these things outside the context of a particular spiritual path, which we are most likely to find within the context of a religious tradition.

Community

Another reason structured religious life and organizations are so important is that they provide community. No individual can grow in isolation. We are who we are because of the contributions our families and communities made in raising us. We have all heard the saying, "It takes a village to raise a child." This is very true. Educational institutions, hospitals, sports, cultural organizations, and religious communities all contribute to the development of a life. North Americans and Europeans in particular are privileged to have so many resources and advantages in this area. The spiritual life, at its most profound, teaches and reveals the interconnection and interdependency of all life.

We need community. But living in community is not necessarily an easy thing. Not only does religious community make demands upon us, it also calls us to do this in cooperation with other people, some of whom we will like, and some of whom we will feel little resonance with. It is one thing to speak idealistically of living in religious community; it is quite another to live that ideal in everyday life.

A fundamental part of spiritual growth entails learning to care for people who are different from us, who may have habits that annoy us, and lifestyles of which we don't approve. But the spiritual vision of life reveals each and every person to be a part of God, as someone with whom we are fundamentally connected to in God. As Jesus said, "Whenever you welcome a child, or give a cup of cold water to a stranger, or visit someone in prison, you do it for me." When we care for each other we care for God. Community calls us to look beyond ourselves. Living in community, being part of a religious community, causes us to grow in awareness, to learn to see all people as expressions of God, as valuable, precious, and worthy of respect.

Spiritual discipline

One of the great values of participating in religious community is that it provides a context and support for our exercise of spiritual discipline. Stephen Covey, in his book *The Seven Habits of Highly Effective People*, makes very clear that our habits, perhaps more than anything else, define who we become as human beings. He says that our character is a composite of our habits and he quotes the maxim, "Sow a thought, reap an action; sow an action, reap a habit; sow a habit, reap a character; sow a character, reap a destiny." Aristotle, too, said, "We are what we repeatedly do."[3]

Spiritual disciplines and practices need to become ingrained habits within our lives. But the reality for most people is that work and entertainment take up the majority of our time. The third of Covey's seven habits is entitled "putting first things first."[4] The majority of people recognize the importance of spiritual study, meditation, group learning, and collective worship, but have a very difficult time making room in chaotic, busy lives for such practices on an ongoing basis. A religious community offers opportunities for spiritual practice, provides weekly habit-forming disciplines, such as Sunday worship, and creates communities of like-minded people who provide each other with support.

Another principle that Covey refers to is the "law of the harvest" or the "law of the farm." This law refers to the fact farmers can't skip vital steps such as preparing the ground, planting the seeds, or tending and cultivating the crop if they want to have a successful harvest. There are sequential stages to growth and development. This is true in all aspects of life, whether one is learning how to play a sport, do a new job at work, or be a new parent. And it is true of spiritual development. Even the Covey organization recognizes that reading books and listening to lectures is not enough to help people establish habits that will make a difference. This is why the organization offers ongoing workshops and an active mentoring process: to help people establish the disciplines they wish to turn into character-shaping habits.

When we become part of a religious community, we acknowledge that we cannot do this spiritual growth all by ourselves. We need other people, other resources, and the support of a community to help us establish the habits that will lead to spiritual growth. Of course, not all religious communities perform this function equally well. And not all religious communities use the same spiritual disciplines and approaches. But the fundamental purpose of religious community is to provide the support people need in order to establish spiritual disciplines and make them into transformational habits.

Opportunities for service

Some time ago, I was in a meeting at the church when our administrative assistant informed me that a young man had just come in from the street and obviously needed to speak to someone. The person I met was clean, well-dressed, but wearing a leather jacket, not the norm for a businessperson or a student. "I'm not here for money," he said. "I just need to talk." After establishing some rapport and doing a little probing, the story came out. He had come from a very violent family. His father had tried to kill him at one point and so he had left home at a very young age. He worked at odd jobs, but then slipped into a life of crime and dealing drugs. He was obviously quite bright and had read a great deal, including philosophy and religion. He was also a fine musician. He had worked with some bands, but constantly resorted to dealing drugs to support his income and his own habits. He had recently lost a job. The wife of the friend he was staying with didn't like him. She locked him out of the house one night. In a fit of rage, he went to collect a drug account from someone he had been dealing with but who didn't have the money. So he took a baseball bat and beat the person up so badly that the man almost died and presently was recovering in the hospital. Now he was feeling a horrible sense of guilt, remorse, and self-loathing. "Pastor, I just wanted to speak with someone before I end it all. I'm sick of my life and I hate who I see when I look into the mirror."

I listened. He ended up sobbing in my arms. I reassured him that despite the darkness and violence in his life, God still loved him and hope was a possibility. I convinced him not to commit suicide until he had had some time to think and I gave him my private phone number so that he could call me if he felt himself slipping towards the brink. I made him promise me that he would not hurt himself, or hurt anyone else, until we had spoken again the next day. He came back the next day. The church provided him with accommodation for some time; various people got involved with him and helped him to become enrolled in a drug treatment program; and saw him start his life over again.

Religious institutions do not only bring people together to worship God; they do not just teach people about spiritual life or support people in a variety of spiritual practices. Religious institutions seek to serve people in their immediate needs, and to address the underlying causes of injustice and suffering. Church people do this not out of a sense of being "do-good-ers," but because they recognize that by caring for others, we are caring for part of ourselves.

As noted in Chapter 8, the gift of service stems from the spiritual vision that in God all people are fundamentally connected.

But service has another component for people in religious organizations, too. As a spiritual discipline, service provides the opportunity to grow past our own self-centeredness, into the vision of the unity of all life, and subsequently into a stance of compassionate love in the midst of life.

Individuals are much less inclined to give of themselves in service without the constant reinforcement, without the constant encouragement and support found in a religious community or other organization. But when such support is present it can make all the difference. A Canadian census study, quoted by the *Globe and Mail* some years ago, revealed that people who acknowledge an affiliation with a faith community tend to be significantly more generous in terms of charitable donations and the offering of services to non-profit organizations than people who acknowledge no connection with a religious tradition. This is because people are most likely to learn about the importance of service and of stewardship in the religious community. This makes such communities invaluable to society at large, as well as to individuals.

Context and meaning for life

I am greatly heartened every time I hear of a new study that confirms that retired ministers and aging people of deep faith tend to live longer than other people of the same age and socio-economic class. One of the reasons given for such extended life is the greater sense of meaning, peace, and happiness that such people experience.

The seriously committed person of faith has a system of meaning in which to situate his or her life. And having this meaningful context cannot be overrated. Without a system of meaning, without a larger context on which to rely for strength, we can feel overwhelmingly lost and alone.

The simple fact is that no matter how exciting life may seem, no matter how many leisure pursuits and friends we may have, at some point life will visit us with some circumstance that is beyond our control. Loss of a job, of health, of a relationship, the experience of death itself, will come our way. Without a meaningful worldview in which to place such experience, we will feel adrift. And recuperation becomes much more difficult.

Some years ago I knew a man named Joe. He was a very active athlete who had competed unsuccessfully for pre-Olympic tryouts in his youth. However, as he got older, he continued to pursue sport passionately. Now in his 40s, and in and out of various relationships, he tore a knee ligament and was laid up from both work and sport for several months. During this time-out from the constant activity of his life, he noticed a deep and unsettled anxiety within himself, a deep feeling of emptiness. Joe had come to realize that living solely for himself was in the end a very lonely and unhappy form of existence. All people crave a certain level of security, financial well-being, and pleasure. But most recognize at some point that life is about transcendence; about giving ourselves over to something larger; about making a contribution that takes us out of ourselves. Ultimately, self-involvement and pursuing only your own life fascinations leads to that deep sense of inner emptiness that Joe discovered. Joe didn't end up turning to religion, but he did have the self-awareness to start contributing his expertise – as a little league baseball coach – and found an entirely new joy in life.

Religion is largely about this process of self-transcendence, of giving ourselves over to something larger than our own life. In the process, we find a sense of meaning and deep joy, far surpassing the pleasure acquired from a night out on the town or a vacation in an exotic holiday resort.

Ideally, commitment to a local church gives us a deep sense of belonging to a community that stands for important values and principles. People are reminded in church that their lives are not just lived for themselves, but for other people. Here they hear the stories of people around them who are hurting, of social causes that need their support, and of a God who calls them to reach out to care for the world.

Dan Wakefield, quoted in Frederic and Mary Ann Brussat's book *Spiritual Literacy*, says,

> Once I began going to church, the age old rituals marking the turning of the year deepened and gave a fuller meaning to the cycle of the seasons and my own relation to them. The year was not only divided now into winter, spring, summer, and fall, but was marked by the expectation of Advent, leading up to the fulfillment of Christmas, followed by Lent, the solemn prelude to the coming of the dark anguish of Good Friday that is transformed in the glory of Easter. Birth and death and resurrection, beginnings and endings and renewals, were observed and celebrated in ceremonies whose experience made me feel I belonged – not just to a neighborhood and a place, but to a larger order of things, a universal sequence of life and death and rebirth.
>
> Going to church, even belonging to it, did not solve life's problems – if anything, they seemed to escalate again around that time – but it gave me a sense of living in a large context, of being part of something far greater than what I could see through the tunnel vision of my personal concerns. I now looked forward to Sunday because it meant going to church; what once was strange now felt not only natural, but essential.[5]

Religious faith is about finding a context for meaning and purpose in our lives; it is about transcending our own self-concerns and preoccupation, and finding a sense of contribution that leads to real joy; it's about becoming part of a community with the values and principles that lead to these things. No wonder people who embody these components of the religious life tend to live longer and healthier lives; not lives free of problems, and struggles, but lives that are more fulfilled and that rebound from struggles with greater elasticity.

In the end, we see that although religion and religious communities contain and advocate a wide variety of spiritual practices and disciplines so important to a whole and growing life, they are about more than that. They provide people with a path, a focus with which to engage spiritual life and practice. They provide a wide range of spiritual practices that suit the individual temperaments of different people, and even more provide the support systems to enable people to make those practices life-transforming habits. They provide community and opportunities for service. And they provide a complete context or framework in which we can live our lives with meaning and with joy.

But this is a most important corollary. Just as we will shop to find a doctor, dentist, or psychologist with whom we feel comfortable, we must take time to find a religious community that is right for us. If we attend a church or religious community in which we do not feel at home, or nurtured spiritually, obviously we will have no incentive or motivation to stay or to grow. People support organizations that are truly helpful. This realization has led religious organizations to become more grounded in a faith that truly speaks to people's lives in practical and down-to-earth ways. Nothing could be better for everyone concerned!

This book has been about the need to retrieve the ancient wisdom present in Christianity, to look at it in the light of contemporary under-standing, and to make it a relevant force for renewal and transformation in our individual and collective lives. If it has contributed to that endeavor in some small way, it shall have served its purpose.

Endnotes

Chapter 1: God

[1] Friedrich Nietzsche, *The Complete Works of Friedrich Nietzsche, Vol. 10*, O. Levy, ed. (London: Allen & Unwin, 1910), 169. The quotation is from "The Gay Science," in Georg Feuerstein, *Holy Madness* (New York: Arkana Books, 1990), 166.

[2] Thomas Barnett and Donald Patriquin, *Songs for the Holy One: Psalms and Refrains for Worship* (Wood Lake Books, 2004).

[3] Sophy Burnham, *The Ecstatic Journey, The Transforming Power of Mystical Experience* (New York: Ballantine Books, 1997), 78–80.

[4] Irina Tweedie, *The Chasm of Fire: A Woman's Experience of Liberation through the Teachings of a Sufi Master* (Rockport, MA: Element Books, 1993), 201.

[5] Jim Collins and Jerry Porras, *Built to Last: Successful Habits of Highly Visionary Companies* (New York: HarperCollins Publishers, 1997), 43.

[6] Huston Smith, *The World's Religions: Our Great Wisdom Traditions* (San Francisco: HarperSanFrancisco, 1991), 273.

Chapter 2: Life

[1] Collins and Porras, *Built to Last*, 146.

[2] Alan Richardson, ed., *A Theological Word Book of the Bible* (New York: Macmillan Publishing Company, 1950), 133–134.

[3] Morford and Lenardon, eds., *Classical Mythology*, 2nd ed., (New York: Longman, 1971, 1977), 215–217.

[4] Quoted by David Suzuki in *The Sacred Balance: Rediscovering Our Place in Nature* (Vancouver: The Douglas and McIntyre Publishing Group, 1999), 16.

Chapter 4: Faith

[1] I am indebted for this description of Niebuhr's understanding to a lecture given by Marcus Borg at the Atlantic Seminar for Theology held in Truro, Nova Scotia in June of 1999, and since expanded in his book *The Heart of Christianity: Rediscovering a Life of Faith* (San Francisco: HarperSanFrancisco, 2003).

[2] Again, I am much indebted to Marcus Borg for his superb lecture on the topic at the Atlantic Seminar for Theology, 1999, and to his book *The Heart of Christianity*.

[3] Frederic and Mary Ann Brussat, *Spiritual Literacy: Reading the Sacred in Everyday Life* (New York: Scribners, 1996). A paraphrase of two different Rumi quotes.

Chapter 5: Prayer & Meditation

[1] Anthony de Mello, *The Song of the Bird* (Garden City, NY: Image Books, 1984), 101.

[2] For a fuller description of the life of prayer, including that of contemplative prayer, see the excellent book by Richard J. Foster, *Prayer: Finding the Heart's True Home* (San Francisco: HarperSanFrancisco, 1992).

Chapter 6: Jesus

[1] Stephanie Nolen, "Give them Jesus, but hold the theology," *Globe & Mail* (2 January 1999).

[2] John Dominic Crossan, *Jesus: A Revolutionary Biography* (San Francisco: HarperSanFrancisco, 1994), 194–195.

[3] Ibid., 18–20. Crossan notes three factors that make it highly unlikely Jesus was born in Bethlehem. He says, "First, there was no such worldwide census under Octavius Augustus. Second, there was indeed a census of Judea, Samaria and Idumea, the territories ruled by Herod the Great's son Archelaus until

the Romans exiled him to Gaul and annexed his lands in 6 C.E. But that was ten years after the death of Herod the Great. Luke begins the story of John and Jesus 'in the days of Herod, King of Judea.' Third, we know from census and taxation decrees in Roman Egypt that individuals were usually registered where they were living and working. They had to return there if they were absent elsewhere. The idea of everyone going back to their ancestral homes for registration and then returning to their present homes would have been then, as now, a bureaucratic nightmare." Crossan goes on to note that the real reason Matthew and Luke place the birth of Jesus in Bethlehem is to connect him with the ancestral lineage of King David, from whom the Israelite people feverishly hoped and believed a new Messiah would come to free Israel.

[4] Ibid., 26.

[5] Ibid., 24.

[6] On October 28, 312, one of the most decisive battles in Western history occurred between two opposing contestants for the leadership of the Roman Empire: Maxentius and Constantine. Maxentius lost the battle and his life, and Constantine became the new leader of the Roman Empire. The night before the battle, Constantine, who had been sympathetic towards the growing Christian religion, is said to have had a pivotal dream in which he saw the initials of the name of Christ and the words, "By this sign you will conquer." He had the monogram ☧ painted on his helmet and on the shields of his soldiers and so, in some sense, he entered the conflict as a Christian. He believed the Christian God had given him the victory. Early in 313, in Milan, what has become known as the "Edict of Milan" was passed granting people full freedom to become Christian. To Constantine's essentially political mind, the adoption of Christianity represented the completion of a process of unification, which had long been in progress in the empire. The empire had one Emperor, one law, and one citizenship for all free men. It should have one religion. See *Williston Walker, A History of the Christian Church* (New York: Charles Scribner's Sons, 1970), 99–106.

[7] Marcus Borg, *Meeting Jesus Again for the First Time: The Historical Jesus and the Heart of Contemporary Faith* (New York: HarperSanFrancisco, 1994), 30–31.

[8] Ibid., 30.

[9] Crossan, *Jesus*, 2–4.

10. Georg Feuerstein, *Holy Madness: The Shock Tactics and Radical Teachings of Crazy-Wise Adepts, Holy Fools, and Rascal Gurus* (New York: Paragon House Publishers, 1991), 138. Feuerstein, a former devotee of Adi Da Samraj, provides a remarkable view into the life of the contemporary mystic Adi Da Samraj and other spiritual geniuses.

Chapter 7: Morality & the Bible

1 Marcus Borg, *Reading the Bible Again for the First Time: Taking the Bible Seriously But Not Literally* (New York: HarperCollins, 2001). See chapter 2.

2 Ibid.

3 William J. Bausch, *A World of Stories for Preachers and Teachers: And All Who Love Stories that Move and Challenge* (Mystic, CT: Twenty-Third Publications, 1998), 260–261.

4 From the original script. Used by permission.

Chapter 8: Service

1 Robert W. Funk, Roy W. Hoover, and the Jesus Seminar, *The Five Gospels: The Search for the Authentic Words of Jesus* (New York: Macmillan Publishing, 1993), 257.

2 Marion Christie, *Growing Up In Bedford: 1914–1930*. First presented at the Scott Manor House, 20 April, 2000.

3 Maria Lopez Virgil, quoted in *The United Church Observer* (November, 1989).

Chapter 10: Suffering & Healing

[1] See *OnLine Etymology Dictionary*, http://www.etymonline.com. O.E. *hælþ* *["health"]* "wholeness, a being whole, sound or well," from PIE **kailo-* "whole, uninjured, of good omen" (cf. O.E. *hal* "hale, whole"; O.N. *heill* "healthy"; O.E. *halig*, O.N. *helge* "holy, sacred"; O.E. *hælan* "to heal").

[2] Ibid., O.E. *halig* "holy," from P.Gmc. **khailagas* (cf. O.N. *heilagr*, Ger. *heilig* Goth. *hailags* "holy"), adopted at conversion for L. *sanctus*. Primary (pre-Christian) meaning is not impossible to determine, but it was probably "that must be preserved whole or intact, that cannot be transgressed or violated," and connected with O.E. *hal* (see *health*) and O.H.G. *heil* "health, happiness, good luck."

[3] Carl Simonton, Stephanie Matthews-Simonton, and James Creighton, *Getting Well Again: The Bestselling Classic About the Simontons' Revolutionary Lifesaving Self- Awareness Techniques* (New York: Bantam Books, 1978), 29–31.

Chapter 11: Sin & Evil

[1] Michael Harris, "The Eerie Normalcy of Psychopaths," *Halifax Daily News*, 8 July 1995.

[2] Ibid.

[3] *Inter Pares* bulletin, June 1995. http://www.interpares.ca/en/index.php

[4] M. Scott Peck, *People of the Lie: The Hope for Healing Human Evil* (New York: Simon and Schuster, 1998), 182–211.

[5] Aleksandr Solzhenitsyn, *The Gulag Archipelago: 1918–1956* (New York: Harper & Row, 1973).

Chapter 12: From Death to New Life

[1] Sogyal Rinpoche, *The Tibetan Book of Living and Dying* (San Francisco: HarperSanFrancisco, 1992), 28.

[2] Brian Greene, *The Fabric of the Cosmos: Space, Time and the Texture of Reality* (New York: Vintage Books, 2005), 18.

[3] Ibid., 393–394.

Conclusion

[1] Borg, *Meeting Jesus*, 37.

[2] Sam Keen, quoted by Sharon Doyle Driedger, in "Soul Searchers," *Maclean's* (16 April 2001)

[3] Stephen Covey, *The Seven Habits of Highly Effective People*, (New York: Simon and Schuster, 1989), 46.

[4] Ibid., 146.

[5] Brussat, *Spiritual Literacy*, 478.

Index

⚡ Northstone Publishing

Northstone Publishing is committed to supporting
and encouraging an emerging form of
Christianity, which recognizes that faith must
evolve with life, and which, at the same time, is
rooted in ancient Christian tradition.

Far from being superficial or trendy, this
commitment is grounded in the Bible (Christian
scripture) and requires us to be dedicated to
spiritual practice and faithful to living out our
values in the world.

We are open and inclusive, and honor the
perennial wisdom and truth contained in all
of the world's enduring religions. We affirm
the equality of the sexes and the godliness of
people of all ages, races, and nationalities. We
believe that the natural world is a sacred part of
creation and needs to be treated as such. We
emphasize the process of transformation rather
than adherence to doctrine or belief.

where spirituality and real life meet

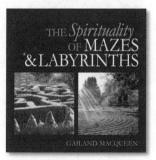
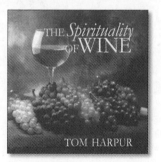

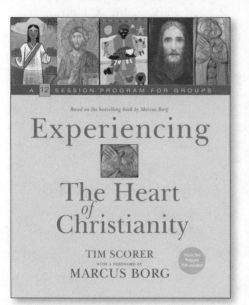

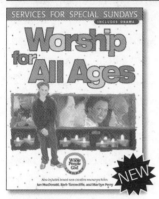

David J. H. Hart is the Lead Minister of Bedford United Church, a large congregation of the United Church of Canada, based in Halifax, Nova Scotia. It is known across Canada for its progressive leadership in contemporary worship, theology, social justice and spirituality. Before coming to Bedford over a decade ago, David worked with various congregations and also served as the Minister for Personnel and Global Justice for the Manitou Conference of the United Church. In that position, he provided extensive leadership in the anti-apartheid movement based in Northern Ontario. During time spent in Guatemala, he helped to strengthen the relationship between the United Church and the Mayan Community within the Presbyterian Church of Guatemala. Today, David is widely known as a highly gifted speaker on the topics of contemporary spirituality and Christian faith.